# CHARLOTTE DESPARD

**Margaret Mulvihill** was born and brought up in Ireland. She studied history at University College Dublin and at Birkbeck College, London. She has worked mainly as an editor of history books and as a writer for history magazines, but *Charlotte Despard* is her first biography.

# Charlotte
# DESPARD

## a biography

*Margaret Mulvihill*

Pandora
*An Imprint of* HarperCollins*Publishers*

Pandora
An Imprint of HarperCollins*Publishers*
77–85 Fulham Palace Road,
Hammersmith, London W6 8JB

First published by Pandora 1989
3  5  7  9  10  8  6  4  2

A catalogue record for this book
is available from the British Library

ISBN 0 86358 213 3

Printed in Great Britain by
HarperCollinsManufacturing Glasgow

# CONTENTS

# LIST OF ILLUSTRATIONS

14   1923: Mrs Despard keeping her lonely vigil at the gates of Kilmainham Gaol while awaiting the release of Maud Gonne MacBride. (*Courtesy of the late Sean MacBride*)

15   Charlotte Despard, suitably unhappy about the company she has to keep, sits beside Ramsay MacDonald as he makes a speech, probably in honour of the 1928 Equal Franchise Act. (*Mary Evans/Fawcett Library*)

16   A happier looking Mrs Despard photographed around the same time. (*Mary Evans/Fawcett Library*)

17   Jack Mulvenna (*left*) with Captain Jack White, who had trained Connolly's Citizen Army in 1914–16. (*Courtesy of Jack Mulvenna*)

18   Mollie Fitzgerald. (*Courtesy of Jack Mulvenna*)

19   Charlotte Despard, now in boots, addresses an anti-fascist rally in Trafalgar Square in 1933. (*National Museum of Photography, Film and Television, Bradford*)

# ABBREVIATIONS

| | |
|---|---|
| COS | Charity Organisation Society |
| CPGB | Communist Party of Great Britain |
| FOSR | Friends of Soviet Russia |
| ILP | Independent Labour Party |
| IWSA | International Women's Suffrage Alliance |
| ISDL | Irish Self Determination League |
| IWFL | Irish Women's Franchise League |
| NUM | National Union of Mineworkers |
| NUWSS | National Union of Women's Suffrage Societies |
| NCF | No Conscription Fellowship |
| SDF | Social Democratic Federation |
| UWM | Unemployed Workers' Movement |
| UDC | Union for Democratic Control |
| WFL | Women's Freedom League |
| WIL | Women's International League (for Peace and Freedom) |
| WPC | Women's Peace Crusade |
| WPDL | Women's Prisoners' Defence League |
| WSPU | Women's Social and Political Union |
| WPI | Workers' Party of Ireland |

For my parents

# ACKNOWLEDGEMENTS

I could not have researched this book without the help of Jack Mulvenna of Belfast, David Doughan of the Fawcett Library, Esther Hewitt of the Public Records Office of Northern Ireland, and my parents, Michael and Peggy Mulvihill, who provided many short-cuts to Dublin references. I could not have written it without the support and encouragement of my husband, Mick Gold. Special thanks must go also to Pauline Cummings, Mary O'Connell and Katy and Susan Gold for minding Katrina during a peripatetic year.

I am more formally indebted to the staff of these libraries and organizations: Battersea District Library (Mr Shaw), the British Museum, the Fawcett Library (Susan Cross), the Greater London Records Office, the Imperial War Museum, the Irish in Britain History Centre (Angela Lynch), the National Library of Ireland, the Public Records Office of Northern Ireland, Save the Children (Jane Button), Trinity College Library, Dublin, and the Vegetarian Society (Pauline Morris).

I am also grateful to the following individuals: George and Ingrid Franks, Nora Harkin, Karen Hunt, Lady Patricia Kingsbury, Candida Lacey, Caitriona Lawlor, Cathy Leeney, Andro Linklater, Edward Lydall, the late Sean MacBride, Mollie Mallaby, Mike Milotte, Gemma O'Connor, June O'Sullivan, T. W. Otway, Marie Quiery, Colette Quinlan, Sir Michael Tippett and Margaret Ward.

It is my sincere hope that *Charlotte Despard* is worthy of such support and that this acknowledgement will cause no one embarrassment.

# CHAPTER 1

# THE VICEROY'S SISTER IN IRELAND: 'A CALL OF THE BLOOD'

On 11 May 1918, at the untender age of sixty-five, Field-Marshal Lord French was sworn in at Dublin Castle as Lord-Lieutenant, or Viceroy, of Ireland. He had greater powers than any of his predecessors and his appointment was, in his own words, 'for purposes of military order and combating German intrigue' in a country that had become virtually ungovernable. Tension had grown in Ireland since the arming of Ulster Unionists in opposition to a Home Rule Act that had been expected to become law in 1914. But the outbreak of the First World War in that year subsumed this local battle into a more gigantic conflict, and so Home Rule was 'hung up' for its duration. Before that war ended, however, Irish republicans and socialists had risen in 1916 to proclaim an independent Irish Republic. But the executions of most of the 1916 leaders boomeranged back on the authorities, who had thought to nip a dangerous fiasco in the bud. Within a year of the Rising's brutal aftermath a more uncompromising movement for national independence had mobilized, under the auspices of a revamped Sinn Fein led by Éamon de Valera. The immediate focus of this movement was resistance to conscription.

Conscription for the Great War had been introduced in Britain in 1916 and, as the haemorrhage of life on the Western Front continued, the man-hungry British war cabinet cast longing eyes on Ireland's male population. It was decided that Home Rule should be put into effect only after Ireland had fought whole-heartedly for King and Empire. The new Viceroy had to restore order and effect conscription, and to Lloyd George's relief he was confident about his mission.

'Johnnie' French was a short man with the bow-legged swagger of a cavalry officer and his florid face made him look permanently angry. A thoroughly military man, his politics were no more sophisticated than they'd been when he had had Boer rebels hanged in 1901, and he treated his delicate mission in Ireland as though it were a cavalry charge. He had approved heartily of the execution of the 1916 men and was sincerely convinced that the new-style Sinn Fein was an incurably violent organization, deriving limited popular support through outright intimidation. This is how the newly appointed Viceroy described the situation to his friend Lord Esher:

> I have loved this country and these people all my life and I would do anything or sacrifice anything for them. But they are so infernally emotional. If they could only be got to realize the true character of such leaders as De Valera – Countess Markiewitz – and Count Plunkett – people steeped to the neck in the violent forms of crime and infamy – and with the smallest possible proportion of Irish blood in their veins. If they would but understand that all these people can do is to *talk* and feed their damnable aggressive vanity – I feel sure that the Irish would cast them out like the swines they are.

While Lord Esher might have wondered what the peaceful forms of crime and infamy were, he would have been in no doubt as to the proportion of Irish blood in his Viceroy friend's veins. Like many an American presidential hopeful, Lord French was well versed in his Irishness and he claimed a special insight into Irish affairs and Irish people on this account. Although his family was only a minor branch of the great Norman Irish family of French, and one that had been settled in England since the eighteenth century, he was nonetheless a great-grandson of John French of High Lake, Roscommon, in turn a descendant of fourteenth-century settlers in Wexford. To this illustrious paternal lineage, the Viceroy added his happy experiences as a horse-loving young officer when his regiment had been stationed in Ireland, and claimed a great rapport with Irish 'society':

'With bright summer weather, the pretty grounds at Ballsbridge presented a more animated appearance than usual at the opening of the Annual Horse Show, the Lord-Lieutenant paying an unofficial call before the State visit. There was a large attendance of Society people.' Fortified by such delightful experiences, Lord French wrote how

> One must try to study what the real Irish national aspirations are, and how to get into and to keep trust with them. But before one can even begin to put the garden in order, one must *weed it out*. My first great effort is to stamp out this German intrigue – many who are implicated have been absolutely *terrorized* by their leaders.

Within days of his solemn swearing-in ceremony an extremely convenient 'plot' between the leaders of the nationalist movement and the German enemy was 'uncovered', which enabled him to get on with the weeding. All seditious persons were rounded up into jail and all subversive organizations, including sporting and language groups, were proscribed. But when the First World War ended in November 1918, leaving the Viceroy with the law and order aspect of his mission, it was followed by a General Election in which the Sinn Fein 'devils' won a landslide victory.

This victory did not deter the redoubtable Field-Marshal Viceroy, who was convinced that the Shinners would desert the independent Dáil, or parliament, which they had set up in Dublin's Mansion House, when they found out that they could not draw their Westminster salaries. Now, however, the Irish Republican Army existed and the first shots of the first phase of the Anglo-Irish War were fired on the same day as the Dáil assembled, 19 January 1919. Soon French was pushed upstairs by other men brought in by the alarmed British government, by Sir Hamar Greenwood, and by General Sir Nevil Macready who was utterly devoid of any sympathy for Irish people. The Dáil went underground and 'Black and Tans' were recruited from demobilized British soldiers as auxiliaries to the 'pacifying' taskforce. These men began to arrive in Ireland in 1920, wearing the composite uniforms of black caps and trousers with khaki jackets that reminded someone of a famous pack of foxhounds and so earned them their nickname.

As the conflict developed into a full-scale war, French himself became personally vulnerable. In December 1919 he escaped an assassination attempt only because he was travelling in the first rather than the second car of a motor convoy:

> In that car a living tool, of England's hated rule.

But now he also had to contend with a personal thorn in the flesh in the thin, gaunt-faced shape of his big sister Charlotte. Eight years his senior, Charlotte Despard, née French, shared her brother's sense of having a special connection with Ireland. In addition to the French family ancestry she was the widow of Maximilian Despard, an Irishman of the county kind, and she maintained cordial relations with her Irish in-laws. Moreover, she chose to live among the poor Irish immigrants of Nine Elms in south London and she was a convert to the Catholic faith.

Charlotte, or 'Lottie', had always adored her only brother 'Jack'. As a well-off married woman and as a wealthy widow she had helped him financially and provided his family with a home while he was sowing wild oats as a young officer. Indeed, until John French's military career had taken off during the South African wars of 1899 to 1902, he had been the black sheep of the French family. He had to be rescued from a socially disastrous first marriage, and his career barely survived financial ruin and an indiscreet liaison with the wife of one of his superiors. But as Jack found his feet and rose to military eminence, the relationship between him and the sister he was so fond of shifted, Lottie taking on the mantle of the black sheep.

Apart from her immersal in the most avant-garde politics of the day, Mrs Despard's taste in dress was hardly that of the aristocratic sister of a general. This is how she was introduced to one little grand-nephew:

> Aunt Lottie, said my mother, was a well-known suffragette called Mrs Despard. Her most salient characteristics were a habit of wearing sandals and a mantilla and a keen desire to be a heroine in the cause of women's suffrage by finding herself in jail. Unfortunately, these two characteristics got in each other's way. Authority apparently decided that it would be unseemly for the sister of the Commander-in-Chief (Lord Ypres) to rot in prison and the order went round debarring

ladies wearing sandals and mantillas from arrest and incarceration. Aunt Lottie began to grow desperate until, tumbling finally to the reason for her lack of success, she sallied out in boots and a bonnet, and, before being identified and ejected, spent one glorious and heroic night in jail.

In such ways Charlotte Despard, who spent more than one glorious night in jail, was written off as a ridiculous and scatty old dear. But her relatives, and her brother in particular, needed to see her in a harmless light in order to remain on affectionate terms with her. Her outspoken pacifism was a problem for Lord French during the First World War but in the case of Ireland it became impossible to separate the private from the public. As the Irish Troubles boiled up Charlotte Despard was drawn in as one of the very people whose activities it was the Viceroy's job to eradicate. Lottie had always mingled with subversives, but now she was emphatically one of them. It didn't help matters that she wrote asking him for repayment of a loan in the very week when the Viceroy was recovering from the attempted assassination.

Few people in the Edwardian Establishment would have credited it, but the outlandish Mrs Despard had a far more realistic perspective on Ireland than her blimpish brother. At least she thought in political rather than purely military terms. For some years from 1909 many perceptive people like Mrs Despard believed that Britain itself faced a social and political crisis of exceptional, possibly even revolutionary, severity. This crisis arose from a convergence of a collection of disputes, each of which threatened the old order: the women's movement, the budget veto of the House of Lords, the waves of strikes and, of course, Ireland. The revolution that seemed to be around the corner before the First World War did actually happen in Russia in 1917.

As a leading suffragette and an active socialist Charlotte Despard was in the thick of this orchestra of struggle. Just before the outbreak of the First World War she had made several successful suffrage speaking tours of Ireland, campaigning for 'Home Rule for men and women together'. Such experiences led to cordial and informed relations with leading Irish suffragists such as Francis and Hanna Sheehy-Skeffington. Meanwhile her involvement with the labour movement acquainted her with

James Connolly, with whom she sometimes shared speakers' platforms. When the vote for women over thirty was won in 1918 Mrs Despard stood as Battersea's Labour Party parliamentary candidate. She did well although she did not win the seat against the 'Jingoes'. But she was pleased by the Sinn Fein victory in that same General Election, a victory which owed much to the enfranchisement of Irishwomen: 'to the ordinary thinker there is no issue: Russia is Bolshevik and Ireland is Sinn Fein.'

She managed, in her seventies, to keep fingers in an astonishing number of political pies. She once confided in her diary, 'It is hard to be out of anything. . . . How ardently would I work here and there, wherever I may be taken and placed.' So it was that in 1920 her special commitment to Ireland, which took the form of active membership of Sinn Fein's British organization, the Irish Self Determination League, and support for Irish political prisoners in Britain, jostled alongside her Nine Elms welfare schemes, Labour and Communist Party work, the Indian independence movement, the London Vegetarian Society, Save the Children work for the relief of distress in post-war Europe, and myriad other local and global causes. When she visited Ireland in the spring of 1919 she was careful to do so in a low-key way, ostensibly a philanthropic rather than a political visitor. Although she ordered a new dress from Liberty's and had her snowy hair done in Bond Street, she avoided the Viceregal Lodge. After visiting her in-laws in County Laois (then Queen's County) she stayed for a couple of days in Dublin at the home of Maud Gonne MacBride, officially as the guest of the Irish Women's Franchise League. At the IWFL reception laid on for her, Mrs Despard met Constance Markievicz and other individuals who inspired her brother's wrath. But that was all. It was the martyrdom of Terence MacSwiney in October 1920 that pushed Lottie into seriously alienating the Viceroy.

Terence MacSwiney, the Lord Mayor of Cork, was arrested in a raid by security forces on the City Hall in August 1920. He was sentenced to two years' penal servitude for possessing seditious documents and within days transported to Brixton Jail in south London. He immediately went on hunger strike, a strategy pioneered by suffragettes, and although he was suffering from tuberculosis his marathon lasted until his death on 25 October. Charlotte Despard was deeply preoccupied by his ordeal and saw a great deal of his sister, Mary MacSwiney, throughout it. She regularly joined the nightly vigils of supporters outside Brixton jail and was shattered by his death: 'Terence MacSwiney, patriot and martyr is dead. That is the one thought.' She joined the procession that escorted MacSwiney's coffin from St George's in Southwark to its entrainment at Euston Station: 'My place was the Battersea Branch of the ISDL. Marched under banner with Miss O'Flynn and a priest from Cork. Never had I seen or felt anything so impressive.'

Then, on 1 November, the day when MacSwiney was buried in Cork, a medical student named Kevin Barry was hanged at Mountjoy Prison in Dublin. Eighteen years of age, Barry had been a member of a party of IRA volunteers which had skirmished with British soldiers. When Charlotte Despard got back to Battersea after an absence of several days 'there was a heap of letters asking for my intercession for the poor boy.' As the atrocities, outrages and sheer terror in Ireland mounted, Charlotte Despard was inundated with such letters. Her Irish friends begged her to intercede with her brother on behalf of republican prisoners. But to all of them she could only offer ordinary solidarity work through the labour movement. She tried, as discreetly as she could, to point out that her brother was cool and carefully distanced from his treacherous sister, and, besides, he was by now merely a figurehead. (Indeed, so removed was the Viceroy from the dirty work that he was free to restore his health with a holiday on the Riviera with his mistress.)

Although the relationship between brother and sister was too strained to be useful, Mrs Despard still enjoyed some propaganda status as the Viceroy's sister. As such, even her presence in Ireland might help. Certainly, Dorothy Macardle, who visited Battersea on the last day of 1920, thought so.

From Miss Macardle a long talk about Ireland. What is worst, she says, is that Sinn Fein has no one policy. Some are propagandists, hoping to convince – some for violence. The young men are almost courting martyrdom. She fears, as I fear, something desperate, then a massacre, followed by a stifling of all spirit. Heaven help our poor country! I promised to go if it would help. We want to start a relief scheme for the unhappy women and children. Goodbye 1920. You have been a year of strange experiences and I do not regret you.

It was a mark of Charlotte Despard's growing commitment to Ireland that she cried out, 'Heaven help *our* poor country!' Despite her continual sense of the special relationship, in 1914 it would still have been *that* country. In January 1921 she got the boat and arrived in Dublin, once again officially the guest of the Irish Women's Franchise League and personally the guest of Maud Gonne MacBride. There were twenty-two years and some political differences between these two friends. Whereas Charlotte Despard had the vocabulary and experience of one who had waged class war and was therefore a socialist republican, Maud Gonne's version of the Irish struggle was more simply romantic and nationalist. Still, the two women had a very similar social background, and they shared their conversion to Catholicism and a great interest in mystical thought. They were also veterans in organizing the relief of distress. But these things did not recommend Charlotte Despard to William Butler Yeats. By all accounts, he found Maud Gonne's elderly new friend irritating and avoided the house on Stephen's Green and the later joint household in Clonskea whenever Mrs Despard was there. At seventy-six Charlotte Despard was hardly a candidate for romantic celebration and she must have seemed distastefully vehement to the poet who fretted about the way in which women could 'give themselves to an opinion as if it were some terrible stone doll'.

On this trip Charlotte Despard set about putting her immunity as the Viceroy's sister to good effect. With Maud Gonne she set off on a fact-finding tour of Cork and the south-western counties, which were under martial law. Her presence gave the motor car a charmed quality for it could sail through road blocks and other official obstacles, into, as Maud Gonne put it, 'places I should never have been able to get to alone in the martial areas'. She was amused by the 'puzzled expressions on the faces of the officers and of the Black and Tans, who continually held up our car, when Mrs Despard said she was the Viceroy's sister'. The Viceroy's sister returned from ravaged Munster with evidence of deliberate terrorism and destruction of property by the security forces. A British Labour Party Commission of Inquiry had earlier investigated Britain's regime in Ireland and reached the same conclusions, but Mrs Despard's account had special publicity value.

But it was the relief of distress in Ireland that called Mrs Despard, especially since the Nine Elms welfare projects that she had pioneered thirty years earlier were being increasingly ratified by the progressive Battersea Council. On Maud Gonne's suggestion, Arthur Griffith had asked the women of Ireland to work with the White Cross, a relief organization for the dependants of Sinn Fein prisoners and other casualties. The White Cross set about creating alternative economic enterprizes, such as clothing co-ops, and raising funds. Then there was the distribution of the funds raised, and of the food and supplies that had been shipped from America. Mrs Despard was an old hand at this sort of work, and she could never resist helping children in need. Moreover there was, despite the daily terror, a buzz in the air, and she wanted to play a part in building a new Ireland.

When she went back to London it was to wind up her life there. Every summer the Women's Freedom League held a special celebration near their first President's June birthday. When she thanked them in 1921 Mrs Despard told the League that she 'could not help' going to Ireland permanently. According to *The Vote*, 'it was a call of the blood! Her ancestry, her late husband, were Irish, and from girlhood she had been a close student of Irish history.' While the treaty between Sinn Fein and the British government was being negotiated at Downing Street she went to Ireland to set up home with Maud Gonne. But the fact that her brother had already left Ireland must have made that decision easier.

On the morning of 30 April 1921 the Viceroy, now Lord Ypres, had stepped on to the mailboat from Kingstown that took him out of official life and into a less than happy retirement. In her memoirs Mary Colum reproduces an anecdote to illustrate his discomfiture in the face of Lottie's antics:

This bewildered gentleman, when driving through Dublin in state with all the trappings of the King's deputy, beheld two beautiful middle-aged women making speeches to an insurrectionary populace. He could not without scandal order their arrest, for one was his sister, Mrs Despard, and the other the woman he once admired, Maud Gonne.

To refer to the terrible twosome as 'middle-aged' around 1920 is a bit romantic, and, other than his Napoleon-like interest in very tall women, there appears to be no basis for the notion that the Viceroy fancied Maud Gonne. But myth is stronger than documentary narratives.

Lord Ypres had hoped to settle in Ireland eventually, to enjoy the country houses he had purchased. Sadly, his advisors told him that his life would be in danger if he did so, and he was left to retire in Britain where he had no home commensurate with his status. A purely honorary position as Captain of Deal Castle, which gave him residency rights, was soon found and there he died in 1925. According to his son, Lord Ypres and Mrs Despard did manage something of a reconciliation just before he died, even though they had failed to meet again.

My father and his sister Mrs Despard had been estranged for many years, but her brother's serious condition brought forth a letter full of warm-hearted sympathy and devotion. She wrote from Ireland where for some time she had been living and trying to assist the cause of Sinn Fein.

My dearest Jack,
    I was in London last week for two days, and called at your hospital and saw matron. It would have given me great joy to have seen you; but the doctors advised it was better not. I find however that you may receive letters and I am sending these few words to tell you how I have thought of you and prayed for you during your illness and what joy it gives me to know that you will soon be on your feet again.
    I wonder if anything will bring you over to this poor sad country once more. It would be more than delightful to see you, and I, who have always been a rebel, know that even rebels — and I see much of them here — thank you kindly. The Lord Mayor of Dublin is one of your admirers and a staunch friend. If, when you are convalescent, you could find time and strength to write to me and let me know what your plans are and where you may be found, it would be a great joy to me.
    I have not given up my hope of meeting you some day at Deal Castle. I expect to be in London early in July.

Alas, the world was rarely so kind. The mind boggles at the thought of Lord Ypres recuperating among the company his sister kept in Ireland. But history has dealt more harshly with the generals of the First World War than it has with 'eccentrics' such as Charlotte Despard. Few people nowadays can see that war as anything but a tragic consequence of political incompetence, whereas most of Mrs Despard's projects are still valid. She was nearly eighty-one when her little brother died, and ahead of her lay another fourteen years with the people she had elected as her kin. If she had never had an Irish impulse she would, in all probability, have lived to become Dame Charlotte Despard, and today there would be some grand public monument in her honour, if not in central London, at the very least in Battersea.

# CHAPTER 2

# A VICTORIAN GIRLHOOD: 'I MUST NOT BE SO DOWNRIGHT...'

When Charlotte Despard looked back at the days of her youth she decided that she must 'always have been independent – more or less a rebel'. This spirit in all likelihood owed something to the fact that as the third daughter in a family that began with five girls, she did not escape the consequences of her father's disappointment. Again and again in their autobiographies, suffragist women account for their motivation in terms of their situation as daughters within their own families. The Irish suffragist Gretta Cousins was the eldest in a family that started with four girls: 'I was so sensitive and intuitional that I knew my little sisters were unwelcome as they monotonously came along. Boys were wanted and expected. I felt acutely the injustice of this attitude and atmosphere.' For Margaret Wynne Nevinson it was, blissfully, the other way round: 'Being an only girl among five sons, I had a warmer welcome at my birth than is generally accorded to daughters, especially from my father. . . .'

Mary French came first, then Caroline (Carrie), Charlotte (Lottie), Margaret (Maggie), Sarah (Nellie) and, at last, John (Jack). The longed-for son and heir was the second last bead to be squashed on to Mrs French's groaning reproductive string for he was followed by a final daughter. Katherine (Katie). They were all born on the estate of Ripple Vale in Kent, which had come into the family through marriage two generations earlier. Some of the money for its upkeep came in the dowry of Charlotte Despard's mother, Margaret Eccles. She hailed from a family of wealthy Glasgow merchants and retained the fervent Presbyterianism of her ancestors. According to French family lore, Margaret Eccles met Captain John Tracey William French when she was visiting a married sister in the West Indies. She was only eighteen when she became his wife in 1842, the same year in which the young Queen Victoria married her beloved Albert. These marriages were more than coincidental. Margaret Eccles was fourteen years younger than her retired naval captain and therefore something of a child-bride. This an unequal partnership, with the 'angel' wife filling up the nursery for her authoritative and in every way senior husband, was entirely in keeping with the domestic ideal of Queen Victoria's early reign. According to his only son, Captain French was 'naturally a man of great strength of character, firm will and self-reliance'. These qualities were hardened and developed by eighteen or nineteen years of strenuous service at sea. As master of his own ship, Captain French lost an eye in the Battle of Navarino and he fought under Sir Charles Napier in support of Dom Pedro during the Portuguese Civil War of the early 1830s. Unlike many naval officers of his class, Captain French enjoyed his active service, but the British Navy after the Napoleonic Wars was not too busy and so he retired to devote his authority and energy to the family estate. But the son, the future Field-Marshal French, who remembered his father so respectfully, in fact hardly knew him, for Captain French died in 1854 when he was two years old and his sister Lottie was ten.

Captain French had not been very interested in his daughters and so until his death the little company of girls enjoyed a relatively unruly childhood. 'We were taught, disciplined, scolded and punished after the repressive fashion of those days; but all that was unimportant to us. Our real life was in our playworld and there we were irrepressibly happy.' They were not allowed to run about on the lawns of the show garden in front of the house but they had their own 'wild corner hidden away behind a large and imposing rockery, with which the superior and alien face never meddled'. There they planned their houses, dug holes to Australia and played smugglers. But this idyll was broken up when some interfering adult – 'we never found out who it was' – reported that the French sisters were communicating 'by means of holes in a tall paling' with some village children outside the estate.

They were then presented with a more easily supervised play area, 'prim box-edged gardens in full view of the library and morning room windows', and for the rest of her days Charlotte remembered her envy of the happy village children 'who could run about as they liked and who did not seem to be troubled by those superior persons, nurses and governesses'. This strict new regime probably began after the death of her father, and she reacted by running away from home. With the money accumulated from 'Sunday tips' she went to the nearest railway station, three miles away, hoping to go to London and find employment as a servant. She was stopped but only after she had gone so far that she could not return to Ripple Vale that night, so she spent it 'alone in a little awe and some importance at a railway station inn'. Back home, lest she infected her sisters with her insubordination, Lottie was put in solitary confinement for three or four days, and then packed off to school. 'That is a hideous time which I never like to remember. Strange to say, however, I was not tamed. My health seemed to be suffering, so after a year of this rough school-life I was allowed to return home.'

Home was now only nominally under the widowed Mrs French. It was not she but probably some male relation of her late husband's who had taken the taming of the girls, and Lottie in particular, in hand. This was because of what her son discreetly referred to as the 'incurable capacity', a euphemism for depression and mental instability, which was gradually getting the better of Margaret French. Captain French had relieved his nervous wife of all responsibility apart from her seven live births and as a widow she was ill-prepared for managing her children and the estate. She therefore drifted on as a semi-invalid until, in 1860, she was confined to a home for the mentally ill.

A great deal has been written about the extent to which middle-class ladies were 'invalided' in the nineteenth century. Almost by definition, they were vulnerable to delicacy, debility and hysteria (literally, 'womb sickness'). That vulnerability was even taken as a sign of breeding and gentility, for factory women had to have a correspondingly 'rude' animal health to justify their direct roles in life. So hypochondria was almost encouraged in Mrs French's day, though it should also be remembered that before modern drugs and contraceptive expertise, death could and did come from colds, chills and from pregnancy.

Sometimes invalidism could be a strategy for otherwise power-less Victorian women. Florence Nightingale, to use the most spectacular example, used her forty-year-long vague incapacity to lobby for reform in Britain's hospitals. By being bedridden she brought the mountain in the shape of politicians and administrators to Mohammed without breaching propriety. Nightingale was a powerful, manipulative invalid but Margaret French was one of the victims whose derangement probably derived from the psychosexual and religious tensions of the day. Victorian Britain abounded with private homes for mentally unstable ladies. For a fictional equivalent of Charlotte Despard's pathetic mother, we might usefully recall Mr Rochester's mad wife in *Jane Eyre* or the wasted woman in *The Woman in White*.

Whatever it is possible to say now about the outlines of Margaret French's story, none of her children seemed to feel able to face their mother's tragedy openly. The two who were to become famous, Lottie and Jack, tended to ignore the immediate Scottish maternal connection, insisting instead on their Irish heritage. Distant Irish forebears on the Eccles side were even added to the French connection with Ireland, which harked back to the Norman Conquest. That was how, according to John French, they derived the 'flow of Irish blood in our veins which develops some curious characteristics'. In seeking by such references to account for his own unruly and on the whole successful career, John French was not unusual. Men and women of his generation habitually explained themselves in terms of their 'ethnicity', much as celebrities these days might employ a Freudian vocabulary. But John French added a more modern insight into his development when he commented that his father's death and his mother's weakness, 'the absence of any powerful directing mind being brought to bear on my childhood and bringing-up', had a 'certain influence' on the rest of his life.

Ditto for Lottie. Although she seems never to have referred directly to her tragic mother, the novels she later wrote are peopled with snowy-haired and wisely compassionate matrons, and it does not seem too much to say that she sorely missed a strong mother. She also acquired a dislike for Presbyterianism, having come 'under the shadow of Scotch puritanism' while with her mother's relatives in Edinburgh, where she went to school for a time.

> Unless we were converted there was no hope of safety in the future; and converted people must keep themselves apart from the world. Opera and theatres and dancers were sinful. Light literature, everything indeed that was interesting and human, must be accepted with great reserve. It was sinful to sew and even open a book of fiction on a Sunday, and anything like pride in dress or appearance was treated with grave suspicion.

Was it any wonder that Miss Charlotte French emerged first as a very ecumenical Christian with theosophical leanings, later as a very individualistic exponent of Popery? Another legacy of Mrs French's demise might have been her daughter's hyperactivism. Right to the end of her life Charlotte Despard was almost obsessively busy. Was she afraid of slipping away like her mother, of losing her grip on reality?

By the time Mrs French had been put away, Charlotte was in her teens. This, according to Leonore Davidoff, was the most awkward age for an upper-class Victorian girl. She had no social place, being neither a wife-to-be nor a child. The only safe contacts outside the home were with a few selected girls from the same background, with clergymen and possibly with 'non-contaminating' charity work such as Sunday School teaching. But Charlotte had her sisters and at home she was responsible for her adored baby brother's elementary education. She taught Jack his letters and told Teresa Billington-Greig, a fellow suffragette, that he was 'dull'. Billington-Greig's memory of that confidence might have been coloured by John French's later military career, but the reader of any of the Field-Marshal's utterances would have to verify that, for all his other talents, he was no intellectual.

A young lady received the education necessary to make her an accomplished companion and a social hostess. There was no question of the French sisters having to work for their living, and, if they acquired more than the usual superficial education, there was a danger of frightening away suitors. Accordingly, 'we were taught a little music, a little drawing, no science or mathematics; but a little literature, geography and history.' And, of course, the all-important 'manners' which Charlotte Despard retained to the end of her days.

Complaints about their education are, again, almost routine in the memoirs of suffragists. (It is significant that Beatrice Webb, who at first shunned the feminist movement, knew herself to have had an exceptionally equal education, and a mother whose intellectual brilliance was legendary.) Poor Lottie could only remember 'incompetent teachers and indifferent learners – nothing thorough'. Like so many others, she thought wistfully, 'what might I not have done had I the freedom and intellectual advantages so largely accorded to men?' She longed to train for a career but no doors were open to women then, even if her family had been sympathetic. 'Moreover I had not been taught to do anything thoroughly. I may say that throughout my life this has been my great drawback. I have indeed taught and drilled myself, and I think I have succeeded in partially over-coming the disadvantages of an inferior, slipshod education.'

The saving grace of this slipshod schooling was literature. The one positive experience in Edinburgh had been the class of a schoolmaster who led her to Milton's poetry. Instead of being horrified at her preference for the noble Lucifer's lines over those of the good angels, he congratulated her on her taste. But when Miss French recited these inspiring lines at a later finishing school poetry class, the lady teacher had a different reaction. 'Yes,' she remarked, 'but these are Satan's lines. You mustn't repeat them.' But Lottie found the good angels as dull as the trim garden of her early childhood.

Milton's Satan of 'Evil, be thou my good!' was the first hero; the second was another literary rebel, Percy Bysshe Shelley. When she was about eighteen a 'discerning boyfriend', who was probably on that account unsuitable, suggested that she read Shelley: 'He would just suit you.' She had studied some of Shelley's shorter poems at school, but even in mid-Victorian Britain the longer poems were considered too 'dangerous' for young ladies: 'So much the better for me – and I entered upon my new delight unbiased.' She would never forget, and her associates were never allowed to forget, the plea of Cythna, heroine of 'The Revolt of Islam': 'Can man be free, and woman be a slave?' Her new reading matter had the effect of 'the lighting of a fire in a room that had been dark and cold'. Milton had made her a radical democrat, but Shelley 'made me a rebel against the existing social order and a profound believer in Utopia.' In Shelley's divine company she shut herself away in her room with 'fierce thoughts and indignant dreams' while other inspirations came from the world outside.

Charlotte Despard's rebellious teens coincided with the stirring events of the Italian Risorgimento, so that Mazzini (after Shelley 'my next master')and Garibaldi became idols in much the same way as Che Guevara was a pin-up for rebellious teenagers in the 1960s. The 'great Garibaldi' was a hero for all British radicals, his popularity enduring in the biscuit (sometimes called 'squashed flies' by children) which was named after him on account of his fondness for eating currants between bread and butter. When he visited London in 1864 he was greeted by the largest procession of workers that the capital had ever seen, the procession in his honour taking six hours to escort him from Nine Elms Station to St James's Palace. Somewhere among the crowd lining this route, twenty-year-old Charlotte French was rapt with adoration, somewhere else the nine-year-old Eleanor Marx, and, on his father's shoulders, the young John Burns. Irish nationalist aspirations also aroused Miss French's sympathetic interest and when she first read about the Penal Laws she thought of them as a 'revelation of evil'. The fact that her late teens coincided with romantic nationalist struggles goes some way towards explaining how, as Madame Despard, she became an enthusiast for Irish republican definitions of liberty.

But she was still hopelessly cut off from the real world. It is not always profitable to read autobiographical intent into works of fiction but we can surely recognize something of the young Miss French in the character of Adèle from her first novel, *Chaste as Ice, Pure as Snow* (1874).

> The mind of a girl of eighteen is, in many cases, more mature than that of a man of twenty. . . . Adèle, with the like luxurious surroundings, had already begun to look past herself, to feel that there was a world of which she knew nothing, but with which, nevertheless, she was very closely connected; a world of want and suffering, where wrong was often triumphant.
>
> She was fond of reading. Perhaps some of these thoughts had crept in through the medium of poet and historian. For

Adèle's insight told her that there were many higher and nobler lives for a man and a woman to lead than that of self-pleasing. She sometimes longed to be a man, that she might do something worth doing, in a world that wanted the active and the strong . . .

Although Lottie resisted the finishing-off process as much as she could, by the time she was twenty her hair was up, her skirts were down, and she was on the marriage market. She was probably too thin and too sharp-featured to be considered pretty by Victorian conventions, but she had a distinctly dignified bearing and fine eyes, and could qualify as a handsome young woman. She also had a, literally, sterling advantage. The Eccles fortune meant that each of the French sisters could expect a substantial dowry, and private means if they failed to find husbands. By now they were settled in London and Mary, who had been twenty-one in 1863, was head of the family of orphans. (Mrs French died, 'quite mad', in 1865.)

The Misses French encountered the cast-iron creed of the day: 'a bad husband is better than none.' A Victorian lady could not take a full place in the adult world unless she was married and from the cradle that achievement was every genteel female's purpose in life. Now Charlotte came up against serious resistance to her rebellious streak. In old age she could still recall the 'sage advice' of her elders: 'You will get yourself talked about my dear. Girls cannot be too particular. Remember what is expected of you.' She was repeatedly exhorted not to be 'so downright' because it was unladylike and would prejudice her marriage prospects. Two of her sisters were prompt in doing what was expected of them. In 1865 a younger sister, Maggie, married an entrepreneurial engineer, Gavin Jones, and went off to live in India, where he was setting up the dominant cotton industry of Cawnpore. Then, in 1867, Mary married a solicitor named John Lydall, and the family began to break up. Brother John went into the Navy and the youngest sister, Katie, was sent to school in Brighton. That left three adult, unmarried sisters: Carrie, Lottie and Nellie. In the year of her eldest sister's marriage Lottie, at twenty-three, was reckoned to be already on the shelf. Later she made the rather optimistic observation, 'that gibe would not worry the modern girl too much!' All might have been well for Lottie with her unconventional expectations had it not been for John Lydall, Mary's husband, who now took on the role of paterfamilias.

The historian of the Lydall family, Edward Lydall, finds it hard to remember anything pleasant about his grandfather. A 'replica of Mr Barrett of Wimpole St', the most pertinent thing about him was his religious fundamentalism, for he had been 'saved' as a young man and had become a devout, yea a fanatical Plymouth Brother. Like the Scottish relatives Charlotte had found uncongenial, Mr Lydall abhorred 'most forms of enjoyment' and was a rigid Sabbatarian. Edward Lydall still recalls how the day started in his grandfather's household, with morning prayers in the dining-room – the patriarch Lydall at the table, the family seated behind him and the servants opposite. At these seances, John Lydall would take advantage of his direct access to the Almighty, 'such phrases as "Lord, thou seest my goings-out and my comings-in" recurring whenever he was thinking what to tell God next'. (Other little Victorians and Edwardians remembered such prayer sessions, when they knelt beside armchairs, as 'smelling the chairs'.)

However, John Lydall's religion was not incompatible with the amassing of a considerable fortune as a solicitor, and more money came with Mary French's dowry. Since Lydall was something of a snob, eager to trace himself 'back to the Conqueror',it would appear that the French genealogy was also much to his liking. At any rate, the two families were to be further connected when Sarah (Nellie) became engaged to his younger brother Wykeham, and for a time Mary Lydall entertained fond hopes that the youngest sister, Katie, would find another Lydall brother as a husband. (Eventually, however, Katie married a Colonel Harley.)

In the meantime, Lottie and Carrie had to find ways of escaping from their born again brother-in-law and so they devoted much of the late 1860s to the most acceptable way of continuing a genteel education – travelling. Languages and culture were seen as inoffensive accomplishments, and the Continent beckoned to young ladies of means. In *Chaste as Ice, Pure as Snow* Mrs Despard describes one such trip made by two young ladies in the company of their aunt chaperon.

My poor aunt! I can hear her now talking about all we should do, the regular hours of study, the steady application. Music was to be taken up in Germany, singing in Italy; languages everywhere. She was far too gentle for the management of such volatile young ladies as we were. Laura and I had pretty much our own way. It was a pleasant time. How intensely we enjoyed the fresh, new life, the constant variety, the enlargement of ideas.

For the first, three-year-long Grand Tour there were three sisters – Carrie, Lottie and Nellie – and, not having an aunt at their disposal, 'a lady was found to accompany us.' In the 1860s the rules of chaperonage were strict. An unmarried woman under thirty could not go anywhere unchaperoned, or even be in a room in her own home with an unrelated man unless accompanied by a married gentlewoman or a servant. An unmarried gentlewoman would not do as a chaperon, though a governess, as an honorary 'spinster', might do. At any rate, it appears that the French sisters abroad with their tame chaperon had pretty much their own way.

The first marathon was very romantic, including Swiss lakes and mountains, the Black Forest, the Rhine and eight weeks in Venice, 'which I remember as a dream of beauty and wonder'. In Milan there were some 'curious adventures in the course of our wanderings', which Mrs Despard does not enlighten us further about. But the novels that later fed from these experiences are full of charming, mysterious foreign gentlemen in pursuit of young ladies, and so we can guess at their nature.

In 1870 – 'a momentous year in the history of the world, and a momentous year in mine' – Carrie and Lottie were in France together without a chaperon. By then Nellie had married her Lydall, and it is a measure of how effectively the remaining older sisters were deemed to have been shelved that they were free to travel together alone. Lottie and Carrie were 'very enthusiastically French', and here something must be said about the long-term consequences of this enthusiasm. French was the language of etiquette and fashion, and it was also something for ladies to be interested in. But this accomplishment incidentally made the internationalism of the later feminist movement all the more feasible. Unlike her 'brothers' in the labour movement, Charlotte Despard could be an Internationalist socialist with ease, attending congresses without the aid of interpreters. Sixty years later, when she was Madame Despard living with Madame

MacBride just outside Dublin, a local bishop expressed his interest in calling on the ladies. Back went a message that they would be happy to receive him but that, since they would not 'sully' their lips with the English tongue, they would only converse in French or Irish. We know that Irish was never mastered by Charlotte Despard, but the French would have presented no problem. Her only brother, who did not enjoy a Grand Tour, had more difficulties when he was trying to liaise with his French military opposite number during the First World War. According to President Poincaré, 'He speaks our tongue with great difficulty.' The suffragists and suffragettes generally had no such problems.

When the Franco-Prussian War broke out Lottie and Carrie hastened down to Paris where the air 'was humming with the Marseillaise, the singing of which had been forbidden for years'. They stayed at a pension where they were 'well known, planning to stay there until the iluminations that were to celebrate the first French victory'. But, 'Alas! no such rejoicings were to be!' and they were still in Paris when news came through of the first French reverse. 'Shortly after that, on the vigorous insistence of our friends, we left Paris.'

Now the Lydall version of this is rather different. According to their records, John Lydall rushed off to Paris on the outbreak of the war and bundled the two renegade sisters home from their 'spree'. Charlotte French never forgave John Lydall for this humiliating 'rescue'. She was to get her revenge by fictionalizing him as the loathsome Mr Robinson in *Chaste as Ice Pure as Snow*. An unscrupulous solicitor, Mr Robinson throws religion into everything and is rather pathetically obsessed with his family tree. 'The quiet ease, the graceful nonchalance, the tone of high breeding, which a fine gentleman possesses, as it were, by instinct, was and would always remain beyond him. And therefore he professed to despise that class.'

Despite his genealogical pretensions John Lydall was definitely bourgeois and relatively self-made. Apart from his religious scruples, he must have been appalled by the headstrong sisters-in-law with their wilful, aristocratic ways. It must be supposed that his own wife, Mary, took after her mother more, perhaps even in terms of the Eccles Presbyterianism. At any rate, she was also fated to die young, of tuberculosis in 1881 at the age of thirty-nine. But the truly venomous portrait of Mr Robinson in *Chaste as Ice, Pure as Snow* is the closest we get to an animated account by Charlotte Despard of someone she obviously disliked. As a mature, secure woman she was, from the biographer's point of view, frustratingly discreet and restrained when it came to anything like gossip.

By 1870 she must have been longing for marriage. Any husband would be better than that brother-in-law breathing down her neck. 'Very young men,' she wrote in that first novel, 'are not, as a rule, passionate admirers of the fair sex.' They were 'full of compassionate condescension', their 'chief cultus is the ego, that is to do and to dare such great things in the untried future'. This tendency, combined with their need to catch up with the more developed minds of young women, would make the ideal husband's age about thirty, with the wife about five years younger. Only then was there a possibility of compatibility. Charlotte Despard was writing here from experience. For in the winter of that momentous year, she found herself a real gentleman to marry.

# CHAPTER 3

# MAXIMILIAN DESPARD: 'AN IDEALLY HAPPY MARRIAGE'

In March 1868 twenty-nine-year-old Maximilian Carden Despard expressed a wish that his husband-hunting youngest sister, Gertrude, would soon hook a 'really good fish'. But, he commiserated, 'they are difficult of finding.' With characteristic self-mockery he added, 'Even the good men of my standing, appearance and fortune are not easily to be attracted into a move for life.' Within a year Gertrude Despard did 'entrap' a fellow 'equestrian' and as Mrs Franks she continued life among the hunting and shooting Irish Quality. No similar destiny seemed likely for her fond brother, who by inclination and physique was decidedly not an outdoor type. But by all the criteria set out in Charlotte Despard's novels, and by her consistently effusive testimonies, Max Despard was an extremely eligible bachelor.

For a start, unlike John Lydall, he was a real Irish gentleman of 'a very ancient and respectable family', which, though it only went back as far as the seventeenth century, complemented the French heritage. The Despards were, to use that unforgettably convenient label, 'Horse Protestants' from the Irish Midland county of Laois, or Queen's County as it was then known. On the male side they produced generations of captains, majors and colonels, military engineers and surveyors, and a sprinkling of Church of Ireland clergymen. But, like many other Anglo-Irish families, they intermarried with their own kind, often with disastrous genetic consequences. No less than three Gertrude Cardens married three George Despards, the last of which marriages produced Maximilian Carden Despard in 1839. Predictably, he was a very delicate child, suffering from a kidney condition that eventually became Bright's Disease. This disability and the absence of any direct or sizeable inheritance in the shape of land meant that Max had to find an untraditional way of matching his pedigree with a suitable income. A clever and determined young man, he went into trade and finance: 'if we had to commence with a true prospect of all future eventualities we would be too disgusted and cast down ever seriously to struggle onward.' Nothing ventured, nothing gained; Max Despard was destined to do both.

Few elites can have been such excellent self-apologists as the Anglo-Irish. They have so successfully attached to themselves as a whole so many of Ireland's most worthy cultural and political achievements that it is sometimes hard to imagine why the natives were so keen on expropriating them. It was from this benign and deeply civilized Irish Raj that Charlotte French liked to think her husband and her new surname came.

But the Despard name had a particular appeal for the Shelley-besotted rebel. One of Maximilian Despard's grand-uncles had been none other than Marcus Despard, the Jacobinical renegade who was hanged and beheaded as a traitor in February 1803 for his part in an aborted republican uprising. As a contemporary pamphlet, in true tabloid style, put it,

> the leading feature of the conspiracy is of so shocking a nature that we cannot insert it without pain and horror. The life of our beloved Sovereign, it seems, was to have been attempted by a division of the conspirators, while the remainder were to attack the Tower and other public places.

Marcus Despard's United Irish sympathies brought him into contact with 'all of the lowest vulgar'. He was to have managed the London end of the plot that was led by Robert Emmet in Dublin. Before this he had enjoyed a distinguished career in the Navy, and Admiral Nelson gave evidence in his defence.

Though not a backwoodsman, grand-nephew Max Despard was no revolutionary. Despite precarious health he made sure he was in the right place at the right time, namely in the Far East in the early 1860s. He went out as the agent of a London shipping firm, and was soon dabbling speculatively on his own behalf in precious stones and in the great opium-tea bonanza. China had been 'opened up' to Western exploitation after the first 'Opium War' of 1839–42, in which Britain crushed a Manchu attempt to stop the opium trade in Canton, then the only point of contact between China and Western money. The resulting Treaty of Nanking (which also gave Britain a foothold in Hong Kong) was the first of a series of unequal agreements that legalized the opium trade and granted trade and territorial rights to Western powers. The way was then clear for British businessmen to sell opium produced in India in exchange for Chinese silks, spices and teas. And young Max Despard was in at the killing.

'If only I could hear from Fitz [his younger brother]', he wrote home from Shanghai in 1864, 'I think that he might make some money by shipping tea from Asia to Victoria [Australia], for the high prices which are paid for such luxuries in that part would leave a tolerably good profit. . . .' The East agreed with Max, and he allayed family anxieties about his health by telling them that he was as 'strong as an ox'. But life in the East was 'dull' so he concentrated on making his fortune. He was shrewd enough to become a founder investor in the Hong Kong & Shanghai Bank, a decision that would ultimately make his widow a rich woman, and by 1868 he was setting himself up in his own right in London.

I have launched into the fresh world of London business and stuck my title over a doorknob – Despard & Company now flourishing in one of the purlieus of the City! I have taken an office, laid in a stock of cigars, and intend to get over some Irish whiskey with which to regale all friends who are likely to transact business with this great merchant! Who knows? Perhaps in a few years time you'll hear of 'the . . . London merchant who commenced on 2/6 but is now worth two millions sterling'! Ain't likely? But, looking afresh, I am really trying my hand and if I only play my cards well I may eventually win the rubber – so here's to success to Despard & Co.

One of the 'rubbers' to be won was marriage which, for a conventional young man of Max Despard's class, implied an income large enough to sustain a substantial, many-servanted household, and unlimited numbers of children. The second half of the nineteenth century saw the much-bewailed phenomenon of the so-called 'surplus women' of the middle classes. These were the single ladies who could not find husbands, and for whom there were virtually no respectable, paying careers. They had to wait on the marriage market for men, who often postponed or abandoned the idea of marrying because of lack of means. Max Despard put off one suitor by telling her that 'the expense of an establishment would weigh me down'. But this must have been a polite rejection because he was simultaneously writing of 'all faces merry as a marriage bell' which, for him, 'at present does not ring'. By the time he met Charlotte French, in 1870 when he was thirty-one, he was capable of marrying in the style which polite society expected. Moreover, Miss French was a modest heiress in her own right so that as a couple they were economically as well as socially compatible.

Soon after that ignominious retreat from Paris she met him at the home of mutual friends in Sussex. These friends may have been associates of her sister Maggie, Mrs Gavin Jones, whose husband was an entrepreneur in the Eastern trade, specifically based in Cawnpore in India. In fact Max Despard invested in Gavin Jones's Muir Mills in Cawnpore. It is possible that Lydall introduced Max to Lottie, but the fact that Lydall disliked Despard intensely makes that unlikely. The Lydall family's image of Max Despard was that of a decidedly shady get-rich-quick character who had made his pile 'supplying dud boots to the soldiery' during the Crimean War. It is hard to recognize the hard-working and sometimes earnest scion of the Irish gentry in this description, though Max does seem to have been a very shrewd businessman.

It must have been a whirlwind courtship, because the marriage took place in the same year, within months of the first meeting. But although Charlotte French had urgent reasons for finding Mr Right, Max Despard had many independent recommendations. He was good-humoured and cultivated, a lover of art, opera and literature – all things frowned upon by those Eccles relatives and John Lydall. When Max Despard learned by letter of his young sister's latest experiments with her hair he wrote, teasingly rather than reprovingly, 'You'll soon rival the Chinese or Japanese beauties who dress their hair, the former in the shape of a butterfly, the latter in the shape of a porcupine. . . .

I hope the suffering necessary . . . will make you repent of your vanity.' Though never a slave to fashion, and indeed a downright ascetic from her widowhood onwards, Charlotte Despard was no puritan and, when he was well enough for them, her beloved husband liked the good things in life.

She revered his intellect, saying that he had 'a much better head for law than many a trained lawyer'. When it came to politics, the Despards were liberal Liberals, supporters of Joseph Chamberlain's radical social policies and of Parnell's campaign for Home Rule for Ireland. Like his wife, Mr Despard was interested in 'questions, and would have answers found' but it was a very sedentary quest. There was no question of giving any public expression to these progressive inclinations. Later, young suffragist friends of Mrs Despard's imagined a discrepancy between her and her late husband on political matters. But, to judge from the perspective of her novels – on such issues as the Indian Mutiny of 1857, for example – Mrs Despard was not herself an outrageous liberal by anything but Lydall standards in the 1870s. For all the serious rebelliousness submerged by a thoroughly respectable front, she was a conventionally progressive woman married to a conventionally progressive man.

Before she set up home as Mrs Maximilian Despard there was one last glorious row to be had with John Lydall. The suspicious solicitor suggested to Charlotte French that she tie up her own money, the Eccles inheritance, in a settlement so that her husband would not automatically own it all, as all husbands did until the Married Women's Property Act of 1882 allowed wives to have independent property. (In fact, Millicent Fawcett, the leader of the constitutional suffrage movement, was partly galvanized by her humiliation when, after her purse had been stolen at Waterloo Station, the thief was charged with stealing 'property of Mr Henry Fawcett'.) Lottie would have none of her brother-in-law's advice, saying, 'I would never marry a man I couldn't trust.' Now since both she and her husband received news of the later Married Women's Property Act with 'solemn exultation', this might seem a surprising reaction, until it is remembered that Lydall, to whom she never spoke again, made no secret of his disapproval of her intended. Moreover, the settlement he recommended was probably not meant on her behalf. Such settlements were usually made by suspicious fathers-in-law as a way of tying up daughters' dowries so that ultimately the money could be kept within the maternal *family's* control. Mr Robinson, alias John Lydall, of *Chaste as Ice, Pure as Snow* is clearly without honourable intentions:

> 'Come now,' he spoke jovially, 'about that fine house of furniture.'
> 'My wife's, I assure you – bought with her money.'
> The lawyer's face fell perceptibly.
> 'Settled then?'
> 'Not precisely, but the same thing; you see it was in fact a wedding present from her father, a man in an excellent position, Mr Robinson.'
> 'Ah!' Mr Robinson showed his teeth, 'law doesn't recognize sentiment, my dear sir – a pity clearly – but so it is. The furniture is yours to dispose of as you will.'

John Lydall showed his teeth to no avail and after their marriage the Despards had as little to do with him and that branch of the family as was politely possible. For their honeymoon, they travelled to Ireland, staying at Westfield House, which was the 'big house' of Gertrude and Matthew Franks. Charlotte Despard liked her in-laws and the Franks were to be lifelong friends. She remembered this first visit to Ireland, and all subsequent ones, with affectionate nostalgia and came increasingly to regard herself as Irish.

For their own household the Despards chose to be in or near London. In due course they purchased 'Courtlands', a large house in a gardenly estate in what was even then a very plush part of Surrey. A photograph from this time, too damaged to be reproduced, shows Mrs Despard in a silk, high-waisted and bustled dress, with luxuriantly braided hair and an expression of benign, reflective intelligence. At Courtlands she cultivated her own garden wilderness, had visiting cards printed and, courtesy of Max's career, offered the finest teas at her 'at homes'. Much later in her life, a suffragette-watcher observed that Mrs Maximilian Despard might have won for herself a position as a leader of society, 'for she has wit, charm, versatility – all that goes to the making of a brilliant social success.' She was established enough in society to be able to offer one motherless Lydall niece, Ethel, a 'coming-out' season in London. But John

Lydall's domestic regime made it impossible for Ethel and her sister to do anything more than minister to their father. Any suitor with nerve enough to make his way to the house was sent packing by the Plymouth Brother, and Ethel turned down her aunt's offer for fear of him. She and her sister diverted themselves by, respectively, practising eurythmics and producing 'plaintive, moaning noises' from a cello. When their father died they celebrated by going to the theatre for the first time in their lives. It was Ethel Lydall who drove Mrs Despard to the count when she stood as a parliamentary candidate for Battersea at the end of 1918.

Aunt Lottie's offer of a season was sincere but it did not mean that she was a committed society lady. After all, as Florence Nightingale pointed out, a single-mindedness about anything else was 'incompatible with the life of "society" '. While her husband carried on making money, Charlotte Despard drilled herself for some worthwhile work. This, of course, was a matter of principle rather than money. When she recalled her 'ideally happy marriage' for a *Guardian* reporter in 1937 she laid great emphasis on her husband's respect for *her* work and its importance for any and every marriage: 'I think it is a mistake for a woman to give up her career in marriage, even when there are children. The very fact that there are children should make a woman more keen to construct a better world for them to live in. . . .'

Since her literary career did not, at least directly, impinge favourably on the welfare of children, Charlotte Despard was probably thinking here about philanthropic or social work. She herself was consistently motivated by her perception of the needs of children, which underwrote all her political work. This commitment was all the more absorbing because of her own childless state. She was twenty-six when she married and it must have been obvious fairly soon that she and Max were not going to have a family. She confided in her prolific sisters and at some stage her sister Maggie Jones, not one to mince words, told her granddaughter that Aunt Lottie's Max was 'impotent'. This debility probably arose from Max's health, which became precarious again quite soon after his marriage. Moreover, as Andro Linklater points out in his biography of Charlotte Despard (*An Unhusbanded Life*), the inbreeding in Max's parentage is likely to have had a drastic effect on his fertility.

So Charlotte Despard had no choice but to be content with a celibate 'marriage of true minds'. She never elevated this into a matter of principle, unlike celibate couples such as Virginia and Leonard Woolf, Beatrice and Sidney Webb, or the Irish Theosophists Gretta and Jim Cousins. The latter couple were explicit about their choice of platonism:

> Something in me revolted then and has ever since protested against, certain of the techniques of nature connected with sex. Nor will I and many men and women of like nature, including my husband, be satisfied, be purified and redeemed, life after life, until the evolution of form has substituted some more artistic way of continuance of the race.

Jim Cousins improvised a swimming costume for himself on a deserted beach and Gretta Cousins couldn't even look at children without recalling the 'shocking circumstances' that had brought about their existence. If Charlotte Despard shared feelings like these, she never expressed them. It seems likely that had she had vehement feelings about sex *per se*, she would have been enthusiastic about Christabel Pankhurst's later purity crusade.

She satisfied herself in the early years of her marriage by being a doting aunt for her multitude of nieces and nephews, for whom she organized massive picnics and outings. Although some adults could perceive her as forbidding, at least in appearance, she never seems to have had any problems with children. Just as her military brother had a way with his ordinary soldiers, so she had an abiding gift with children, of every class and any nationality. To this day, Sir Michael Tippett, whose mother was a cousin of Mrs Despard's and also a prominent suffragette, recalls Charlotte Despard as an especially 'kind aunt'.

But she first made a name for herself as a writer, an occupation that could travel with her and Max. He was only well in England in summer and so for the rest of the year they travelled. There were trips to North America, cruises in the Mediterranean and extended visits to India, where she had her sister Maggie and they both had many friends. Writing was not a surprising choice of distraction for a nineteenth-century lady of means. Then, as now, women were avid readers of fiction, and a corresponding importance, even a political importance, was attached to that taste. The pioneering Irish trade unionist Louie Bennett, who was born in 1870, started her public life as the author of *The Proving of Priscilla* and *A Prisoner of His Word*. At a time when there were precious few role models for women with worldly ambition, for aspiring writers there were the Brontë sisters and George Eliot. Fuelled as she had been by literary rebels such as Shelley, it was almost inevitable that Mrs Despard should have first expressed her own rebelliousness in works of popular fiction.

It must be said that the seven published Despard novels are not in the Brontë-Eliot class, possibly because their author's high-mindedness overwhelmed all other urges. In fact, they are very hard going and one can only be thankful that Charlotte Despard's literary career was a short one. They represent precisely the type of 'three-volume novel' of 'more than usually revolting sentimentality' which Oscar Wilde pokes fun at in *The Importance of Being Earnest*. Miss Prism, the author of the work found by Lady Bracknell in the pram instead of her nephew, explains, 'The good ended happily, and the bad unhappily. That is what fiction means.' Mrs Despard's fictions reached their readers through the private circulating libraries, chiefly Mudies, which catered for leisured lady readers. With a bit of drastic editing they would fulfill the requirements of modern formula romances. Take this for a reunion between a young Rajah and his golden-haired Grace: 'He rushed forward, flung himself on his knees beside the couch, and, with a look of infinite yearning, held out his arms. For a moment she drew back, in the next his love had conquered.'

Mrs Despard's heroines invariably have faces 'pure as an angel's', 'bell-like' voices and 'sparkling eyes'. Their male counterparts are impetuous young men, made into perfect gentlemen by the vicissitudes encountered in the course of wooing their angels. These ladies and gentlemen often boast mysterious parentage. Like Clara Dering of *Outlawed* they are 'the inheritor from unknown parents of unusual talents, unusual beauty, and exceptional physique'. And just to gild the lily of their beauty and accomplishments, they usually end up with great wealth. Jonas Sylvester, of the novel of the same title, finds treasure 'enough and more to restore the shattered fortunes of the Sylvesters'; while the Rajah's heir manages to set up his worthy old mother in style, in a mansion of his own design, though 'folks say' that she prefers the humble cottage. Here are the young lovers of *Wandering Fires* – their romance having been thwarted by a series of melodramatic misfortunes – reunited at last on a gondola in Venice:

> 'Erick,' said the young girl softly, 'I am *too* happy. I feel as if my heart would break.'
> 'Eat,' he answered, 'eat, my love, and your heart will find room for this happiness and more.'
> He steeped a roll in the milk and offered it to her piece by piece. They might have been little children in their simplicity; and very childlike were the sympathic lookers-on – the two gondoliers, who loved their young master, and would have gone through fire and water for his beautiful lady, and the kindly Italian matron, whose rosy, sunburnt face hid a warm and tender heart.'

Mrs Despard's novels abound with racial and cultural stereotypes. The Irish characters are usually kind, lively and humorous, the French and Russian ones mercurial, the Italian ones irrepressible, and so on. In *Chaste as Ice, Pure as Snow* we are reminded that L'Estrange, the abductor of a misunderstood young 'widow's' only child, is not an Englishman: 'There is, I think, a certain oneness of nature about the Anglo-Saxon race, that renders it very difficult for its members to understand the emotional, impulsive, two-sided character of the Celt, the Latin or the Greek.' Mrs Despard's plots are thickened with abductions, cases of mistaken identity, ecstatic reunions and swooning death scenes, and the locations would delight any modern commercial film-maker. They range from London slums to Cornish castles, from Swiss chalets to tsarist palaces and, in *The Rajah's Heir*, include azure-blue miniature lakes and glistening pavilions. Virtue is frequently signalled by flowers, the heroines being particularly fond of arranging and sniffing them.

These romances offered Mrs Despard an outlet for her finest feelings. Like so many of her heroines, she was undergoing what might today be called a 'personal growth'. As early as *Chaste as Ice, Pure as Snow* (1874), when she was probably still smarting from memories of Presbyterian Sundays and John Lydall, she wrote of the character Adèle,

Her religion was the growth of her loving heart; she had no particular doctrines, for so-called theology always seemed too hard to be understood; but she believed, in the full simplicity and truth of her young soul, what many religionists, by their harsh doctrine, practically deny – that God, the Father of all spirits, is a merciful God.

By the 1880s this compassionate agnosticism was evolving into something more consciously eclectic, and in all probability Mrs Despard's mystical journey matched her awareness of Max's fragility. While in India with him she devoured as much as she could of Buddhist thought, finding particular solace in the theory of the transmigration of souls.

Her Indian experiences found expression in her most successful novel, *The Rajah's Heir*, which was published in 1890 and enjoyed a critical success, with citations in the *Saturday Review* and the *Pall Mall Gazette* as one of the books of the year. Basically, the soul of an old Indian Rajah enters the body of a young Englishman as part of a divine plan whereby the unlikely heir will combine in him a Western education and an Eastern sensibility. In claiming his extraordinary legacy the heir comes to self-knowledge (and great wealth), and, in addition to the love interest, the Indian Mutiny is an enlivening background. The young Rajah's courtship of one Grace is frustrated by the fact that, of course, her parents don't realize that he has such exotic 'prospects'. In any case she dies fairly soon after the romance's ecstatic non-consummation. But before Grace expires, as beautifully as expected, she relays the truths imparted to her by the Hindu priest, Vishnugupta. He has told her that there is going to be a new Redeemer, for which the world should prepare by 'slaying the self':

He says they have known it here for thousands of years. . . .
They are expecting another revealer. He will be different from any who have gone before him, for the sphere will be larger. New lights have been dawning upon the nations, and new truths, forced painfully from the silence by the higher minds, are waiting to be shown to the people. He will know all this. He will be of the West by his training, of the East by his nature. He will have the science and learning of the New World, and the self-forgetting passion of the Old.

Grace's reverie was in tune with the 'alternative' atmosphere of the late nineteenth century. In Britain a vogue for Eastern religious thought found expression in the popularity of the Theosophical movement. This organization had been co-founded by Helena Blavatsky, a Russian woman once described by W. B. Yeats as being like a 'sort of peasant Irish woman with an air of humour and gay audacity' (by James Joyce as 'a nice bag of tricks'). Whatever her charlatan qualities, Madame Blavatsky had a great gift for synthesis. The impact of Darwinism on traditional Christianity had left a vacuum and the Theosophical fusion of elements of Buddhist and Hindu thought with an ecumenical Christian morality filled it for many. It was also sensational in a period when detailed knowledge of other cultures was not yet generally available. It is hard to describe a phenomenon as vague as Theosophy, but, broadly speaking, the movement had three aims. First, there was the object of universal brotherhood; second, the comparative study of religion, philosophy and science as 'interdependent phases of the Life within all lives'; and, third, the study of the 'deeper laws of nature and their application in the development of one's powers beyond the present normal. . . .' Such was Theosophy's appeal that when Madame Blavatsky died in 1891 there were 100,000 avowed members of her movement and a paper that sold in London, New York and Paris. Her leading disciple, and eventual heir, was Mrs Annie Besant, another household name of the late nineteenth century.

Mrs Besant (who pronounced her surname to rhyme with 'pleasant' so as to further separate herself from a very nasty ex-husband) 'converted' to Theosophy after reviewing Blavatsky's *The Secret Doctrine*. Before her Theosophical career took off she had had two successive careers in the secularist and socialist movements. Like Mrs Despard, she rejected notions of the Almighty as a power 'indifferent to the pain of sentient beings' and she had always experienced herself as a rebellious woman. She was also of part Irish extraction and Charlotte Despard, who was alert to Annie Besant's every move and who later got to know her, must have been aware of many personal parallels with her own development. Indeed, it is not going too far from the evidence, of which none is concrete, to say that had Charlotte French not met her Max there is every reason to suppose that she might have come out earlier in her life as an outlaw like Mrs Besant. There had been a paucity of challenging female role models for unconventional young women in Charlotte Despard's youth. But middle age offered the inspiring progress of Annie Besant.

Although her incessantly travelling lifestyle made it difficult for Charlotte Despard to be more than a long-distance recruit to fin-de-siècle mysticism, it was a sympathy that could be pursued in relative isolation. In fact the psychic aspect of the business positively demanded isolation. The Cousinses were enchanted by Theosophy, eventually going off to India themselves, and Jim Cousins was an unusually supportive husband when it came to his wife's special psychic gifts. He bought his Gretta a planchette one Christmas. This castor-mounted board was bought by many Victorians as a game (ouija board), but for Gretta Cousins and Mrs Despard it was an 'accessory to enquiry'. Experimenting with a purple pen, Gretta found that she could be 'used' by some extraneous force for the 'receiving of interpretations of myths, Bible stories, visions and what were called communications on general matters, and illuminations on higher matters'.For example, the planchette told Gretta that St Paul's attitude towards women was 'intelligible' if Corinthians was read as a 'symbolical and psychologically wise' instruction to bring the formulating intellect (symbolically the husband) to the aid of the receiving intuition (the wife) for expression.

To her credit, Mrs Despard never tried to rehabilitate St Paul on her planchette, preferring to remind people that 'by his own admission he sometimes "spoke foolishly".' The spirits who chatted with Mrs Despard were unusual, chiefly Mazzini and Garibaldi. (Confused perhaps by her rather Sibylline references to such communications some of Charlotte Despard's friends thought that she had actually met with these higher minds.) But, as yet, the planchette was Charlotte Despard's private eccentricity, perhaps an accessory in her psychological preparations for Max's imminent death. He was clearly drifting over to what she called 'the other side' and on the return voyage from India in 1890 his condition deteriorated rapidly. At Tenerife he was taken ashore, only to be put aboard the next England-bound ship, on which he died on Good Friday, April 1890. To the rest of Charlotte Despard's days Good Friday retained an extra quota of tragic significance and she never spoke of her husband without a prefix of affectionate lamentation.

# CHAPTER 4

# WIDOWHOOD AND PHILANTHROPY: 'A VERY NOBLE-MINDED ROMAN CATHOLIC LADY'

The Victorian cult of mourning reached its height from about 1870 to 1880, and the conventions attached to it were still powerful in the year of Mrs Despard's bereavement. Widows went into the deepest and longest mourning. 'First mourning', which meant all black clothes, sometimes covered with crepe, no jewellery and a widow's cap with veil, lasted for a year and a day; 'second mourning', black with less crepe and possibly jet ornaments, lasted for the next twelve months; while the third year saw the introduction of grey or mauve to the basic black. Thereafter, some widows chose to remain in mourning for the rest of their lives, but this was not necessarily a measure of their grief. An aunt of the writer Laurence Housman (brother of the Shropshire lad), who was 'well over seventy years of age', confided that she found her weeds 'such a protection'. From what, Housman condescendingly failed to enquire, but we can suggest that his aunt might have found in her mourning outfit a convenient turn-off to wealth-hunting suitors.

One very welcome dimension of the widow's status was the relative freedom that came with it. A widow was often economically, to a large extent socially, independent, without any of the opprobrium still attached to spinsters. And widowhood suited

Charlotte Despard well because the conventions of mourning complemented her slaying of the self. From 1890 until the end of her life she wore extremely plain, often black clothes and instead of the hat, which was almost a biological female characteristic, a flowing black lace mantilla crowned her head. Her clothes, and particularly the dramatic mantilla, are the first things that anyone who met her ever mentions. Margaret Bondfield and Teresa Billington-Greig were enthusiastic about her strangely appealing clothes and her 'tall, straight figure'. As a child growing up in Surrey, Vera Ryder remembered the 'shiny white hair, which shone through a flowing black chiffon veil' and the sandalled feet which peeped out from beneath 'voluminous black skirts' – 'really most attractive for a "witch" '. These sandals, of which more later, and the mantilla became for Mrs Despard the saintly socialist what the wheel is to St Catherine.

Her friends celebrated the 'chosen simplicity' of her unconventional clothes, but most of her relatives were not so sanguine. Even today, one grand-niece remembers the horrified reaction to Aunt Lottie's appearance at a family wedding, shuffling down the aisle in her sandals and hygienic robes. But this reaction must be seen against well-bred fin-de-siècle ladies' taste for conspicuous consumption. Mrs Despard emerged as a secular nun in a period when hats were enormous edifices requiring servants to hoist them on, when ostrich feathers, bustles and quantities of lace were *de rigueur* and when outfits were changed for morning, afternoon and evening, as well as for outdoor and indoor activities.

But it should be pointed out that for all her ascetic Bohemianism, Mrs Despard was never slovenly. Every week she had a professional shampoo at an expensive hairdressing establishment and from the crown of her head to her naked toes she was always immaculately groomed. She took a tepid bath first thing every morning and Alice Schofield Coates, who went with her to a Labour Party conference in 1917, remembers her companion's reaction when their landlady responded to a request for a bath by having a conventionally hot one filled: 'She was not pleased.' Sean MacBride, who only knew Mrs Despard as an old lady, also recalled how, even in the woolly socks that she wore in winter with her sandals, she was a paragon of neatness. Once a lady, always a lady.

In the immediate aftermath of Max's death, Mrs Despard's appearance did not perturb her relatives unduly because she did not go out at all. She was so grief-stricken that she shut herself away at Courtlands and communicated only with the great souls encountered by means of the planchette. By her own account, she was first pulled out of this lonely reverie by the Duchess of Albany. This august personage was installed at magnificent Claremount and, in the environs of Esher, passed for a neighbour. A servant in full livery, green tailcoat with gleaming buttons and cockaded top-hat, stood to attention at the gates of Claremount, where the Princess Charlotte had died in childbirth in 1817.

The Duchess was herself a more conventional widow; in Vera Ryder's words, a 'stout, dumpy, old lady in a black silk dress and a black bonnet'. But she knew just the thing to drag Mrs Despard back into society. Weren't women, as another popular, though more famous, woman novelist, Mrs Humphrey Ward, had put it, 'made for charity'? Sustained activities of the charitable kind had not been possible for Mrs Despard on account of her peripatetic married life, but she had in the past obliged the Duchess's project, which was called the Nine Elms Flower Mission. Her Grace now asked Mrs Despard to become one of her horticultural missioners, kind ladies with enormous gardens who delivered hampers of flowers to the people of a slum in Battersea, south London. This suggestion amounted to a royal command, and Mrs Despard was a keen gardener, so she climbed out of herself and got involved with the real world again.

The Nine Elms Flower Mission is only intelligible in terms of a Victorian debate about how the well-off could get through the eye of the needle without actually encouraging the poor to be paupers. This debate had been won by the Charity Organization Society, which saw its role as the checking of 'superfluous effort' and 'untrained emotions' when it came to philanthropy. The rich had to be restrained from spontaneous hand-outs to beggars and dossers. Instead, actual funds should be channelled to the 'deserving', that is seriously vetted, poor through the Charity Organisation Society. Meanwhile, the 'undeserving' – people who didn't measure up in terms of middle-class morality, such as widows who cohabited with men, or alcoholics – would be left to the untender mercies of the Poor Law, that is, the workhouse. But flowers wouldn't 'demoralize' the poor, and by placing them in humble homes the horticultural lady missioners incidentally had an opportunity of observing how deserving they were.

As a young girl in York Charlotte French had visited local slums, and as a rebellious young Miss in London she had ventured to the East End.

> How bitterly ashamed I was of it all! How ardently I longed to speak to these people in their misery, to say, 'Why do you bear it? Rise as the men and women of Argolis did under Saon and Cythna. Smite your oppressors. Be true and strong!' Of course I was much to shy to say anything of the sort. I returned home feeling useless and wretched.

She tried to feel more useful and less wretched by inserting her political feelings into her novels, even the most unabashedly romantic of them. But one in particular, *A Voice from the Dim Millions* (1884), gives an indication of how inevitable Charlotte Despard's later career was. This novella purports to be the 'true history of a working-woman', simply 'edited' by Mrs M. C. Despard:

> God knows this is no fiction I am telling. God knows that lives sadder than ours are being lived out every day. Here – in this rich, and free, and prosperous country – men and women groan daily in a slavery from which there is no rescue but death.

The setting for this multiple case history is Nine Elms and, one by one, the working-woman's family is picked off by injustices such as the sweatshop system, disease, cyclical unemployment, drink and prostitution. But it would not be a Despard novel without a reasonably happy ending, however tempered by ghastly experiences. With her 'fallen' but now redeemed sister the working-woman ends up as co-manager of a model sewing shop:

> We are told by some that we are spoiling the labour market. I may be very unphilosophical; but when ever I hear that said,

I am seized with an ardent wish to have a large enough business to spoil it for good and all.

Charlotte Despard's sensitivity to such 'social questions' as the sweating system or the ravages of unemployment was not unique. Indeed the social and economic crisis of the 1880s, which saw the rise of new unions for the unskilled and the mobilization of unemployed workers in London, also saw a great 'consciousness of sin' among the better-off. Like Charlotte French, Beatrice Webb, née Potter, was an intelligent heiress and she took to 'social work' to salve her conscience. By day she 'East-Ended' as a lady rent collector in a model housing project, by night she West-Ended as her widower father's hostess. Soon she was helping her cousin's husband, Charles Booth, in his monumental survey of *London Life and Labour*. This enormously detailed survey began as a response to the socialist H. M. Hyndman's contention that one quarter of London's population was destitute. Using COS criteria, and data collected by COS agents, Booth eventually had to agree that the problem was even worse. In some parts of London, such as Tower Hamlets, 35 per cent of the population could be described in sober 'scientific' terms as destitute. All of this data was then mapped, the streets in black being 'lowest class', those in blue 'very poor' and those in pale blue suffering 'moderate poverty'.

The area to which Charlotte Despard brought her hampers of flowers was very black on Charles Booth's map. The population of the district known as Battersea had increased from nearly 7,000 in 1841 to nearly 169,000 in 1901. It was bounded to the north by the Thames, to the east by Wandsworth, to the west by Vauxhall, and to the vaguely defined south by Tooting, and Nine Elms was its poorest slum. It was said that you could smell Battersea before you saw it, and the Battersea that smelled was the Nine Elms part. Here, the air was heavy with coal dust and greasy with fumes from the railway depot, the gasworks and local industries. The men were chiefly employed in railway jobs and at the gasworks; the women at the cigar, pencil, soap and candle factories, as well as in the laundries. (Gasworkers' wives took to laundry work in summer when their men were slack, while builders' wives took over in the winter.)

Charles Booth's investigator described Mrs Despard's fief as a place of 'very degraded poverty'.

The houses are two-storey and flush with the pavement, with no backs to speak of. The streets, with the exception of a bit here and a bit there, all show the usual signs of squalor in an exaggerated form: broken windows, filthy cracked plaster, dirty ragged children and drink-sodden women. Several of the children were without shoes and stockings, one girl of five with nothing on but a shirt (it was summer), and the police say it is quite common to see small children running about stark naked. The place is almost completely isolated. In hot weather the people often bring out mattresses and sleep in the open, for the houses swarm with vermin.

Many of the inhabitants were old residents. Some families have been here ever since the streets were made, about thirty or forty years ago. Engaged on the railway, or at the gasworks, many of the men, though perhaps irregularly employed, earn good wages; others are costermongers of the unsatisfactory class who take to street selling as a last resource. Destitution, when it occurs, is usually the result of drink.

Mrs Despard first rented a house on the Wandsworth Road, near but not in Nine Elms proper. She gradually integrated herself with the local slum-dwellers through the children, for whom she funded and staffed (with a nurse) a drop-in clinic on the ground floor of this house. But this first-aid was only the tip of the iceberg and before long she was running a full-scale community centre. At first the Nine Elms women resisted help because they thought it only natural to have 'borne twelve and buried seven'. But they soon lost their suspicions, so that in addition to a youth club and clinic, Mrs Despard was hosting 'mothers' meetings', providing good food cheaply and arranging for baby equipment – cots, layettes and so on – to circulate around the neighbourhood.

When the first Despard Club was established, another was started up. In 1891 a corner house fell vacant in Currie Street, which was right in the middle of the Nine Elms rookery. She bought this, moved in and began to live above her 'shop'. She was, on her own rather than on any COS-determined initative, gradually building up what amounted to a mini welfare state for the area. Her fame became more than local when Mr Booth's investigator into 'religious influences' made his report on her clubs in 1898:

> Mrs Despard, a very noble-minded Roman Catholic lady, gives her life to these people, and especially to the young among them, and the people recognize her devotion. The boys' club she has made her home: or, perhaps, one might better say, her home is their club. She does not find them unmanageable. They submit readily to her gentle force. 'You hurt me,' cried a big strong fellow, but he did not resist when she took him by the arm in the cause of order. She laments the stunted growth of the lads and the early age at which they become their own masters. They are allowed to smoke in the club; it might be better for their growth that they should not, but they will have their 'fags' and it is felt that to forbid smoking would be unwise. There is a Sunday 'conference', which, although religion has to be run lightly, is in fact a Bible-class. In truth the work is ostensibly more social than religious in character, and there is no trace of the propagandist spirit, for, though herself a recent convert, Mrs Despard never proselytises, and the representative of the Church of England himself says that if some do adopt her religion it is from admiration of her character.

Mrs Despard had chosen to live her 'simple life' not in some rural Tolstoyan commune but in an urban wilderness. But it was not surprising that by 1898 Catholicism had been added to her very individual cluster of belief-systems. To some extent her conversion was an anti-Establishment gesture, congenial to one who had grown up to resent Protestant fundamentalism. There was even a nascent feminism to her conversion because before *Humanae Vitae* the Catholic Church was less easily identifiable as a virulently patriarchal version of Christianity. It allowed, via the cult of the Virgin Mother, for the centrality of women and of womanly values in religious discourse.Most importantly, Charlotte Despard's new faith, which was always discreet and never very strict doctrinally, brought her closer to her overwhelmingly Irish neighbours.

Booth's investigator noted that Battersea as a whole lacked alien foreigners, 'except for a few chance waiters and German bakers', but Nine Elms was one of Britain's many 'Little Irelands'. Mrs Despard found her Irish women friends' way of dealing with their own regular bereavements very comforting, the fact that, as she makes an Irish character in one of her novels say, 'We can laugh with the tears on our faces; and I thank God for it.' The narrator of *A Voice from the Dim Millions*, which probably was inspired by Mrs Despard's first taste of Nine Elms through the flower mission, marries a sober, second-generation Irishman called Gerry, whose accent 'had none of the vulgarity which we disliked in the people around us'. From the start Mrs Despard's attitude towards the slum Irish was very different from that of, say, Margaret Wynne Nevinson in the East End:

> The Irish, we found, fully lived up to their reputation as difficult tenants. I learnt by bitter experience not to believe in their optimism. They were always expecting work or money, if only they might rub a week longer. 'And what a beautiful baby yours is, Madam. . . .'

Simply doing her job as a lady rent collector Nevinson often got the considerable 'length of their tongues', but Mrs Despard would appear to have had a happier relationship, possibly because of her sympathy with Ireland to start with and even more so on account of her religion.

Mrs Despard's opinion matched that of the Battersea priest who told Mr Booth's investigator that his Irish flock were very 'independent', that they did not beg much and that serious crime was rare. When crime did occur, alcohol was usually behind it, and on this issue Mrs Despard was almost vehement: one of the villains in *A Voice from the Dim Millions* is a shebeen-keeper and she frequently describes the impact of the demon drink as a 'maddening poison', particularly on the Irish. According to her, drink and gambling were the local vices,

> and the quarrelling apt to follow excessive drinking make up, she says, the greater part of the indictment that could be brought; although we hear once more of the curse of 'loaning'. Some of the worst harpies are women who make it their business to tempt others, generally younger than themselves, first to drink and then to borrow.

Like so many other radicals of her day, including Keir Hardie,

Mrs Despard was an enthusiastic advocate of temperance, but even as she dealt with the 'soaker' women around her there was a decided absence of squeamishness. This attitude contrasted with Margaret Wynne Nevinson's, who put in two years as a voluntary 'good example' slum-dweller in the East End:

> No one can stand it for long, especially in Buildings. The uncouth ugliness, the noise, the smells, the sense of countless multitudes of men, women and children, all jammed together in indecent proximity, above all, the triumphant march of vermin, produce a sense of nausea and disgust. The longing for silence, for windswept plains, for the sea and the green things upon the earth becomes almost an obsession.

Mrs Despard's visitors from the genteel world marvelled at her survival in malodorous Nine Elms, but she always kept a country bolt-hole for herself. For the first years she had Courtlands to retire to at weekends and, when her brother and his family occupied that mansion, she had her own cottage in its grounds. Lottie's new vocation and her absorption in Battersea affairs was very convenient for her brother's family in the early 1890s. But she was entirely glad that this was so. Her always especially affectionate relationship with Jack had deepened since he too had fallen foul of his Lydall big brother-in-law. In the year of Charlotte's marriage, John French had left the navy in order to enter the army. Though a desertion of the immediate paternal tradition, this transfer was in keeping with the French family sense of Irishness. Not only did the Anglo-Irish Ascendancy act as a stable for officers, but by that paradox whereby the victims of empires become its defenders, something like 14 per cent of the British Army's rank and file was Irish-born in 1891.

But John French's decision was frowned upon because, unlike naval officers, army officers were not expected to live on their pay. Although he had inherited an Eccles fortune, John French dissipated much of it in various sporting and amorous adventures, and even pawned the family silver. Of all army careers, the cavalryman's life was notoriously extravagant, and that was what Jack wanted. He tried to join a flash Irish regiment, the 8th Hussars, but, possibly because he was not tall enough, he ended up in the 19th Hussars. For part of the 1880s this regiment was based in Ireland, where the hunting and steeplechasing

French was in his element and probably became friendly with Mrs Despard's in-laws. One of his duties while in Ireland was giving military protection to the volunteers who made the notorious Captain Boycott's hay in the summer of 1880. Charlotte and Maximilian Despard probably felt ambiguous about that particular duty, but they frequently helped Jack financially, and this show was to run and run.

What finally alienated the prudent John Lydall from his wife's only brother was the decidedly furtive and definitely unsuitable marriage that he made in 1875. Lydall rescued French from this *mésalliance* by finding a 'co-respondent' for the obligingly 'guilty' (and presumably well-paid) first wife and so securing a divorce. But this incident permanently and inalienably soured relations between Jack and John Lydall, so that their respective children were brought up to regard each other's families as 'not nice to know'. For all his later success, John Lydall could only perceive John French as a 'sorry fellow'. But the whole divorce episode was very efficiently covered up and John French soon made a very suitable marriage to a 'Belle of Bletchley', one Eleanora Selby-Lowndes. But he was not a solidly married man for long. His roving eye, especially for tall, dark women, still got him into hot water.

John French's family settled in Courtlands when the 19th Hussars were posted to India, where the climate was considered unsuitable for English children who were in any case usually educated in the home country. But by the summer of 1893 French was back on half-pay and under a cloud. After an affair with the wife of a fellow officer, which gave a new resonance to the term 'French leave', he was cited as the co-respondent in the ensuing divorce case. With his family at Courtlands he was therefore at something of a loose end and made up for the absence of horses by learning to ride a bicycle and generally doing his bit as a good family man.

The family installed at Courtlands was obliged to humour Aunt Lottie's schemes, even when they meant regular invasions by her Nine Elms friends on the outings she arranged. This is the recollection of one of her nephews:

> It was certainly amusing to some extent, but it had its trying side. For instance, they came equipped with several barrel organs, which of course they never ceased playing from the

time of their arrival to their departure. Their womenfolk accompanied them, and dancing went on during the greater part of the day on the lawns and on the drive. My father, if I remember rightly, threw himself nobly into the breech and helped to organize sports for the men. He possessed a most acute sense of humour and I think he was more amused than anyone at the extraordinary antics of the invaders of our peace and quietness. They swarmed all over the place, and when evening came and they set out on the return journey to London, we at any rate were not sorry that the entertainment had at last come to an end.

John French's good humour matched his sister's, for they both had the common touch. Though his military expertise is still a matter of debate, it has always been agreed that soldiers liked French and that he had a way with them. Ditto for Lottie, who always got along with 'ordinary people' despite her aristocratic bearing and clipped accent. In his momumental *Outcast London* Gareth Stedman Jones suggests that the hard-headed 'professionalism' of the Charity Organisation Society partly derived from the overwhelmingly middle-class background of its instigators and administrators. Lawyers, businessmen, doctors and clergymen approached the problem of poverty and pauperism in a business-like, cost-effective way. This contrasted with the more open-handed paternalism of the rural upper classes, who at some level actually knew their local paupers. Indeed, the massive social problems of the East End and areas like Nine Elms were sometimes blamed on the absence of supervisory local elites. So Mrs Despard's establishment in Nine Elms can be seen as an imitation of the rural order, and her attitude towards her constituents was correspondingly less censorious, less distrustful than that of professional middle-class women such as Margaret Wynne Nevinson or Beatrice Webb (née Potter). Her situation was always going to be one of giving and hoping, rather than one of giving and insisting.

It was her sympathetic brother who, in 1892, escorted Charlotte Despard to the door of the Wandsworth hall where she made her first public speech to a large audience. As he turned to leave her she was overcome by nervousness and told him that she wished to return home. But he nudged her in, saying, 'Only nervous people are ever of any real use.' This was the beginning of a new public identity, one which her darling brother would gradually find it less easy to support her in.

# CHAPTER 5

# SOCIALISM AND THE WORKHOUSE: 'IS THERE NOTHING BUT THE BUTCHER?'

Mrs Despard never rested on her philanthropic laurels. Battersea's secular Mother Theresa felt that she was caring for children whose general deprivation derived from the brutal contradictions of capitalism as much as from deficiencies in the milk of human kindness. But just as she never preached her religion, so she preferred to apply her increasingly radical politics as practically as she could. In the Booth report on the Despard boys' clubs, the socialist dimension of the 'noble-minded lady's' good works is only hinted at: 'As the boys become men the problem of "after" presses upon her. She is something like the possessor of a pet lamb who wonders what is to be done when it is a sheep. Is there nothing but the butcher?'

Wealth and cast-iron respectability gave Mrs Despard access to local workhouses, the abattoirs of late Victorian society. She first entered the workhouse as a lady 'visitor' to the elderly inmates, a role which was akin to that of the Duchess of Albany's flower missioners. With its associated infirmary, mental asylum and children's homes, the workhouse was still the only welfare safety net for the poor, whether 'able-bodied' or not. In practice the Poor Law catered for the aged, the sick, the disabled, for children and their mothers. The inoperable rigidity of the Charity Organisation Society's division between the 'deserving' and the 'undeserving' was shown by the plight of old people. A good half of the respectable poor over the age of sixty ended their lives in the workhouse, the majority of them women (as indeed the majority of adult recipients of Poor Law Relief were) because although subject to chronic ailments, they still had a longer life expectancy than men. The 50 per cent who were not driven to the workhouse were not necessarily any better off. When old age pensions for 'deserving' over-seventy-year-olds were introduced in 1908 the demand far exceeded official estimates, causing Lloyd George to comment on 'a mass of poverty and destitution which is too proud to wear the badge of pauperism'.

Whatever the dire circumstances that sent individual paupers through the workhouse gates, once inside they were subject to a punitive regime. The over-sixties were separated from those younger, women from men, boys from girls, and all children over the age of two from their mothers. Life was controlled by the bells that tolled for work, meals and rest. The inmates had to wear their paupers' uniforms and they could not leave the premises, or even receive visitors, without written permission from the authorities.

To live up to its deterrent reputation as a place of last resort, the workhouse kept its able-bodied inmates busy: stone-breaking, wood-chopping, corn-grinding and general maintenance work for the men; domestic work, sewing and oakum-picking for women. Oakum-picking, the beating and unravelling of pieces of old rope to make a re-usable loose hemp, was the most ignominious work of all. Unmarried mothers and prostitutes were often delegated to this most shameful task. As a Poor Law Guardian, Mrs Despard was to ensure that skilled needlewomen were not put to oakum-picking when the taskmistress had nothing else to offer. Even fit old people were employed, though as helpers in the kitchen and supervisors of child inmates, they could enjoy the wider contacts afforded by their chores. Despite an increase in specialized provision for children, old people and lunatics, the workhouse of *Oliver Twist* was alive and well in the 1890s.

Mrs Despard's friends in the Independent Labour Party (founded in 1893) persuaded her that she could serve the socialist cause well as a member of the Lambeth Board of Guardians, within whose jurisdiction the Wandsworth Road premises fell. (The Currie Street centre lay within the Wandsworth Poor Law Union.) Local Guardians were elected every three years by ratepayers. In 1894 the property qualification for Guardian candidates was abolished and though this did not affect the wealthy Mrs Despard's eligibility, it meant that she stood as the Guardian for the Vauxhall section of the Lambeth Union at a time when many more women, and some working men, were also intervening in the administration of the Poor Law. In fact, she had served as a Guardian for Esher in 1892–93, but had resigned after a year of less than whole-hearted involvement with a Poor Law Union whose problems were far less urgent than those pressing upon the Lambeth Union, which was the largest in London.

When Mrs Despard went to her first meeting of the Lambeth Board of Guardians in January 1895, she was armed with her knowledge of the workhouse system from its consumers' point of view, and she meant business. But what a tedious, undynamic (and unpaid) business it was. With the long weekly meetings of the full Board, the sub-committee meetings and the inspections and the rounds of local institutions, the active Guardian had what amounted to a full-time job. By the mid–1890s the Poor Law Unions were divided between those trying systematically to limit relief; those who stuck to their old, and in rural areas often more relaxed ways; and those Unions adopting more generous policies. Poplar in East London was becoming celebrated, or notorious, for paying 'outdoor relief' (i.e. not in the workhouse) to respectable able-bodied paupers such as widows, deserted wives and unemployed men. But there was little chance of 'Poplarism' in the Lambeth Union, which was known for its illiberalism and its inefficiency. Among fellow Guardians who were at best philanthropically minded, at worst local 'wire-pullers', and most concerned with keeping the poor rates down, Mrs Despard was alone. George Lansbury, a Poplar Guardian, confessed that it was a 'mystery' to him why the 'Guardians of the Poor' were so called when they were really Guardians of the Law. Another woman Guardian in another urban Union, Margaret Wynne Nevinson, described the job as 'always saying no when you would rather say yes'. Mrs Despard rarely wanted to say 'no'. But to extract the odd 'yes' from her Board she had to prove her benign instincts in terms of efficiency. Frank Briant, a fellow socialist, who joined her as a Guardian on the Lambeth Board in 1898, recalled how they struggled together to get the better of 'corruption'. He described

Mrs Despard as his 'chaperon' on the Board, for she was then a 'veteran' of three years, from whom he learnt 'that supreme form of courage which does not falter in the face of over-whelming opposition'.

Female eligibility for Poor Law Guardianship in a period when women were denied political citizenship seems surprising until it is remembered that 'lady Guardians' were often seen as housekeepers for the ratepayers. A sense of thrift and managerial expertise, which the clubs and clinic showed that Mrs Despard, had, were in theory very welcome. At her first meeting she duly proposed that the lady Guardians constitute 'a separate committee for the control of purely domestic matters'. That upstart suggestion was shot down but it was Mrs Despard who brought to the Board's attention the 'inferior' material bought for workhouse shirting, which would be 'worthless after once washing'; who commented on the rotten potatoes served out at Infirmary meals; and who suggested that outdoor relief parcels should be issued in instalments rather than once a week so that the food would not be stale and therefore wasted. But Mrs Despard's vigilance was always applied on the paupers' behalf – indeed she preferred to use the word 'person' and persuaded the Board to remove the word 'pauper' from the Relieving Officers' forms.

It is impossible to imagine Mrs Despard commenting, as Margaret Wynne Nevinson, who resigned on account of 'extravagant and illegal expenditure of public money', did, on waste within the workhouse *per se*: 'food is weighed out daily on the ration system, as in prisons and in the army, regardless of the fact that many of the inmates are aged and toothless. Appetites being mostly small, the allowance is in most cases much more than required . . .' Mrs Despard's perspective told her that once rations were reduced, the system would mean that they were reduced for one and all.

Probably on account of the aged females whose plight had first galvanized her into Guardianship, Mrs Despard seems to have had it in for the Master at Renfrew Road Workhouse, one Mr Ayles. She suspected his integrity – there were grounds for believing, for example, that he had some kind of a deal with the Norwood butcher who took left-over bread from the workhouse kitchen every day – and she knew his inhumanity. But she could only challenge Mr Ayles's regime by insisting on the procedures laid down in Local Government Board memoranda and circulars. Even his trivial breaches of national policy, such as the omission of evening prayers, were a means of keeping Mr Ayles on his toes. But most of her queries were more serious. When Mr Ayles 'punished' some aged females by putting them on a diet of bread and water, she wanted to know whether he had first sought the Medical Officer's approval. When Mr Ayles eventually satisfied the Board that he had, she wrote over their heads to the Local Government Board, asking for guidance on fit punishments for the elderly. Such gestures infuriated her fellow Guardians.

They were also annoyed when Mrs Despard sought out Martha Richardson, aged thirteen, who had lost part of a finger in the workhouse bread-cutting machine. It had already been decided, officially, that this accident was the girl's own fault because she was not supposed to be using such a dangerous machine. But Martha Richardson told Mrs Despard that she had been asked to use the machine, 'and her statement was corroborated by two other children.' Who else would trust the victim's testimony, or rely on corroboration from other children? Mrs Despard also reported the 'bad temper' of Miss Hancock, the workhouse taskmistress, and the rough ways of a Nurse Hewitt. But the other Guardians, 'having seen Nurse Hewitt and heard her statement, decided not to pursue the matter'.

Sometimes there were little victories. Mrs Despard succeeded in providing her elderly protegées with 'small comforts' such as individual towels and rations of sweets and tobacco, and she introduced a lady reader to the blind aged females who until then had been left in darkness for much of the day (the blind men already had a reader). Apart from what she observed on her regular rounds of the workhouse, she continued to have uninhibited contact with inmates through the treats she provided: day trips to the country for laundrywomen, needlewomen or aged females, teas at her clubs and entertainments within the workhouse.

The aged females were the most powerless paupers but married women generally suffered most under the system because legally they were 'something akin to his [their husband's] pet monkey'. Mrs Despard's special concern with their vulnerability emerges from the dry and dusty minutes of the Lambeth Board of Guardians and it influenced her ready adoption of the suffragette cause.

> ... my sister women – those who, in discouragement, nay, sometimes in despair, are struggling with Social problems; and those who slave all their lives long for the community – some as shop, factory, and domestic slaves, earning barely a subsistence and thrown aside to death or the parish when they are no longer profitable; some as mothers, bearing and rearing children, seeing them go forth to their work in the world, and spending their own last years lonely and unconsidered in the cheerless wards of a workhouse. These I tried to help, tried all I knew; but alas! how futile were my efforts! Turn which way I would, I knocked my head against a law to which neither my sisters nor I had consented, and which, though we were bound to obey it (at the risk of being where I am to-day) we had no chance of getting altered. The thought of all this nearly made me wild.

That was how, from Holloway Jail in July 1907, Mrs Despard described her feelings. But despite her understandable sense of inadequacy she did have some small victories. For example, she successfully moved a resolution that pregnant women, 'whether married or unmarried', should be seen by a committee of women Guardians and not the full Board when they presented themselves for admission to the lying-in hospital. Up in Manchester, another female Guardian who was to become famous, Mrs Emmeline Pankhurst, highlighted the case of workhouse girls who had no underclothing and no nightdresses because the matter had been considered too delicate to be raised before an all-male Board. But Mrs Despard did not succeed in her plea for one Emma Mitchell to be allowed to leave the workhouse with just one of her children, so that she could set up a home and gradually provide for all of them.

Mrs Mitchell's predicament was a common one. As late as 1908 feminists agitated on behalf of a married woman who wished to leave the workhouse but was refused permission while her husband was still inside, even though she was skilled and therefore a potential supporter of the whole family. Even a deserted wife within the workhouse could not leave without all of her children. There was no room for flexibility, or any realistic awareness of what the problems were. To give an idea of the cases coming up before Charlotte Despard's Board, we can describe one particularly famous one, that of the 'sons of Charles Chaplin'.

Charlie Chaplin was born in 1889. His father did not support his family by his first marriage, and was to die of alcoholic excess at the age of thirty-seven. But the Chaplin circumstances were moderately comfortable because Mrs Chaplin earned a good living as a music-hall dancer and singer. 'Winter' came when Mrs Chaplin's career began to falter on account of ill-health. She took to religion and so qualified as a deserving recipient of soup tickets and relief parcels, but eventually a solicitor advised her to throw herself and her young sons upon the support of the Lambeth Board of Guardians. That was the only way of putting the legal machinery into effect which would make Mr Chaplin contribute to the family's support. Sidney and Charles Chaplin were separated from their mother within the workhouse. In *My Autobiography*, Charlie Chaplin recalled his sadness on the first visiting day, 'the shock of seeing Mother enter the visiting-room garbed in workhouse clothes. How forlorn and embarrassed she looked!' Mrs Chaplin regained her composure, smiled at her sons' cropped heads and from her apron produced some sweets, which she had bought with the proceeds from some lace cuffs she had crocheted for a work-house nurse. Chaplin also recalled a grandfather in the infirmary who used his kitchen chores to provide the family with the presents of illicit eggs that were stashed in his bedside locker.

After about three weeks, the Chaplin brothers were sent to the Hanwell School for Orphans and Destitute Children, which was outside the Lambeth area. Once there, they could not see their mother at all, unless she took the drastic step of signing them all out of the Poor Law administration: 'this ruse was her only means to be with us.' Having retrieved their crumpled, unpressed private clothes, the family ambled out through the workhouse gates early in the morning.

Sidney had ninepence tied up in a handkerchief, so we bought half a pound of black cherries and spent the morning in Kennington Park, sitting on a bench eating them. Sidney crumpled a sheet of newspaper and wrapped some string around it and for a while the three of us played catch-ball.

At noon we went to a coffee shop and spent the rest of our
money on a twopenny tea-cake, a penny bloater and two
halfpenny cups of tea, which we shared between us. . . . In
the afternoon we made our way back to the workhouse. As
Mother said with levity: 'We'll be just in time for tea.'

There, the whole admissions procedure began again, and after
another three weeks the boys went back to Hanwell. Such 'ins
and outs' infuriated the workhouse authorities. Mrs Despard
thought that the problem would not arise if women in Mrs
Chaplin's position were not separated from their children in the
first place, and she tried hard to ensure more regular 'interviews'
between mothers and their children.

Sidney and Charles Chaplin escaped from the 'after' promised
by the Poor Law. Sidney ran away from the training ship
*Exmouth*, where he was supposed to have served his sea apprenticeship, and both brothers eventually found their vaudevillian
feet. But other Lambeth boys were not so street-wise or talented,
and Mrs Despard was their champion. It was usually she who
intervened in cases such as that of the boy apprenticed to a
bootmaker who was being made to do menial domestic work
instead of being trained. Her special interest in boys was
reflected in her appointment in 1901 to the Council of the
Association for Befriending Boys.

She was fortunate enough to be able to put money where her
conscience was. When she got involved in the campaign to
provide meals at school for pupils too starved to learn anything,
she prodded a local school by providing the kitchen facilities.
Her clinic supplemented the workhouse medical care, and she
could indulge in 'head-hunting' from the workhouse, in 1898
recruiting workhouse matron Rosalie Mansell to be her resident
nurse in Currie Street. But one of the more spectacular follow-
ups made by Mrs Despard was the six-week journey she made
to Canada in the summer of 1902 to see what had become of
the Lambeth boy paupers sent there as farm apprentices under
the aegis of Dr Barnardo's junior emigration scheme.

Although Mrs Despard crossed the Atlantic with members of
the Catholic Emigration Society, her concern about the fate of
boy emigrants was also political. Like other activists in the
labour movement, and Canadian trade unionists, she worried
lest the Lambeth Board was merely 'cheapening labour and

pouring a helot class into Canada', having heard that the 'better class' of Canadian farmer took children from their own orphanages. But the Catholic Emigration Society was not guilty of such offloading. She approved of its elaborate system of enquiry and inspection, which meant that the children emigrated under its auspices found healthy, caring homes, where they had a real chance of an agricultural training. Moreover, the Catholic children were always placed within reach of a church, a place of refuge and a 'court of appeal' in case of need, and no children were sent to the far west.

The same could not be said for Dr Barnardo's organization. Although the formal part of the business was well done, the Barnardo's agency in Toronto was a 'very poor place'. Some of the Lambeth boys were living very far away from school; some had been moved from place to place two or three times; and one had been lost sight of altogether. When she ventured to the farms in the west she found more to depress her. Here, the households were often a hundred miles apart and at one farm her buggy driver spontaneously commented that 'he would not have placed his boy in such a home'. There was no support network and little chance of schooling: 'One must not forget in considering the case of our child emigrants to the Far West, the awful loneliness of those scattered farms in the long Canadian winter.'

All this was in contrast with Dr Barnardo's well-publicized follow-up visit of 1900 when he met with a thousand of the 10,000 young people who had passed over his 'Golden Bridge' to the New World. He met only with 'well grown, stalwart, muscular fellows, bronzed and bearded and altogether so changed that I usually quite failed to recognize in them the puny, half-starved, homeless waifs that had come under my care in England, twelve, fifteen or twenty years before.' By contrast, Mrs Despard heard a number of complaints about the physical and moral condition of the Lambeth children, and their 'habits': 'This seemed rather strange to me when I remembered the care that had been taken in selecting these children, and the healthy appearance they had presented when they bade us farewell.'

The Lambeth Board received Mrs Despard's report with thanks, and it was agreed that future pauper export schemes should only be undertaken by agencies with standards of inspection that matched those of the Catholic Emigration Society. In the face of Mrs Despard's diligence the Board could do little else, even though her connection with the progressive scene outside the boardroom was by now challengingly overt. Indeed, before she had left for her Canadian trip another Lambeth Guardian, Mr Bayliss, gave notice that at the next meeting of the Board he would propose.

'That in view of the statements alleged to have been made at a meeting on Sunday morning the 9th June, by Mrs Despard in Brockwell Park, reflecting upon the Guardians, this Board is of the opinion that such statements should be either proved or withdrawn.

But the lady philanthropist was not for recanting. The hopelessness of the whole Poor Law business.

and the ocean of misery through which I was compelled to wade made me search desperately for some remedy. Party politics held out no hope. I saw the terrible problem of the people's necessities played with. I heard promises made to them which I knew would not be fulfilled . . . At last, sick of all these, I determined to study for myself the great problems of society. My study landed me in uncompromising socialism.

Although Charlotte Despard and Frank Briant were embattled voices on the Lambeth Board of Guardians, the world outside was reverberating with the sounds made by their allies. Keir Hardie's Independent Labour Party had been formed in 1893 while the Social Democratic Federation, which had emerged as a militant champion of the unemployed in the turbulent 1880s, was dynamic in south London. More sedate, in theory and practice, was the Fabian Society, which had also emerged in the 1880s. These and other radical political groups complemented the 'new' trade unions in which unskilled or low-status workers – dockers, gasworkers, factory workers, clerks and shop assistants – were organizing themselves.

It must be said that at the time of Charlotte Despard's radical education the word 'socialist' had a very general currency. The introduction of death duties in an attempt to curb landed wealth in 1895 prompted Sir William Harcourt to exclaim, 'We are all socialists now.' This remark testified not so such much to a radical concensus as to a ruling class realization that the labour movement was at least threatening enough to be bargained with. But the very promiscuity of the label 'socialist' meant that highly idiosyncratic versions of the idea were permitted. Henry Mayers Hyndman, for example, the founder and leader of the SDF, was a wealthy stockbroker and cricket enthusiast, while one of the SDFs more colourful supporters, the Countess of Warwick, was not embarrassed by the private train which she hired to take her to London meetings.

Had Charlotte Despard found herself in, say, Sheffield, in this perid she might well have joined the group of ethical socialists around Edward Carpenter. Like her, he thought in moral as much as political terms, of socialism within as well as without. Indeed, there were many grounds for the self-denying widow's compatibility with this homosexual exponent of the 'simpler life'. Born in the same year (1844), and the many-sistered son of an ex-naval officer, Edward Carpenter was a poet and a poetry lover, and an exponent of Eastern religious values. Between the 1880s and the 1900s he lectured all over Britain, and Charlotte Despard's kinship with him probably began at one of these meetings. Carpenter sent the sandals he made himself to friends all over the world and it seems likely that it was he who first incited her to 'freedom from boots'. Her first pair of sandals – which with that mantilla were her trademarks – probably emanated from the workshop of the Sheffield libertarian.

But Charlotte Despard didn't live in Sheffield and she chose to become involved with the Social Democratic Federation which, in the words of its founder, Hyndman, had no time for 'old cranks, humanitarians, vegetarians, anti-vivisectionists and anti-vaccinationists, arty-crafties and all the rest of them. . . .' Hyndman's pessimistic estimate of the state of London's working class – an optimistic estimate by his own revolutionary criteria – had prompted Charles Booth's massive enquiry into the capital's life and labour. The SDF leader's interpretation of the Marxists texts then available made him contemptuous of all reformists and of stepping-stones to a socialist world. His organization would have been a very unlikely beacon to the mystical Charlotte Despard had it not been for the often forgotten fact that the SDF was never Hyndman's creature. In practice, especially at local levels, SDF branches were actively involved with all the issues of concern to working men and women: with the struggle for the eight-hour day, for minimum wages, for less punitive treatment of the unemployed under the Poor Law, with meals for needy schoolchildren, and so on. And despite Hyndman's sectarian personality, there was a considerable overlap both in membership and in solidarity between the SDF and other socialist or radical groups, especially outside London. As a member of both the Independent Labour Party and the Social Democratic Federation Charlotte Despard was not unusual.

In London in the l890s the SDF was very vigorous. Its 'scientific' (i.e. avowedly Marxist) socialism was consistent with the capital's traditions of secular radicalism. Its insistence on a revolutionary agenda, however long-term, and its refreshingly internationalist perspective attracted the very *crème de la crème* of London's young activists. Though the SDF had a very high turnover in membership – in Yvonne Kapp's phrase, it was a veritable 'revolving door' for apprentice revolutionaries – it was a membership of high quality, These were the thinking, reading working men and women so admired by Charlotte Despard. For her and for many of them (e.g. George Lansbury and Margaret Bondfield) the experience was often a political education. There was even an Irish dimension to Charlotte Despard's urban, revolutionary affections because many of the London SDF cadres were Irish or of Irish extraction. The dockers' strike of l889, for example, in which Cardinal Manning had been an intermediary, had as its headquarters an Irish riverside pub. In that formative struggle, Tom Mann, Ben Tillett and John Burns had been prominent. The last-named never earned Charlotte Despard's respect for reasons which come later, but Mann and Tillett were 'sons' and 'pals'.

She contributed money and time to the SDF, spoke at many meetings, and put her first club on the Wandsworth Road, now known as Social Hall, at the disposal of the SDF and the local labour movement. At the International Socialist Workers' and Trade Union Conference in 1896 she was the delegate representing the Ilkeston SDF, presumably because that Derbyshire branch could not afford to send someone to London, and Battersea was thick with representatives. Without benefit of the microphone Eleanor Marx did her best as an interpreter for a veritable Babel of delegates, the distinguished foreigners including Clara Zetkin, Georgi Plekhanov and Jean Jaurès. We have to picture a grey-haired, be-sandalled and fifty-two-year-old Mrs Charlotte Despard among that crowd, singing the '*Auld Lang Syne* in the British fashion' (with crossed hands clasped) after days of debating such issues as the 'Agrarian Question', 'War' and 'Education and Physical Development'.

Eleanor Marx and her 'free union' partner Edward Aveling were SDF stars in this period, and Charlotte Despard, who joined them regularly on local speakers' platforms, was friendly with both of them. With Will Thorne, Eleanor Marx had had a key role in the organization of the gasworkers, a union which gave equal rights to its male and female members. The gasworks were the largest employer of men where Charlotte Despard lived and she probably joined the union's eighth anniversary celebrations in Battersea Park in 1897. The brilliant, dedicated Eleanor Marx was well loved by the London socialist scene, but her consort was another matter. Bernard Shaw described Aveling as 'quite a pleasant fellow who would have gone to the scaffold for socialism or atheism but with absolutely no conscience in his private life.' We must assume that Aveling, who has come down to us as one of history's arch cads, was at least 'quite a pleasant follow'. How otherwise are Annie Besant's infatuation with him, Eleanor Marx's fourteen-year-long devotion, to be explained? The Marx-Avelings shared a passion for theatre. Eleanor seriously considered a career on the stage and Aveling was an inveterate writer and producer of plays, as well as an amateur actor. He gave 'elocution and dramatic lessons' at Social Hall, and probably also lent Mrs Despard a hand with those workhouse 'entertainments'. But what would have particularly recommended Aveling to Mrs Despard, who was not vulnerable to his sexual charm, was the Irishness that he claimed by way of his mother's and his paternal grandmother's ancestry.

January 1897 saw Aveling at Social Hall, supervising a 'dramatic entertainment' in aid of the SDF science classes held in the Strand. In this production a young amateur actress by the name of Eva Frye distinguished herself with a rendering of 'Love's Old Sweet Song'. Six months later, using his *nom de plume* of Alec Nelson and a false address, Aveling secretly married Eva Frye. This marriage was to be explained, according to Yvonne Kapp, 'only by the supposition that the young lady refused to go to bed with him unless he married her, alternatively

that she was pregnant, or said she was'. But its discovery was
the final blow in a series of betrayals for Eleanor Marx. In
circumstances that made Aveling at least complicit, she poisoned
herself in March 1898. The owner of Social Hall has been
allocated a small role in the mythology of the Marx-Aveling
tragedy. 'Some have it that he [Aveling] was distraught with
grief and flung himself into the arms of Mrs Despard: others that
he was unmoved to the point of total and shocking indifference.'
Whatever happened, and Charlotte Despard's lips were always
sealed when it came to sensational gossip, it is extremely hard
to imagine her giving any physical consolation to Edward
Aveling. She just might have stretched to a cup of her rather
superior tea.

Had Eleanor Marx lived longer she would have been among
those other SDF members, those ILP-ers, Fabians and trade
unionists who gathered, almost unnoticed amid the jingo of the
Boer War, at the Memorial Hall in Clerkenwell to form the
Labour Representation Committee in 1900. This group, which
by 1906 was the Labour Party, aimed at getting a 'distinct
Labour group' into Parliament 'who shall have their own whips
and agree upon their policy'. Although the SDF formally separated itself from this initiative after a year because revolution
was not put firmly on the new party's agenda, its official position
was benevolently neutral and at the grassroots level actively
supportive.

The new Labour Party had as its guiding principle the idea
that the interests of the working class were intrinsically different
from those represented by both the established parliamentary
parties, the Liberals and the Conservatives. At the forefront of
the minds of men like Keir Hardie and women like Charlotte
Despard was the disappointing example of John Burns, 'labour's
lost leader'. A brilliant demagogue, John Burns emerged as a
national figure during the dockers' strike. After 'no victimiz-
ation' and the dockers' tanner (sixpence per hour as the
minimum rate) had been won, his effigy was on display at
Madame Tussaud's. He left the Social Democratic Federation
in that same year and viewed the ILP with contempt. Although
he still styled himself as a socialist, Burns furthered his own
maverick career both on the London County Council and as
Member of Parliament for Battersea between 1892 and 1918 by
bargaining and compromising with the Liberals. The difference

between the 'king of Battersea' and Keir Hardie was symbolized by their respective dress when they entered Parliament in 1892. Whereas Hardie insisted on his famous cloth cap, Burns wore an exclusive suit, paid for by his supporters.

Burns ran official Battersea politics with the aid of his own machine, the Socialist Labour League, which, despite its title, was really the plebs' version of the local Liberal Association. By the time the new Labour Party had twenty-nine members of Parliament, in 1905, Burns was in the Liberal Cabinet as President of the Local Government Board. He should have been in a position to effect from above what progressive Guardians such as Mrs Despard had been trying to do at local level. Instead he allowed himself to preside over an investigation into corruption at the Poplar Union, which was patently an attempt to discredit its radical Poor Law initiatives. Beatrice Webb summed up John Burns thus: 'A man of splendid physique, fine and strong intelligence, human sympathy, practical capacity, he is unfitted for a really great position by his utter inability to be a constant and loyal comrade. He stands absolutely alone.'

Few people earned Charlotte Despard's direct disapproval, but John Burns was one and Ramsay MacDonald was to be another. Perhaps because she herself was, as the incomparably precise Beatrice Webb would have said, 'a lady by birth', Charlotte Despard was harsh on those who were 'traitors' to their class. But any consideration of her political orientation in the 1890s and 1900s must take 'Honest John's' utter domination of Battersea into account. Early in 1903 she resigned from the Lambeth Board of Guardians because by no longer having a residence at Social Hall she was no longer eligible, and for a year she served on the Wandsworth Board, which her Nine Elms premises made her eligible for. But the Wandsworth Union was dominated by Burns, and he was then President of the Local Government Board, so she did not feel able to get involved and resigned after a year. She nonetheless kept a beady eye on the man who had waved the red flag and who now played the bosses' tune, and who cordially returned her dislike. In 1910 Burns delivered the Christmas speech to the inmates of the Wandsworth workhouse, a 'statistical *hors d'oeuvre*' according to a local newspaper. At a meeting in Battersea Library Charlotte Despard was reported as feeling deeply for the old folk who had to listen to his statistics which they did not understand. All the comfort he gave them was by saying that sixty years ago a great many more of them were there than that day. They had to listen to his silvery tongue, and feel not the least anxious about their dinner. If no other Liberal was thrown out, she hoped Mr Burns was not returned as he had been a traitor to his class, and because of his overwhelming vanity.

But by then Burns was becoming an irrelevant thorn in the flesh of the labour movement, which was increasingly defined by the Labour Party. But because the Labour Party emerged as a governing political party and because Britain never had an SDF-style revolution, the political boundaries of the Edwardian period are often seen as less fluid than they were. And since the SDF fed many of its members and traditions into the later British Communist Party, a senior Labour Party politician like Margaret Bondfield was careful to distance herself from it when she came to writing her memoirs. She said she disliked the SDF emphasis on 'bloody class war', that the rumours of 'citizens drilling in Harry Quelch's backyard' had made her uncomfortable and soon she had transferred her energy exclusively to the ILP.

To the best of her ability, Charlotte Despard was a loyal 'joiner'. She did not, like John Burns, want to be a leader of mere followers. But, perhaps because she came to politics as an aristocratic widow of independent means, she did not, until 1906, experience her membership of the Independent Labour Party and of the Social Democratic Federation as irreconcilable, any more than she found her Catholicism hard to square with the tenets of the Theosophical movement. Probably by virtue of her age and her utter sincerity, she was tolerated by people more single-minded than she was and especially by young people. Above all, she was seen as incorruptible. For the feminists and communists of the 1920s and the 1930s, she was a grandmother figure; for the socialists and suffragists of the 1890s and the 1900s, she was a mother, always 'Mrs Despard' rather than Charlotte Despard. Margaret Bondfield never forgot how

many years ago, when a sick and sorry young trade union organiser, she was lent a room in Mrs Despard's house, in which to hold a meeting of underpaid shop girls; how nobody turned up; and how, when on the verge of heartbreak, Mrs Despard had talked to her like a mother, and showed her that disappointment was not failure or defeat, but was the call to that increased effort which gives the strength necessary for victory.

For her, Mrs Despard was a 'guide, philosopher and friend'.

In the midst of their drab surroundings it was Mrs Despard who had given them a glimpse of a social life, then entirely strange. Young shop assistants, clerks, and factory workers had entered Mrs Despard's home, and that home, poor and simple enough to its owner, to many who entered it gave the first introduction to good taste, surroundings of culture, and the loving kindness which emanates from a gracious hostess.

Like other 'lame dogs and tired workers who needed rest and soul refreshment', Margaret Bondfield was invited for weekends to the Surrey cottage at Oxshott. Such young men and women noticed that their hostess herself ate most sparingly and they were politely fascinated when she told them about her table-rapping communications with Mazzini. The Bondfield image of Mrs Despard is one that many people recognized: 'on her knees, weeding her garden at sunrise, she seemed to me a saint at prayer'. Now acknowledged saints are invaluable supporters of any campaign, and before long the Blessed Mrs Despard was enlisted for the cause that would make her a household name.

# CHAPTER 6

# THE SUFFRAGETTES:'CAN THIS BE THE BEGINNING?'

Early in 1906 two young women from Manchester by the names of Annie Kenney and Teresa Billington-Greig made their way to Currie Street, Nine Elms. They went as agents of the Women's Social and Political Union and their mission was the recruitment of Charlotte Despard to *the* Cause.

Of course, Charlotte Despard had never been indisposed towards the idea of votes for women. Back in the 1880s she had briefly worked with Liberal Party women to that end, but found them 'inspired by men for the ends of men'. By 1906 her commitment to full democracy was expressed through her membership of the Adult Suffrage League, which campaigned for a wholesale reform of the electoral register. As a convinced socialist, she believed, like Margaret Bondfield, that the goal of female enfranchisement was inseparable from the goal of universal suffrage. In 1906 even men had to be householders, or at least registered house-occupiers, before they were eligible for the electoral roll. Therefore, to struggle for votes for women on the same terms as men currently held the vote was to struggle for political rights for middle-class and relatively wealthy women.

Mrs Despard's forebodings about any distinctly feminist strategy appeared to have been borne out by the style of the constitutional suffrage movement led by Mrs Millicent Fawcett, which for several decades had been lobbying Parliament. Though wholly admirable and, in a demure way, heroic, Mrs Fawcett herself often illustrated the shortcomings of the 'votes for ladies' movement, from a socialist point of view. In the very year of Kenney and Billington-Greig's first visit to Currie Street, the *Daily Mail* sponsored a Sweated Industries Exhibition in London, where the work done under appalling conditions for abominably low pay by women was revealed to the public at large. The agitation around this issue was led by associates of Mrs Despard's: Mary MacArthur, Margaret Bondfield and Susan Lawrence. Yet, when the Bryant & May matchgirls had gone on strike in 1888, Millicent Fawcett, a shareholder of that company, had taken a shareholder's line on that working women's battle.

But the movement represented on Mrs Despard's doorstep by these two young women promised something different. The *Social* part of the Women's Social and Political Union, which had been founded in the northern radical capital of Manchester by Mrs Emmeline Pankhurst late in 1903, reflected its real affinities with the Labour Party (or Labour Representation Committee). Mrs Pankhurst was the widow of a nationally respected radical lawyer, Dr Richard Pankhurst. He had never carved the Sunday joint and belonged to the feminist tradition of J. S. Mill, and the Pankhurst domestic regime had hinged around the principle that 'every struggling cause shall be ours'. Mrs Pankhurst was an able and extremely attractive woman and, unlike Mrs Fawcett, she seemed to be in a great hurry. In just two years she and her galaxy of daughters had brought a new dimension to the Woman Question, an issue that until then had seemed polite and peripheral to politics in general.

The eldest and, in 1906, the most prominent ('anointed') daughter, Christabel, had been induced to follow up the family's political heritage by Esther Roper, Secretary of the North of England Society for Women's Suffrage, and Eva Gore-Booth, Secretary of the Manchester Women's Trades Council. They coaxed Christabel, who was then by temperament an unlikely political debutante, out into the feminist daylight and persuaded her to study law even though that was not a strictly vocational training in a period when women could not practise as lawyers.

For the first eighteen months or so, the WSPU did the propaganda work that was typical of single-issue organizations, acting in tandem with the labour movement. But late in 1905 they set the national heather on fire with an action that was calculated to rouse women as they had never been roused before. Christabel Pankhurst and Annie Kenney disrupted a prestigious Liberal meeting in Manchester, at which Sir Edward Grey was the main speaker, with the repeated question, 'Will you give votes to women?' After their forcible ejection from this meeting Christabel and Annie were jailed. Quite deliberately, they had both earned instant martyrdom. The WSPU also benefited from great publicity with the new popular newspapers with their large pictures and big type, taking an unprecedented interest. Even women who had no natural sympathy with the Pankhursts were mobilized. Helena Swanwick, who joined a Fawcett-style suffrage society soon after the Manchester incident, was typical:

> Their challenge had this effect on me (as it had on countless other women), that, believing in the enfranchisement of women, I could not keep out of this struggle at this time. It did not attract me; it bludgeoned my conscience. I could do no other than become one of those who were heaving the wheel of reform out of its rut.

Charlotte Despard's feelings were less qualified:

> I confess there was something in this society which, from the beginning, appealed to me. The youth of many of the members; the fact that they had come together in womanly frankness and love, not for political ends, not to further the candidature of party men for public place and power, but for social and political ends which would affect themselves and the world; the dashing courage of the little band, their selflessness, their quiet endurance of the results of their lawless action – these things attracted me. Sometimes I asked myself, 'Can this be the beginning? Is this indeed a part of that revolutionary movement for which all my life long I have been waiting?'

The Pankhursts had given fresh meaning to the word 'militancy' and Mrs Despard, who always thought of herself as a revolutionary, was with them. The suffragettes (as the *Daily Mail* soon labelled them) were only doing things that the Irish and the unemployed had done, but they were females and, what was more, respectable females. Even though their militancy was, by later standards, quite mild, it was sensational. Mrs Fawcett compared her well-behaved constitutional movement with the Irish parliamentary party under Isaac Butt, 'who achieved nothing', that of the Pankhursts with Parnell who successfully mobilized extra-parliamentary forces and filibustered Parliament to get 'practically anything he wanted short of Home Rule'. So the boldness of the WSPU initiative, which made some suffragists wary, was wonderful to Mrs Despard. When she later referred to 'my militant days', she was not talking about her SDF activities or her Irish experiences, but about those thrilling suffragette years before the First World War.

Though still involved with multiple commitments arising from her Battersea secular mission, Charlotte Despard was relatively free to take up a new campaign in 1906, and it did not take Teresa Billington-Greig and Annie Kenney long to woo her. She and Annie had been sent to London to set up the WSPU in the capital, so that it could focus more directly on Parliament. Until the summer Mrs Pankhurst was detained in Manchester by her job as Registrar of Births and Deaths, and Christabel by her legal studies.

As a former cotton factory worker Annie Kenney personified the WSPU's broadly based support. But she was, first and foremost, a personal protegée of the Pankhursts, who was unworried about being nicknamed 'Christabel's blotting paper'. Billington-Greig was an altogether more formidable and, for Charlotte Despard, convincing character. She had worked as a schoolteacher and was a committed ILP supporter. With her considerable intellectual and oratorical gifts, Billington-Greig was Christabel Pankhurst's main rival as the young star of the suffragette movement; she was also the first suffragette to enter Holloway Jail. 'TBG' represented the dashing, bike-riding elite of young women, who had emerged from the institutions of higher education newly opened to them only to find inferior status, restricted job opportunities and lower pay as teachers, doctors, civil servants, journalists and office workers.

Teresa Billington-Greig described the meeting that clinched Mrs Despard's enlistment at a high level into the central London branch of the WSPU. According to her, the Battersea grande dame's main commitment was to 'humanism – a devotion in which the most distressed and weak and burdened might have priority – but the whole human family must be served'. Billington-Greig, who was an ex-Catholic, had done her homework well. At Eustace Miles's café, where 'best light and sustaining lunches for brain-workers' were served, she agreed with Mrs Despard's humanist sentiments. (A Battersea worker had told TBG that although Mrs Despard's flock did not understand a word she said, they knew her to be their 'eternal friend' and one 'poor wife' had spontaneously confided, 'If only God would give *her* power.') Wouldn't Mrs Despard agree, TBG suggested, that

'the most distressed, the most denied must be uplifted first – if the whole was to be uplifted. To secure full humanism, feminism must take priority for women reformers. To such men as could realize that the human race was dual, the other so-called humanist reforms had often only emphasized the subjection of women. I said, 'women the first!' Were they not the worst sufferers in her little corner at Nine Elms?

At the final session between the two women in Nine Elms, this argument went down well. 'She knew this was true. Also, the sweated industries figures were beginning to be quoted.'

Feeling quite exhausted but very pleased with her work, Billington-Greig spent that night in Battersea. She remembered that the windows were left open and that she slept 'like a child', having experienced Charlotte Despard's 'goodnight' as a kind of benediction. In the morning, through the bedroom wall, she could hear her hostess reciting and correcting herself, and beginning again a speech she was scheduled to deliver. TBG returned to the WSPU offices in a jubilant frame of mind: 'We might not carry with us the echo women of the extreme left – trade union or Marxian – but we could carry their "sainted pillar of integrity", their "lady of human service".'

The WSPU had moved its headquarters to London in the wake of a massive victory by the Liberal party in the General Election of 1906. Although no political party had votes for women as part of its policy until the Labour Party formally included this demand in their programme in 1912, it was known that many Liberal and Labour Members of Parliament, and some Unionists were in favour of it. Indeed, the Prime Minister,

Sir Henry Campbell-Bannerman, was sympathetic to the suffragettes and had seemed to offer encouragement when he told the WSPU to keep on 'pestering'. Most important, from Charlotte Despard's point of view, was the fact that Keir Hardie and George Lansbury were outspoken supporters of the principle of fighting separately for women's political rights. A man of commanding integrity, Keir Hardie's views carried great weight with Charlotte Despard. He was a close family friend of the Pankhursts, later on what the Edwardians would have described as 'the most intimate of terms' with Sylvia Pankhurst.

But it was not as simple as saying 'yes' to votes for women. If the vote were to be granted to all women over twenty-one, it would also have to be given to men on the same terms. But the abolition of the householding principle would effect universal suffrage, which threatened the whole status quo and so made Conservative supporters of female enfranchisement very nervous. But Labour men were not happy with the idea of giving the vote to women householders and wives of householders, a measure that would only confirm the deficiencies of the 'votes for ladies' movement. The Pankhursts offered a new line on this dilemma, which men like Keir Hardie could accept:

> Our main concern was not with the numbers of women to be enfranchised but with the removal of the *stigma* upon womanhood as such. Even if the vote were to be given only to women with black hair or to woman of a certain height, it would mean that the barrier against women had been broken.

The logic of this position ultimately led to a split within the 'advanced women's movement', but for the time being it made the Cause easier to plead.

The Cause had to be a powerful plea because no government was obliged to take account of women's feelings. In 1906 it was a matter of bludgeoning the consciences of individual Members of Parliament and of the male electorate, of making the enfranchisement of women an issue of national importance. By the summer of that year the senior Pankhursts were in town. By then Charlotte Despard, with a young science graduate called Edith How-Martyn, was joint Hon. Secretary of the London WSPU. The offices in Clement's Inn were managed, and largely funded, by one of those super-efficient, super-dedicated, feminist couples, Emmeline and Henry Pethick-Lawrence. (They had been recommended to the Cause by Keir Hardie.) As WSPU branches sprang up all over Britain, Mrs Fawcett's movement enjoyed a parallel growth, and the real fight began.

The WSPU decided to take advantage of an ancient right to petition the monarch about a grievance; and since women were voteless it was decided that they should exercise this right by going to see the King's Members of Parliament in person. Accordingly, October of that year saw Charlotte Despard and about twenty women in the central lobby of the House of Commons. When that area was full of MPs, Mrs Pethick-Lawrence observed 'little Mary Gawthorpe' mounting a settee beneath the statue of Lord Northcote and beginning to address the men. As soon as she had been 'removed' by policemen, Mrs Despard stepped into her place: 'Neither her age nor her standing carried any weight with the police. She was immediately lost to view.' We might add that Mrs Despard, the habitual muncher of dry biscuits and fruit, literally carried no weight, but her 'standing' in the world outside the House of Commons explained why, unlike Mrs Pethick-Lawrence and ten other women, she was not arrested on that occasion.

From Mrs Dora Montefiore, another suffragette with SDF connections, we have a slightly different and mildly self-glorifying account of the same occasion. She saw Mrs Despard at the top of some steps with a policeman just behind her.

> Feeling that a woman of her age might be injured by the rough and tumble efforts which the police, under orders, were executing, I called out to some of the members [of Parliament] and onlookers who were mixed up with the women at the foot of the stairs: 'Can you stand by and see a venerable woman handled in that way in which we have just been handled?'

But Mrs Montefiore only drew attention to herself, for just then another policeman called out, 'Take Mrs Montefiore in; she is one of the ringleaders.'

At some level Charlotte Despard resented the protectiveness of her sisters and the reluctance of policemen to select her for arrest. Teresa Billington-Greig liked to think that Mrs Despard's immunity was due to the authorities' fear that the arrest of the

Queen of Battersea would have an explosive effect on turbulent south London; others thought that this immunity also derived from her relationship with Sir John French, the man being mooted as the next Inspector-General of the Armed Forces. Whatever the reason, Mrs Despard knew that her conspicuousness did not help, because even the most inexperienced policeman could keep an eye out for the older lady in the mantilla and sandals. So, on the next likely occasion for a real penalty for her convictions, she donned a motoring hat with a streaming veil. This disguise is probably the origin of the family version of Aunt Lottie's longing for prison glory. But it did work.

The occasion was the first 'rush' on Parliament after the King's Speech of 12 February 1907. On that day some 400 women assembled in nearby Caxton Hall, and the WSPU speakers on the platform included Mrs Despard. When the word came through that there had been no mention of women's suffrage in the royal speech, which traditionally outlines the British government's programme of legislation, the cry of 'Rise up Women!' from the platform was met by shouts of 'Now, now!' In small groups, one of which was led by an umbrella-brandishing Charlotte Despard, the women hastened to Parliament Square. There they were met by an army of policemen, including the mounted variety, the 'London Cossacks'. A Glasgow delegate to Caxton Hall, Mrs Moffat, saw Mrs Despard surrounded by horses and slipped between the animals to be 'by the old lady's side, saying "I will stay with you." "Oh, I'm quite safe," replied Mrs Despard, "I love horses." ' But in the ensuing 'crowd control' exercise, in which the official brutality towards the women had a nasty sexual dimension, Charlotte Despard was arrested. She refused to pay her fine and within days began to serve a twenty-one-day sentence in Holloway Jail, along with thirty-one other women.

The suffragettes who were imprisoned usually went into the 'second division' as ordinary female criminals. And although most of these political prisoners were very shocked by conditions inside, for the 'scrubbers' the arrival of lady prisoners meant improvements: 'It ain't the same place as it was before you ladies came.' But if anyone was able to deal with the squalor, discomfort and grim discipline of prison life it was the ascetic Mrs Despard who usually ate sparingly, who favoured cold-to-tepid baths and whose clothes, though far more clean and comfortable than prison dress, were decidedly unconventional. Moreover, she had immense reserves of spiritual strength to draw upon and even in prison her whole aura meant that, relatively speaking, the authorities had on kid gloves.

During another imprisonment, in 1909, Mrs Pethick-Lawrence happened to be in Holloway at the same time. She was in the sick ward when she saw a new bed being prepared:

> I heard that communication had come from the Home Office that Mrs Despard was to be expected that evening. As her trial had yet to take place, it seemed that the Home Office had arrived at a foregone conclusion. Later that day I was thrilled to see that stately and commanding figure enter the ward, looking, if possible, more dignified than ever in the quaint uniform of the criminal. Her first act was a calm refusal to take the medicine the doctor had prescribed. 'I have never taken medicine in my life – I do not propose to begin now.' Her word was immediately taken as law. All the officers appeared to be in awe of her.

On this occasion Mrs Despard's imprisonment was too politically hot to handle and she was released after a couple of days: 'My health, which was perfectly good, being given as the excuse.'

Gretta Cousins, soon to be prominent in the Irish suffragist struggle, chanced to be in London on Theosophical business in 1907. Her path crossed Charlotte Despard's at several points, for apart from suffragism and Theosophy, she was also involved in the Irish vegetarian movement. (The Irish Vegetarian Society aroused some mirth because of the names of its chief officers: President Mr Henry Ham, Vice Presidents Mrs Maud Joynt and Mrs Jonathon Hogg.) Mr and Mrs Cousins found themselves on a crowded pavement near Parliament Square and watched a small band of women being led off to a police station by a bevy of Peelers.

> They were, we were told, the leaders of the suffrage movement. In their simplicity, respectability, and dignified demeanour they were deeply impressive. I was so hurt by the indignity to which these fine educated women were subjected that I cried for hours that night before I could get to sleep

through an intuition of the struggle that women would have to make to secure any freedom from the subjection which they had had to endure through the ages. I suffered the insult in my own soul in sympathy with those self-sacrificing women whom later I met and knew and worked with, Mrs Pankhurst and Christabel, Mrs Pethick-Lawrence, noble elderly Mrs Despard, and others.

With typical resourcefulness, Charlotte Despard used her jail experiences to advertise the plight of women prisoners generally. With Mabel Collins, she revived her skills as a popular novelist to produce *Outlawed*, which was published in 1908. This melodrama, which, thankfully, does not run to three volumes, has familiar ingredients: thwarted young love, mysterious parentage, confusion of identity. They heroine, one Beryl, ends up in Holloway on account of her uncanny resemblance to a murderess. But she cannot reveal her innocent identity because she is simultaneously playing dead on the odious husband she has married out of duty: 'George Faulding with that look of gratified power and expectant tyranny on his face – that smile, that look, in comparison with which the nethermost depth of hell was a Paradise.'

Beryl's first day in prison may serve as a sample for many others; for in prison day follows day with monotonous regularity. The same hours, the same meals, the same inspections, the same soul-deadening sense of separateness – of having passed into a world where you are an outlaw and an outcast.

But Beryl's experience is alleviated by a kind doctor, a sympathetic and fellow-Catholic Irish wardress and two 'pet' books – a collection of Shelley and Thomas à Kempis's *Imitation of Christ* (which also presumably consoled Charlotte Despard). 'She opened the pages at random. Some of the passages were marked. Here was one! "For Thy life is our path, and by Holy Patience we walk unto Thee Who art our crown." ' This makes Beryl spring to her feet 'with her cheeks burning and the blood coursing like liquid fire through her veins' and she cries out, 'But one may have too much patience. *They* have.' In her despair she vows that if and when she is released she will fight for the rights of imprisoned women. This happens, courtesy of the motor car that comes downhill at full speed to kill the odious Faulding in the company of the real murderess, and Beryl finds true love in the arms of a young painter suitor who has become fabulously successful. 'Yes,' says Beryl's aristocratic sponsor, 'yours is going to be a good marriage because he will have his work, and you will have yours. And Beryl, I have some strange news for you today. Power is to be given into your hands. You are rich my child.'

Via Beryl, Mrs Despard tried to broaden the value of her imprisonment, but her incarceration was immediately good value for the movement. The *Daily News* expressed the pay-off from the outlawing of the like of Mrs Charlotte Despard succinctly: 'such social reformers as Cobden's daughter [Annie Cobden Sanderson] and Mrs Despard cannot be condemned as oppressed with a desire for silly self-advertisement.' Charlotte Despard was right to think that serving prison sentences was something she could do usefully. Other women, for example Virginia Woolf, confessed, '. . . I could neither do sums or argue or speak, but I could do the humbler work if that is any good.' Mrs Despard preferred the front line. Besides, she was, according to Helena Swanwick and TBG, 'no good at all on a committee, where she found it impossible to bring her mind to bear on a resolution'. As we shall see, this vagueness was to be a source of strength to the later Women's Freedom League. Right from the beginning of her militant days Mrs Despard had a unique appeal. Brilliant manipulators of the media, the Pankhursts sold her as the mystical, sybilline component of their dream ticket.

In *The Case for Women's Suffrage*, a collection of articles published in 1907, Mrs Pankhurst's contribution kept strictly to the political points in hand, while Christabel Pankhurst's summary of female legal disabilities was brisk. It was left to Charlotte Despard to ramble on about Isis of Egypt, Athene Pallas of Greece, Juno of Rome, the Virgin Mother, the medieval abbesses who sat on state councils, and great saints such as Catherine of Siena and Theresa of Avila who were consulted on public matters. For this author 'life itself would be but a small price to pay' for the joy of being a pioneer in a movement whose aim was 'to prepare and reveal' the New Woman and the New Era of peace and glorious co-operation between the sexes.

By all accounts Mrs Despard was great crowd-puller. At a

meeting in Hyde Park, where the 'Irish-born visionary' was one of the principal speakers, a policeman told Christopher St John,

> 'Some of the platforms, you see, have only got a handful. But Mrs Despard has got a big crowd; but that's nothing. He jerked a white-gloved hand in the direction of that which was nothing' . . . 'Mrs Despard – she always gets a crowd.'

Against the trees St John saw her with her arms raised,

> Cassandra-like; the whole thin, fragile body seemed to vibrate with a prophecy, and, from the white hair, the familiar black lace veil streamed back like a pennon . . . the selfishness and materialism of the crowd, its indifference to its own improvement, its deafness to the misery of others, seemed to shrivel before this woman's look.

There is no doubt that in another era Charlotte Despard would have ranked as a saint. Her fans rated her quasi-religious qualities far above the conventional political expertise of other leading suffragettes. For Gretta Cousins she was

> a leader of the highest quality, an aristocrat who was the most democratic of the political thinkers amongst us. She was one of the rare Catholics who were Theosophists. She looked as old as the hills and twice as wrinkled, but her heart was eternally young. She was a warrior – and a pacifist. Her type of mind appealed to me most of any of the suffragettes.

Mary Colum also compared Mrs Despard's style favourably with that of other suffragettes: 'the Pankhursts fought magnificently but when they made speeches they talked like lawyers and politicians. Mrs Despard's speeches had warmth and poetry, and that intellectual reality mixed with emotional intensity which I have always thought is a Celtic quality.' Teresa Billington-Greig was not always charmed by the prophetess and the 'Shelley ad nauseam', while Helena Swanwick referred to an absence of directed logic in those mystical speeches. But everyone acknowledged Charlotte Despard's warmth and good humour, qualities that are not always evident in the hawk-like profile she presents in official portraits.

In these exciting years the woman who had grown up among sisters discovered the joy of political sisterhood. Though her new friends perceived her as old, she herself felt young among them: 'How beautiful this new pride in womanhood is!' As she explained in 'Why I became a Suffragette' (*Women's Franchise*, 1907):

I had sought comradeship of some sort with men. I had marched with great processions of the unemployed, I had stood on platforms of Labour men and Socialists, I had tried to stir up the people to a sense of shame about the misery of their lives, and the degradation of their women. I had listened with sympathy to fiery denunciations of Governments and the Capitalistic system to which they belong. Amongst all these experiences, I had not found what I met on the threshold of this young, vigorous union of hearts.

Now the Nine Elms base served the Cause and Rosalie Mansell joined her employer to become a dab hand at organizing jumble sales – 'men's, boys' and children's clothing welcome – but no hats please'. In summer the Oxshott cottage was also at the disposal of the movement, sometimes being the venue for London branch committee meetings. (It should be remembered that in southern England the word 'cottage' often means a small country house, so that Mrs Despard's retreat had room for several overnight guests and facilities for large tea parties.) When Vera Ryder was a little girl she was sometimes taken to tea with family friends who lived near Earnshaw Cottage:

Perhaps the most exciting thing that came our way on our outings was the possibility of meeting a certain lady who lived further up the road towards Oxshott. She was a Mrs Despard, a militant suffragette. Occasionally the even more notorious Mrs Pankhurst, and her daughter, Christabel, came to stay with her.

The little Ryders could not understand why grown-ups disapproved and why 'Nannie hurried us past the little house as though it were a fever hospital with germs jumping out of it', and imagined that Mrs Despard was a witch. But when they did pass the infamous lady, in her full regalia, they decided 'from surreptitious glances beneath lowered eyes' that she was 'really most attractive for a witch'. Charlotte Despard would have been very flattered by nannie's insistence that nonetheless she was 'a very dangerous person'.

# Chapter 7

# THE WOMEN'S FREEDOM LEAGUE: 'MOTHER OF THE LEAGUE'

The first 'split' within the WSPU, which happened late in 1907, was achieved with little long-term bitterness. Indeed, faced with the degree of solidarity sustained between the different suffragist societies before the First World War, it becomes easier to understand why so many of the women involved sincerely trusted that female enfranchisement would usher in a New Order of permanent world peace.

Back in the WSPU's shoestring Manchester days a Labour man had been cynical about Mrs Pankhurst and her eldest daughter: 'Really the pair are not seeking democratic freedom but self-importance. . . .' More tellingly, Eva Gore-Booth, who had been a political godmother to Christabel Pankhurst, became critical when, in the wake of the first famous act of militancy, she began to behave like any other hack politician: 'Now she is out in the open. She cannot fit her explanation to her audience. . . . She either deliberately invited imprisonment or she was a victim. . . . She can't tell one tale in Manchester and another in Oldham.' As the senior Pankhursts hit the metropolitan limelight, other Manchester pioneers shared Eva Gore-Booth's alienation. Alice Milne was discomfited by the tone of the London WSPU's weekly 'At Homes', where interested (and hopefully moneyed) ladies met the increasingly elegant Christabel.

We found the place full of fashionable ladies in rustling silks and satins ... if any of our Adult Suffrage Socialist friends could have looked into that room, he would have said that more than ever ours was a movement for the middle classes and upper classes. What a fever our Union members in Manchester would have been in, if such ladies had made a descent on us in Manchester.

Not without justification, the Pankhursts felt that the militant movement was theirs rather than 'ours', and they did their best to keep it that way. Partly because she was Christabel's main rival in talent and popularity, Teresa Billington-Greig was soon sent away from London to Scotland to organize the WSPU branches there, a 'Siberia' which, with typical panache, she soon turned into an alternative powerbase. But when the Pethick-Lawrences got a suffragette newspaper going, TBG was offended by the fact that she was not asked to contribute to it, 'not even a message welcoming its appearance'.

Meanwhile, bourgeois London was lionizing the Pankhursts. Their susceptibility to heroine worship and nice clothes did have some political value, because the movement's image was all-important in attracting media interest and sympathy. They had a very modern instinct for what makes good copy and they made sure that they were always photogenic. It was all very well for eccentric saints like Charlotte Despard to go about in 'rational dress', but otherwise suffragettes had a duty to present themselves as smartly as possible. Apart from propriety, the Pankhursts were determined that they and their followers would not be slagged off as cranky unmarriageables.

Dora Montefiore took this public relations thing very seriously. When younger members of the WSPU were pushed into the waiting room at Cannon Row Police Station with their hair down and their clothes torn, she took it upon herself to make them 'once more presentable'. Though a generation younger than Charlotte Despard and therefore not yet venerable, Mrs Montefiore was also something of a political veteran. In pre-WSPU days she had avoided paying imperial taxes on the principle of 'no taxation without representation' (local taxes could be paid because some women had votes in local government). But she got no media mileage out of her lonely troubles. For the WSPU-backed 'Siege of Fort Montefiore' in the summer of

1906, when her Chiswick house was barricaded and festooned with suffragette banners in readiness for the distraint bailiffs, Mrs Montefiore did hit the headlines.

But Dora Montefiore's centrality to the early London WSPU did not earn her the Pankhursts' undying loyalty or affection. By her own account she was 'choked off' when she began to query the secrecy surrounding the amount and the use of WSPU funds and to become uneasy about the prison-martyr cult, by which young suffragettes were being encouraged to physically resist the police. But the excuse for offloading Montefiore came when she supported the eligibility of the wife of a Liberal MP for the secretaryship of the Westminster WSPU branch, which she was instrumental in setting up. Having thereby banished Montefiore, the Pankhursts and their coterie reminded themselves of Mrs Montefiore's moral deficiencies, namely her liking for cocaine lozenges.

Dora Montefiore's extraordinary career was by no means over when she found herself 'not wanted' by the WSPU. Nevertheless, she consoled herself by identifying 'poor Mrs Despard' as a 'stalking horse' because the letter invalidating the Westminster society's status as a WSPU branch bore her typed signature.

Charlotte Despard was no more immune to Emmeline and Christabel Pankhurst's star qualities than she was to be to that of the equally charismatic Maud Gonne. But although she enjoyed their vitality, she was never putty in their hands. By way of illustrating such a condition, we can quote Annie Kenney, for whom Christabel was 'the idol, the loved and honoured one . . . we were conscious that she was the woman of the age, and that she alone could lead us to the land of political freedom.' Charlotte Despard had not spent the previous fifteen years schooling herself into a self-denying commitment to mass-based, mass-accountable political movements just to become a Pankhurst client. While she agreed with the principle of tactical independence and accepted the logic of harassing the Liberal government and the Liberal Party, she was with them. Nevertheless, as she told the newspapers after her release from Holloway in 1907, if she had been free she would have helped 'Labour men only' in the London County Council elections.

The Labour Party justified the support of Charlotte Despard and the benevolently neutral attitude of the WSPU when, at its Easter Conference in 1907, Keir Hardie's resolution was passed in favour of votes for women as a goal that was separable, rather than a mere appendage of, the goal of universal adult suffrage. Mrs Despard and Mrs Cobden Sanderson thanked the conference with a pledge of loyalty to the Labour Party. But this pledge was interpreted in its narrowest terms by Emmeline Pankhurst, who rose to say, 'We are not going to wait until the Labour Party can give us the vote.' This repudiation of the spirit of the Despard-Cobden Sanderson pledge could be seen as a necessary affirmation of suffragette autonomy, were it not for the fact that Emmeline and Christabel Pankhurst were by now moving to the right. In two recent by-elections the WSPU had intervened to the detriment of both Liberal and Labour men, and this strategy was making them responsive to the blandishments of the official opposition, the Tories. But the growing misgivings of women like Charlotte Despard were not simply informed by loyalty to the Labour Party.

Teresa Billington-Greig's kinship with the Labour Party was by now historic and she was openly critical of the stance of socialist women such as Margaret Bondfield: 'We fail to see why it should be so very virtuous to fight against class-aggression, and so very wicked to fight against sex-aggression.' But the Pankhurst effort to distance the WSPU from its radical origins had implications which TBG would not put up with. It had been she who had drafted an ILP-style constitution for the WSPU back in Manchester. As the WSPU went national it was supposed to be controlled by this constitution, which allowed for an annual conference composed of delegates entitled to vote on tactics and for the members of its executive council.

By such procedures it was hoped that the rather too freelance Pankhursts would be monitored by their supporters, and not surprisingly, they were having none of it. They professed to be alarmed by the 'newcomers pouring into the Union'. The WSPU was a militant, combative organization – like an army – and soldiers shouldn't debate their orders. As that good trooper, Annie Kenney, put it,

> Christabel, Mrs Pankhurst, Mr and Mrs Pethick Lawrence and I all realized the futility of such action [conferences and the like] in a revolutionary movement, a movement whose actions were decided not after hours of debate, but were acted upon the moment the idea presented itself.

At a meeting of London WSPU members in September1907 Mrs
Pankhurst tore up the constitution document and announced
that, henceforth, the WSPU would be replaced by a new organization with an executive committee answerable only to herself
and Christabel (who was preserved from any overt dirty work).
With a coolness worthy of Lady Macbeth Mrs Pankhurst further
declared that her anti-constitutional putsch had been motivated
by the need to defeat a conspiracy to shackle the WSPU to the
Labour Party. As TBG noted acidly, 'The aggressors cloaked
themselves in the mantles of saviours who had boldly nipped
an insidious conspiracy against the Union's independence in the
bud and had saved the Union at the cost of their most cherished
principles. . . .'

But the 'conspirators' felt that it was absurd as well as wrong
for women campaigning for democratic rights to deny them
within their own movement, and they went ahead with the
constitution conference. These women included most of the
suffragettes of any prominence outside the Pankhurst-Pethick-
Lawrence coterie, representing about one-fifth of the WSPU's
original membership. Noting the seniority of the defectors,
newspapers saw a generation gap in the 'Split'. Margaret Wynne
Nevinson, a Liberal Party woman and no socialist, who was
usually nominated when the future Women's Freedom League
was asked by Conservative women's organizations for a speaker,
was one of the splitters. There were many others of her calibre.
Hannah Mitchell, a working-class suffragette, was hurt by the
Pankhursts' indifference to her illness in 1907; 'not even a letter
of sympathy was forthcoming.' By contrast, Charlotte Despard
found the time to visit her, and paid for her to have extra food.
The recovered Hannah Mitchell then joined the splitters.

They first based themselves in an office near the Strand, with
a year's rent and expenses up to £100 guaranteed by Charlotte
Despard. 'Then we began almost literally to live in it. What jolly
"scratch" teas we had on the bare office tables and what startling
plots and plans we hatched round them.' After less than a year
the conspirators had emerged as the Women's Freedom League,
and although the role of President was not formally created or
ratified until 1909, from the start Charlotte Despard acted it.
But as the League's figurehead she did not behave, as Mrs
Wolstenholme Elmy, a truly ancient suffragist who was a
Pankhurst fan, predicted:

1. Miss Charlotte French (*British Library*)

VOTES FOR WOMEN.

Mrs. DESPARD.

2. Mrs Despard as a leading light in the Women's Social and Political Union. (*Mary Evans/Fawcett Library*)

3. Mrs Despard addresses a meeting outside Parliament. (*Mary Evans/Fawcett Library*)

4. *Above* Charlotte Despard and Anne Cobden-Sanderson outside 10 Downing Street, 1909. The famous sandals are just visible beneath the long black skirt. Shortly afterwards they were arrested. (*National Portrait Gallery*)

5. *Left* Charlotte Despard as President of the Women's Freedom League. (*Mary Evans/Fawcett Library*)

6. *Above* With the executive of the WFL, possibly photographed after one of the summer birthday parties. Teresa Billington-Greig is sitting on the left of Charlotte Despard. (*Mary Evans/Fawcett Library*)

7. *Right* Dressed, as all suffragettes who could afford it were advised, in white for the occasion, Charlotte Despard leads the WFL contingent on a summer demonstration in 1911. (*Mary Evans/Fawcett Library*)

8. Charlotte Despard orates on Labour Day 1920 in Hyde Park. (*Syndication International Limited*)

9. Lord French inspects the Royal Irish Constabulary and says goodbye to Ireland, April 1921. (*BBC Hulton Picture Library*)

10. Maud Gonne, 1895, pin-up of the Celtic Twilight. (*National Library of Ireland*).

11. *Below* Maud Gonne MacBride. Her habitual, French-style widow's headpiece complemented Charlotte Despard's mantilla. (*National Library of Ireland*)

12. *Below right* Sean O'Sullivan's drawing of Maud Gonne MacBride. This is how she looked when she became friends with Charlotte Despard. (*National Library of Ireland*)

13.  *Above* Madame MacBride, Madame Despard and Dorothy Macardle inspect the remains of a Balbriggan hosiery factory burnt by the Black and Tans, 1921. (*Courtesy of the late Sean MacBride*)

14.  *Left* 1923: Mrs Despard keeping her lonely vigil at the gates of Kilmainham Gaol while awaiting the release of Maud Gonne MacBride. (*Courtesy of the late Sean MacBride*)

15. Charlotte Despard, suitably unhappy about the company she has to keep, sits beside Ramsay MacDonald as he makes a speech, probably in honour of the 1928 Equal Franchise Act. (*Mary Evans/Fawcett Library*)

16. A happier looking Mrs Despard, photographed around the same time. (*Mary Evans/Fawcett Library*)

17. Jack Mulvenna (*left*) with Captain Jack White, who had trained Connolly's Citizen Army in 1914–16. (*Courtesy of Jack Mulvenna*)

18. Mollie Fitzgerald. (*Courtesy of Jack Mulvenna*)

19. Charlotte Despard, now in boots, addresses an anti-fascist rally in Trafalgar Square in 1933. (*National Museum of Photography, Film and Television, Bradford*)

I expect Mrs Despard will lead the dissidents into the arms of the SDF. . . . the whole idea of superseding the Pankhursts, who have created and sustained the movement, by Mrs Despard, who has neither political knowledge nor practical wisdom, is too monstrously silly, to say nothing of its vile ingratitude.

But this lack of conventional 'political knowledge' was one of Charlotte Despard's greatest assets in her new role. Although the constitutionalists were legally entitled to the WSPU's name, office, funds and literature, she appealed, 'as she always does', to the 'highest feelings', and recommended a totally new organization in the name of feminist unity. TBG, the real first leader of the League, was not very happy about going out into the wilderness alone because of Mrs Despard's scruples, 'making a free gift of the funds, name, prestige and achievements, which had been acquired by the efforts of all combined.' But in the end most people agreed that it had been a decision for the best. The Women's Freedom League was never guided by Charlotte Despard into the unlikely arms of the Social Democratic Federation. Although it would never, unlike the WSPU, insist on its members' exclusive loyalty, it sought co-operation with every other organization sympathetic to women's suffrage, especially at a local level. Soon after the WFL's foundation, friendly overtures were made to such groups as the Women's Co-operative Guild, women's trade unions and the Men's League for Women's Suffrage. Even WSPU meetings were advertised in the League's newspaper *The Vote*.

Before long the League had a distinct identity as the *other* militant suffragist organization, or, because of its place between the more militarily militant WSPU and Mrs Fawcett's National Union of Women's Suffrage Societies (NUWSS), the 'constitutional militant' society. The influence of Charlotte Despard can be discerned in the League's perception of votelessness as the root of women's oppression generally. Accordingly, its members and its newspaper were actively concerned with the treatment of female crimes such as infanticide, as well as with female vulnerability in male courts. Their agitation over such *causes célèbres* as that of Daisy Lord, a nineteen-year-old jailed for killing her baby, is reminiscent of contemporary feminist campaigns. The Leaguers kept a vigilant eye on all legislation affecting the lives of working women, and of mothers in particular. Mrs Despard's Poor Law experiences found expression in her critique of the 1910 Children's Charter, which sought to protect children via compulsory fireguards and cots without regard for the realities that forced poor women to 'neglect' them in the first place.

The WFL's motto was 'Dare to be Free!' and the telegram address was simply and significantly 'Despard'. At each annual conference a militancy that broke no 'moral law' was ratified, which meant that the WFL concentrated on propaganda work. In WSPU days, TBG, a brilliant tactician, had felt frustrated by the fact that the Pankhursts had only taken up her petitioning and protesting strategies. Now other tactics could be exercised. A typical wheeze was the League-inspired boycott of the Census of 1911, when thousands of women refused, by dint of removing themselves from their normal places of abode on Census Night, to be enumerated in symbolic protest against their absence as full citizens.

Mrs Despard justified the WFL's illegal strategies by saying, 'There are times and seasons in human history when civil disobedience is the highest duty we can offer to our generation.' Late in 1909 she met the man who was to become most famous as an exponent of the politics of passive resistance, Mahatma Gandhi. He was generally impressed by the suffragette campaigns and met both Mrs Pankhurst and Mrs Despard. But he had a special affinity with the latter: 'Mrs Despard herself is a wonderful person. I had long talks with her in London, and admire her greatly, and much appreciate her advocacy of "spiritual resistance".'

Tax evasion was played by the League to maximum effect, Mrs Despard suffering the indignities of distraint on many occasions. Once, when her Nine Elms furniture had been seized by bailiffs in lieu of unpaid taxes, she went along to the auction rooms. 'By courtesy of the auctioneer Mrs Despard addressed the people in the sale rooms to explain the protest.' When her piano was 'burgled' while she was away on a speaking tour of Scotland, *The Vote* kept its readers informed of its whereabouts, and sympathizers, against Mrs Despard's wishes, often purchased her personal belongings in order to return them to her.

Women who lacked means could refuse to pay their dog

licences and those who felt shy of public speaking could wear the League's propaganda sandwich boards, made comfortably economic by the use of cardboard rather than wood: 'It must be a shock for many a well-bred person out for a morning's shopping to meet her friend unconcernedly strolling up Regent Street between sandwich boards. . . .' There was an unintimidating cosiness to the League's style, from *The Vote*'s commercial advertisements – 'humanitarians can wear our lovely ostrich feathers with a clear conscience' – to featurettes about the daily lives of prominent Leaguers: 'Mrs Snowden makes pastry'; 'Mrs How-Martyn makes jam'; 'Alison Neilans cleans the stove'; and Mrs Despard, photographed in a rather austere room, 'knits a comforter'.

But the League also had its more adventurous members. The Australian Muriel Matters floated over London in a hot-air balloon and kept herself warm by hurling her 'votes for women' pamphlets overboard. A Miss Moloney earned immortality as 'La Belle Moloney' when she followed Winston Churchill during a Scottish by-election with the clang of her muffin bell. With another Leaguer, Muriel Matters chained herself to the *grille* that screened off the Ladies Gallery in the House of Commons. Even Millicent Fawcett, who couldn't condone such stunts because of the offence against property, said that looking through this screen used to make her cross-eyed. While supporters chanted 'Votes for Women!' this odious grating was removed with the women still attached to it. They sat in a committee room until a locksmith was found to separate them from the thirty-foot-long *grille*, which never returned to the Ladies Gallery.

The *grille* protest worked well but other stunts, planned with equal care, went horribly wrong. Alison Neilans and Mrs Chapin spilled a chemical into the ballot boxes at a polling station in Bermondsey, intending to destroy the votes inside. They had experimented beforehand to make sure that the substance, which in the event did not even destroy the voting papers, was harmless to humans. But when some of it splashed into the eye of a polling booth official, his panicky colleagues rushed to his aid with ammonia, which did cause him considerable pain. As a result, Alison Neilans and Mrs Chapin were jailed for several months.

It was getting harder and harder to even ask for the vote

because in April 1908 the encouraging Campbell-Bannerman had been replaced as Prime Minister by Herbert Asquith. He was personally hostile to female enfranchisement, believing that it amounted to votes for more Tories. In any case, he was preoccupied with the steering of government legislation through a hostile (mainly Conservative) House of Lords. Following his refusals to meet suffragette deputations, the League set up its 'Great Watch' on Parliament from summer to November of 1909. More than 14,000 woman-hours were put in during all weathers for this mute and morally touching vigil in Westminster. H. G. Wells fictionalized its impact in *The New Machiavelli*:

> There were women of all sorts, though of course the independent working class predominated. There were grey-haired old ladies ... north country factory girls – cheaply dressed suburban women – trimly comfortable mothers of families – lank hungry creatures who stirred one's imagination – one very dainty little woman in deep mourning, grave and steadfast, with eyes fixed on distant things. Some looked defiant, some timidly aggressive, some full of the stir of adventure, some drooping with cold and fatigue ... I found that continual siege of the legislature extraordinarily impressive – infinitely more impressive than the feeble-forcing 'ragging' of the more militant section.

Hostile passers-by made remarks that according to the super-respectable Margaret Wynne Nevinson were calculated to raise 'a blush to the cheek of modesty' and she hoped that the younger unmarried members wouldn't understand. Friendly passers-by sometimes brought chocolate and cups of tea, and worried about whether the ladies would spoil their complexions in broiling sunshine.

But there was nothing cosy about the effort to keep the vote on the political agenda as the government began to arrest women even before they made any significant protest. Charlotte Despard's second imprisonment in 1909 happened after she took part in a deliberately small and low-key deputation to Downing Street to protest about the routine omission of the vote from the King's Speech. At her trial she made great capital out of her snowy hair: 'I am an old woman and I have tried all my life to fulfil loyally the duties of citizenship. I simply wanted to see the Prime Minister and for this I was arrested and ignominiously taken through the streets to a police station.' But the presiding magistrate decided that although 'she could not use much force . . . she evidently tried her best'. Off to Holloway she went, though only for a few days on account of the authorities' mysterious concern for her health.

On another, similar occasion, Mrs Despard, Mrs Cobden Sanderson and Mrs Hicks had their fines paid anonymously before they could make a prison protest:

> No personal friend [of Mrs Despard's] would have dared to do this, knowing her strong feelings on the subject of fines. It was a significant fact that the fines of all three had been paid on the same day, and before it was generally known that the warrants were about to be issued. They could draw their own conclusions as to who paid the fines, whilst also bearing in mind the fact that it would not have suited the Government at the present time to have certain members of the League in prison.

Meanwhile the prisons, notably Holloway, were filling up with suffragettes. With the first outbreak of window-smashing WSPU militancy had taken a new turn, which was a response to the unparalleled brutality with which one of their demonstrations had been broken up. In July 1909 a WSPU member, Marion Wallace Dunlop, became the first suffragette prisoner to go on hunger strike. Her early release encouraged imitation and within a few weeks the emaciated window-smashers were also released. Later that year the government authorized a dangerous and painful method of forcible feeding whereby liquid food was poured into a hunger-striking prisoner's stomach by means of a rubber tube clamped to the mouth or nostrils. (By 1913 public feeling was so outraged that the government had to introduce the 'Cat and Mouse' Act, which allowed for the temporary discharge, and re-arrest, of hunger strikers.) Soon the Women's Freedom League had its quota of hunger-striking prisoners and its own award for gallantry. The 'Holloway Badge' was presented by Mrs Despard, 'the mother of the League'.

But the evangelical work went on. In the summer of 1908 a League team took to the country roads of southern England with a horse-drawn caravan for 'an interesting and health-giving form of propaganda'. The horse was named 'Asquith' because he was 'driven by women to assist the cause of votes for women'. It was sent off from Mrs Despard's Surrey cottage with the intrepid Muriel Matters as the first travelling star-speaker. Amids cornfields scarlet with poppies, she wrote about how difficult it was to feel 'strenuous-minded or militant'. But at other times the torrential rain forced the caravan crew on to the hospitality of local sympathizers. The political conditions encountered by the WFL roadshow were frequently variable: flowers and 'opera star' treatment at one village, violence or, worse, apathy, at the next. Mrs Despard described her first six-week stint with the caravan as a life 'full of contrasts', her typically euphemistic description of what was at times an extremely hazardous venture.

Open-air speakers were always vulnerable and the picture hats so beloved of otherwise defiantly hatless suffragette speakers often served as shields for their eyes against whatever came to a hostile audience's hands. But the mantilla-crowned Charlotte Despard was a very experienced public speaker and adroit with hecklers. Her age usually commanded some respect and in London she also benefited from her status as a friend of the working man, of the working Catholic Irishman in particular. It sometimes helped that the League's colours of green, white and gold appealed to Irish men. In the Edwardian period this affinity had nothing to do with the Irish tricolour, which, though it can be traced back to the Young Ireland move-ment of the 1840s, was not then identified as the national flag. But the gold (or yellow) and white colours were the same as the Pope's. At a street meeting recalled by Margaret Wynne Nevinson, when the WFL platform was decorated only with gold and white ribbons because of a shortfall of green ones, the speakers were protected from threats by the shout, 'Don't touch them, they're Catholics,' and 'a huge Irish coster forced his way to the front and stood beside us with clenched fists.'

But it is possible that Margaret Wynne Nevinson was unaware of Irish sympathies for Mrs Despard, which were extended to her Women's Freedom League. While on her caravan duty at Canterbury, Wynne Nevinson and her party were again saved from a mean and moody crowd by the intervention of an Irish soldier: 'Shut your dirty mouths, that lady reminds me of my mother and, begorrah, she shall have a hearing – I'll fight the first man that interrupts her.' But no Irish gallants were at hand when Charlotte Despard and the caravan hit Maidstone in Kent. As she rose to speak she was met with a shower of broken granite and pebbles, some of which struck her in the face and caused her to bleed profusely. But she climbed back on to her chair and began to speak again, until the crowd made a rush for her.

> Fortunately, she was able to get upon her feet on the ground, but the chair was smashed up, and things looked indeed very dangerous. A little body of working men tried hard to protect us and fought valiantly on our behalf. Stones, granite and missiles of all kinds were flying around us.

And all the while some 'so-called gentlemen' onlookers stood by, 'many of them smiling with evident satisfaction'.

Like the early Christians, the women usually stayed their ground to earn a chastened and attentive audience at the next meeting in the same place. But such brushes with physical martyrdom enhanced Charlotte Despard's saintly image, and she seems to have colluded with her own personality cult, for in a suffragette Pageant of Women she donned a wimple to play Saint Hilda.

> Justice (Miss Edythe Olive), in a glory of gold against a sombre background of green, hears the case of the shackled Woman (Mary Webb) against prejudice (Nigel Playfair), and as witnesses for the Plaintiff come a glittering array of the flowering of woman in the past and present. Prejudice will have it that women have no wit or learning, and crowding in to give him the lie come Hypatia, St Teresa, De Scudery, De Stael, Georges Sand, Madame Curie, girl graduates in cap and gown, and a host of others. He denies that holiness or philanthropy is theirs, and St Hilda, Elisabeth of Hungary, with many others confront him. They have no art, he says, and straight appear to Woman's answering voice, Rosa Bonheur (Edith Craig), Nance Oldfield (Ellen Terry), who does her talking for herself and flouts the boaster. . . .'

Such events boosted flagging morale as the women's campaign

appeared to lose momentum in the face of Asquith's diehard opposition and intensifying repression. More than before the massive summer demonstrations served to simultaneously keep the movement's spirits up and to warn the world that women were on the threshold of power. The women brought a new animation and an extraordinarily charged atmosphere to the traditional march-meeting. Their demonstrations were huge moving pageants, with a forest of vivid and often exquisitely embroidered banners on themes ranging from the mystical recall of heroines past to the roles of women in the modern world: 'Vashti, Queen and Woman', 'Black Agnes of Dunbar', 'Joan of Arc'.

On all-suffragist marches the WFL contingent was usually led by Mrs Despard:

> It is arranged that I, as president, shall lead, and I am naturally anxious that our contingent shall be worthy of its place in this great pageant . . . Mrs How-Martyn, in cap and gown, will lead the doctors, professors, and graduates. Nurses in uniform . . . will have a section of their own. Our prisoners, each bringing her own special banner, will form another . . . the pharmacists, I hear, have applied for a banner, which promises to be attractive. . . . To give an additional brightness and unity to our march the organizers hope that very many of our processionists will wear white with the regalia of the Women's Freedom League, which can be had (price 2s.) at our office.

At the front of the WFL, Mrs Despard would enjoy almost royal acclaim. Here, a working man would rush from the pavement in order to kiss her hand; elsewhere, there would be spontaneous shouts of 'Up Lambeth!' or, from groups of soldiers, 'Up French!' and 'She's one of the best!' By now in her late sixties, she seems to have had no trouble marching right through central London to begin speaking either at Hyde Park or the Albert Hall. And when the 'truce' of 1910 came, and she found herself regularly on platforms with Mrs Fawcett and Mrs Pankhurst, she often enjoyed the most impressive reception from the crowd. This happy, expectant, but all too brief 'truce' situation arose from a very complex set of developments after the Budget of 1909 had been thrown out by the House of Lords.

In the ensuing 'People versus Peers' General Election early in 1910, the Liberals were returned to government with a very reduced majority. In that summer, which was marked by really magnificent suffrage monster-demonstrations, a 'Conciliation Bill' for women's suffrage was drawn up by an all-Party parliamentary committee. It would have given the vote to women who owned the freehold or leasehold of property valued at £10 per annum. Married women were not excluded, being assigned a vote on the same terms as widows and spinsters, provided that husband and wife did not claim their franchise in respect of the same property. This bill, and successive Conciliation Bills, was in fact doomed and it wouldn't have given anything to 'the millhand, or the housewife tied to a drunkard in the Mile End Road'. But it was a start, a concession to be further worked upon. As such, the Conciliation Bill was hailed by all the suffragist organizations and leaders, and a truce with regard to militant activities was declared. (This truce wobbled after the brutal events of 'Black Friday' 1910, when a WSPU protest march against Asquith's cynical abandonment of the first Conciliation Bill was broken up with such violence that two women actually died as a result of their injuries.)

But the first months of the truce were Mrs Despard's heyday, when she could regale her listeners with the promise of the 'triumph of reason' and the 'coming of the golden year'. During this time Laurence Housman, a prominent male supporter of women's suffrage, had what he called the 'delicate task' of preparing a toast at a celebratory dinner to which Mrs Fawcett, Mrs Despard and Miss Christabel Pankhurst, the guests of honour, were to respond in turn. Mrs Despard was usually up there with the other widow women who are today better remembered as the leaders of the Cause. But few contemporary commentators realized that although Mrs Despard's shining hour had come, her venerable show had another quarter of a century to run.

# CHAPTER 8

# THE EDWARDIAN CRISIS: 'IT IS HARD TO BE OUT OF EVERYTHING'

The parliamentary Conciliation Committee was to propose a number of suffrage bills over the next few years, all of which faltered. Dependent on Labour and Irish support, Asquith's Liberal government was, as *The Vote* put it, 'between the devil and the deep sea'. Since the Labour devil was by now firmly in favour of women's suffrage, Irish affairs and Irishwomen became of great interest to the Women's Freedom League:

> All those members of ours who have friends or relatives in Ireland, or who are themselves in touch with Irish affairs, should immediately place the information they have got at the disposal of the Organizing Department. The preliminary work in Ireland has already begun, and no time is to be lost.

The League had established a foothold in Ireland with the branch started in Bangor in 1908 and soon Dublin had an outpost based in Grafton Street. A leading light in this Dublin WFL was the daughter of the Lord Chief Justice of Ireland, the Hon. Georgina O'Brien. In 1910 Miss O'Brien hosted a suffragette reception at her family home, Airfield, where a fashionable gathering was introduced to Muriel Matters. But the Leaguers were not proselytizers and they sought a broad solidarity with progressive Irish forces rather than an organizational conquest. By contrast, the WSPU irritated Irish suffragist activists when it began recruiting independently, 'trying to run the suffrage movement in Ireland on purely English lines'. The WFL's ecumenism reflected its President's respect for the autonomy of Irish politics, and her old connections with Ireland were now very relevant to the success of the suffrage Cause.

Charlotte Despard's sense of Irishness, deriving from the paternal ancestry, the late husband and some spiritual sense of kinship, intensified from 1910 onwards. Just as she saw the liberation of humankind as a corollary of female emancipation, so she saw Irish national independence (then perceived in terms of Home Rule) as a corollary of the emancipation of Irish women. In *The Vote* there are frequent wishful thoughts along these lines:

Irish women have great traditions behind them to guide them in the future – greater in some ways than those of their Anglo-Saxon sisters. There are the old Brehon annals records of women doctors and of women lawyers. There was even one Brigit who became a judge and whose wise decisions were followed as precedents for hundreds of years. Women Hospitallers and Abbesses without number brought honour to Erin in the grand old days.

In the effort to support the first Conciliation Bill some sixty-nine English town councils sent resolutions in favour to Parliament, as did nearly a hundred trade unions. The Lord Mayor of Dublin, Tom Kelly, whose wife was to become Dublin's first woman mayor, took advantage of an ancient right of his city to petition the House of Commons in its support. In the full scarlet and gold regalia of his office, bearing a white wand and with an attendant carrying the Irish mace and sword of state before him, he addressed the House. Afterwards, at a dinner in the Connaught Rooms in Mayor Kelly's honour, Hugh Law MP and Charlotte Despard, 'an Irish leader here', were the main speakers. On this, as on most such occasions, she affirmed her commitment 'heart and soul' to getting votes for women into 'any and every Home Rule Bill'. At the same time, she urged the importance of working independently for women's rights through the Conciliation Bill, 'or any other bill the English parties might introduce either before or during all contemporaneous phases of the 700-year struggle for the freedom of Ireland'.

Her letters to the leader of the Irish parliamentary party, John Redmond, also sought to reconcile the two aspirations of women's suffrage and Home Rule.

My lifelong sympathy with all peoples struggling for liberty makes me the more confident in approaching you with this appeal. In all the struggles that Ireland has waged for its ideals, your countrywomen have rendered valuable service and sacrifice, and have in fact paid a heavier price than their brothers.

The Irish cultural revival often celebrated the essentially 'feminine' nature of the Celt, as opposed to the rationalist, capitalist and male nature of the Teuton. This language was very congenial to Charlotte Despard. She was a great admirer of 'AE' (George Russell), the chief guru of the mystical strand within the Celtic Twilight, and embellished one of her little diaries with inspirational quotes from his writings: 'I shake my heavy fears aside and seize the flaming sword of will.' Her own spiritual fluency went down a treat on her speaking tours of Ireland. Even Louie Bennett, who thought of herself as a down-to-earth, practical woman and was to become the leader of the Irish women's trade union movement, noted the special appeal of Mrs Despard's 'type of personality' in Ireland. She organized the spring speaking tour of 1912, which was so successful that immediately afterwards a 'Despard Fund' was started to bring her back in September.

On the last night of that spring tour Mrs Despard reportedly held her Dublin listeners enthralled for nearly an hour:

It was with deep regret that they saw the chairman remind her that her time was up and that she must bring her speech to a close as she had to leave to catch the Holyhead boat . . . she left the Hall amidst a tremendous ovation of cheers and applause, many of the audience pressing forward to touch her hand as she passed . . . her beautiful personality and beautiful selfless self has roused in us the spirit of hero-worship, and the opportunity for even a fleeting sight and sound of her is an inspiration and encouragement.

And after the succeeding autumn tour, 'Two Irishwomen' wrote with equal rapture to *The Vote*:

> The vision which she sees, the vision towards which she stretches out arms of longing and hope, is akin to that which greeted the dying eyes of Faust. A vision of a free people standing upon the ground which they have wrested for themselves. . . . One of Mrs Despard's great gifts is that she can impart a dim impression of this vision and stir other souls in pursuit of it.

But Mr Redmond's soul remained unstirred by the 'height that is higher'. He wished to avoid any issue that, by precipitating a General Election or the resignation of a Cabinet minister, might get in the way of Home Rule, so tantalizingly within legislative reach after the taming of the House of Lords. Some Irish parliamentarians had a more principled perspective on the issue. John Dillon MP, for example, believed that votes for women would usher in nothing less than the ruin of Western civilization: 'It will destroy the home, challenging the headship of man, laid down by God.' Others, notably Tom Kettle, whose wife was one of the Sheehy sisters, was active in support of the Cause. But when all was said and done, Home Rule was the thing and most of the Irish MPs fell into line behind Redmond.

Suffragist hopes, so often raised, were cruelly and conclusively dashed in November 1911 when Asquith 'torpedoed' the current Conciliation Bill by announcing that he was about to introduce a Franchise Bill that would abolish all property-based voting qualifications, but for men only. There was the technical possibility that votes for women could be tacked on to this as an amendment, but in practice Asquith's proposal was a way of shelving the issue. The WSPU response was open warfare, and so began the real militancy of poisoned golf greens, cut telegraph wires, wrecked sports pavilions, slashed pictures and arson, and all against the grim background of hunger-striking prisoners and the Cat and Mouse Act. The Women's Freedom League decided to hold its militant options in reserve: 'we can use it; or we can refrain from using it. When, with full recognition of the sacrifice entailed, we do deliberately make use of militancy, we make clearly evident the logical necessity behind it.'

Mrs Despard's cryptic little diaries record her distance from

WSPU-style militancy just before the First World War. On arson, 'news today of the burning of a beautiful church, how piteous'; on the slashing of the *Rokeby Venus*, 'news of poor Miss Richardson's smashing of Velazquez' *Venus*. When is it to end?' When Emily Wilding Davison threw herself under the King's horse in the 1913 Derby, Mrs Despard commented on it as a 'wild action'. But despite her disapproval of such militancy she was actively concerned about the fate of Mrs Pankhurst, who between July and December of 1913 was arrested and imprisoned six times under the Cat and Mouse Act. She did join the whole movement in making Emily Wilding Davison's funeral procession one of the most moving moments in the history of the Cause.

During the torpedo crisis Asquith agreed to meet a deputation of leading women to repudiate the accusations of bad faith being made against him. According to the cool, calm and collected Helena Swanwick, the WSPU women insisted on speaking first, and the others agreed to 'get 'em out of the way right off'. Christabel read most of a 'halting speech' and was followed by Emmeline Pethick-Lawrence. But they were not very impressive since 'both depend enormously on an applauding or interrupting crowd'. By contrast, Mrs Despard, who was not immune to Swanwick's critical scrutiny, was 'remarkably effective' and, whether she appreciated it or not, the two government ministers 'liked her hugely'. 'I have never heard her so good. She was brief and very moving. . . .' But though she must have been tired that day, Christabel Pankhurst's position was clearest because she was single-mindedly a suffragette above all else. By now that single-mindedness meant that she was overtly Tory in sympathy, which also meant that she was anti-Home Rule.

Within months of that deputation to Asquith the Pethick-Lawrences were excommunicated from the WSPU. They became critical of the WSPU militancy as it entered its kamikaze phase, and eventually Sylvia Pankhurst, who had not responded to an order from Christabel to burn down Nottingham Castle, also had to make a public break with her mother and elder sister. In London's East End, Sylvia Pankhurst's career paralleled that of Charlotte Despard in Battersea. There, her fellow suffragettes were for the most part working women and her struggle for the vote was closely allied with socialist and trade union struggles. The senior Pankhursts were sniffy about Sylvia's involvement with working-class women – the 'weakest and least intelligent of their sex'. There were many opportunities for Christabel to castigate the working classes during the years of the constipated Conciliation Bills because this was also the time of the 'Labour Unrest'. Between 1911 and 1914 dockers, seamen, railwaymen and miners all struck. With 1,450 strikes recorded in 1913, as compared with 380 in 1908, votes for women were being pushed from the headlines. Alongside the traditional demands for better pay and conditions, these disputes were also expressed in Syndicalist terms, whereby the strike and industrial sabotage were political weapons in class war. For Christabel Pankhurst it was nothing short of 'scandalous' that men should resort to such 'childish, uncivilized methods, depreciating the value of the vote for which women were struggling, and undermining the State which they were so keen to uphold'.

But for the President of the Women's Freedom League the Labour Unrest was not a rival to the suffragist struggle but another aspect of the Coming of the New Order. As the WSPU leadership drifted into a politics of despair, Charlotte Despard was reclaimed by socialist politics. Her Currie Street corner became the headquarters of Battersea's striking railwaymen. During other local disputes it was the place where distress committees met, where demonstrations and fund-raising events were planned, where the wives of strikers held clothes-making sessions and where strikers' children were fed. When the women of Bermondsey's jam, pickle and perambulator factories – Bermondsey was a kindred area to Battersea – came out in sympathy with the dockers in 1911, Mrs Despard put her resources at their disposal.

Ireland shared in the Labour Unrest and the leaders of the Dublin Lock-out of 1913 were respected acquaintances. James Connolly was Jim to Charlotte Despard. Indeed, Louie Bennett recalled the Irish labour leader's preference for the militant sections of the suffragist movement, which in all likelihood meant socialist feminism, such as that espoused by Mrs Despard and Eva Gore-Booth.

Meanwhile the Theosophical/vegetarian aspect of the Despard show continued. Mrs Despard had no problem in addressing a meeting of Battersea labourers one moment and in the next lecturing ladies on the connections between the women's movement and Theosophy. In her oft-expressed dream, the women's movement and the anti-capitalist movement were in the same direct line of spiritual evolution, twin preparations for 'the divine event towards which the whole creation moves'. In November 1913 Gretta Cousins, living in Liverpool as the first leg of a journey to India, had what she called the 'spiritual enrichment' of a visit from Charlotte Despard. A report from the *Liverpool Express* gives the flavour of this typical visit:

> In recognition of her twenty years' labour for food reform, a luncheon was given today to Mrs Despard by the Liverpool Vegetarian Society. . . . Their guest, said Mrs Cousins, Mus. Bac., the president, was an arch-reformer and pioneer of the cause of freedom. Many of them looked upon her as being the real Queen Mother of Freedom, from the soles of her feet, where she wore sandals, to the top of her head, where she did not wear a hat (laughter and applause). She had as great a love for the freedom of the animal as for men and women, and was the freest woman she (the speaker) had ever met (applause). Mrs Despard expressed the opinion that vegetarianism was really at the base of a great many things. Food seemed only a humble thing, but if they realized what did and might go into them through the body, then perhaps they would think the question of food was one of the greatest importance.

But while Gretta Cousins sighed with appreciation others were decidedly testy about the Despard personality cult. Mrs Despard's prophecies, her ubiquitousness and her postcard portraits went down well with the WFL rank and file, but some members of the League's executive committee felt that the President was not applying herself enough to the day-to-day, nitty-gritty business. Apart from the demands of her ongoing Battersea projects, she was often embarrassingly individualistic from the official WFL point of view. As TBG put it, 'for her own guidance she took council with her own soul', and 'so sure a soul did not make for easy co-operation'.

> As a result we saw a non-political [i.e. non Party] organization whose president would appear making speeches on extreme rebel platforms and though there might be nothing in those speeches to which any rebel feminist could object whatever

her political bent, their locale caused some public confusion and some internal protest.

In any case, worn down and made ill by her own hectic career in previous years, Teresa Billington-Greig resigned from her leading position in the League in 1911. A certain fatigue with Charlotte Despard's reign is also evident in the comment of an otherwise sympathetic suffragist-watcher, the journalist H. N. Brailsford. He coupled the League's president with Mrs Pankhurst, saying that both the venerable queens should be 'tugged to a haven of quiet rest like the *Téméraire*, or given two chapels in the Abbey and left there for adoration'.

Back on the Battersea front, Rosalie Mansell did her best to manage things during her celebrity employer's frequent absences. But the strain of this work and the cumulative effect of her addiction to laudanum triggered off her complete collapse in 1912. Addiction to laudanum, an opium derivative which was used as a painkiller and a tranquillizer, was something of an occupational hazard among Victorian women in general, and Victorian nurses in particular. While on the Lambeth Board of Guardians, Mrs Despard had had to consider the state of a charge nurse who had commenced taking opiates under medical direction 'for an internal complaint and allowed the taking of them to become a fixed habit'. It is probable that Rosalie Mansell's habit started in similar circumstances.

But this crisis had one rather intimate consequence for Rosalie's employer because she had cared for a ten-year-old girl named Vere Foley. Rosalie Mansell had been the effective foster-mother of this illegitimate daughter of an army officer and a nurse who had met during the Boer War. But, probably because baby Vere's existence had been brought to her attention by John French, Charlotte Despard was her legal guardian. Although she was in regular touch with Vere's natural parents, even after Rosalie's crisis there appears to have been no question of their being directly involved with the child's upbringing.

Over the next eight years or so, Vere was to be an onerous responsibility for 'Granny' Despard because, apart from the fact that in 1912 she was sixty-eight and more used to dealing with rough Battersea 'lads', the 'dear darling, so strangely thrown in my way' was quite a handful. Given the circumstances of her early childhood, it was hardly surprising that Vere Foley was not a well-adjusted or academic little girl, and many of the scrapes she got into are piteously intelligible to the modern reader. At the same time, the well-meaning elderly lady who worked so hard for so many nameless children and yet found it difficult to care for her own ward does command a certain sympathy. Charlotte Despard's hectic diaries are littered with Vere-induced hiccups:

> I think it was on Tuesday . . . that I received the shock of hearing that my Vere was sent back from the school where I had placed her. It was not altogether the poor child's fault. She had been gossiping idly and boastfully – her father a colonel, her sister an actress. Miss Oakley took alarm . . . I knew nothing until it was all over.

Between editing *The Vote*, the day trips to Holloway, the speaking engagements all over Britain and the punishing Battersea schedule, Charlotte Despard also had to find time to lecture Vere on manners and to kit her out for yet another school. With this, as with her strictly suffragette and philanthropic ventures, she had the support of a new close friend.

Mrs Kate Harvey gave Granny Despard the benefit of her experience as the mother of three teenage daughters. Her devotion to the Cause was largely motivated by her concern with the welfare of children: 'the Cause that is nearest to our hearts, the Cause of women – and children, they are inseparable'. At Brackenhill, her rambling house in Bromley, Kate Harvey ran a home for sick and handicapped children, some of whom were referred from Nine Elms and paid for by Charlotte Despard.

Mrs Harvey was an extremely efficient and courageous woman. Despite her virtual deafness she played a prominent role in the WFL, as press officer, organizer of *Vote* sales and a fund-raiser, and as a heroine in the passive resistance campaigns. When she refused to pay her gardener's insurance stamps on the no taxation without representation principle, the case enjoyed national publicity because the man's name happened to be Asquith. Brackenhill was repeatedly barricaded against the distraint bailiffs and the 'Siege of Brackenhill', for which its owner was sentenced to two months in Holloway, entered the League's annals as a particularly glorious chapter:

Brackenhill siege will bring good cheer
To those who hold Freedom dear
And fight the good fight far and near.

Kate Harvey was the first person to replace the 'dear departed' Max as an intimate friend and constant companion. The two women shared a love of gardening and of nature, Mrs Harvey being an exponent of the open-air school movement. It was fitting that, in a Christmas letter to her very old, old friend more than twenty years later, Kate Harvey described their friendship in terms of flowers: 'Yes, we had many many lovely days of work and pleasure together, and we have memories that we may have roses in December. Ours have lovely colours and the sweetest scents.' For the work – on the streets, in courtrooms and outside or inside Holloway – Mrs Harvey and Mrs Despard were inseparable. In the summer of 1913 they went together as delegates from the WFL to the seventh Congress of the International Women's Suffrage Alliance in Budapest.

Eight hundred of the participants, including Despard and Harvey, travelled the last stage of their 'delightful' journey by steamer down the Danube from Vienna. At the Hungarian capital the 3,000 suffragist delegates from all over the world were treated with lavish hospitality by the Austro-Hungarian authorities. There were banquets, an official reception in a palace above the Danube, a gala performance of *The Magic Flute* and an army of boy scouts to act as helpers and messengers. Mrs Harvey energetically sold *The Vote* and the WFL delegates were gratified by the reception given to their President by the Congress, which was equalled only by that accorded to the IWSA president, the American, Carrie Chapman Catt.

Mrs Despard took the opportunity to visit Hungarian schools, crèches and children's clinics. She was thrilled to find that 'in Hungary, at least, no child need die of hunger or neglect, and no young mother need be driven to despair'. As a whole, the Budapest Congress of 1913 was an exhilarating experience. Existing connections with Irish delegates such as Louie Bennett and Hanna Sheehy-Skeffington, were renewed and new friendships were forged. The internationalist stance of so many suffragists during the First World War owed something to the contacts made at Budapest. From then on *The Vote* contained an international section with items relating to progress in several countries, edited by the 'Head of the International Department', Mrs Harvey. Specifically, Charlotte Despard's happy memories of the facilities for orphans and children in Hungary before the war intensified her awareness of their privations after it.

With Kate Harvey, there were also Theosophical receptions to be enjoyed, and holidays to the seaside with the children or, for Christmas 1913, to Switzerland.

> There is not much variety in our life here – sports, talks with some of the English people who form the principal number of guests now, letters, papers, reading. Sunday visits to the little village, looking over winter work – this constitutes our day. The mountains are glorious. I never knew how snow could take so many colours, or that its shadows could be so soft and mysterious. I am in love with this dry clean snow. I long to bathe in it. The cold we do not feel much. This evening, Percy French, an Irishman, gave an entertainment for the Waifs & Strays, lightning sketches, very amusing.

It was a measure of Kate Harvey's powers of persuasion and Charlotte Despard's affection for her that she could set aside time for such a relatively leisured holiday. In general, Kate Harvey tried to look after her friend, organizing her correspondence and speaking tours, sending the 'motor' to collect and deliver her to railway stations, sorting out the Nine Elms accounts when, as frequently, they were 'in a mess', and even giving dancing lessons to Nine Elms children. She was unmistakably one of Mrs Despard's greatest fans as well as a friend. In March 1914 it was Mrs Harvey who organized a dramatic performance in aid of the Nine Elms clinic:

> So far no response has been made to my appeal, sent to the London branches, that we should take this opportunity of showing our appreciation of the help given to us freely and untiringly by our beloved President. It will speak badly for us if both performances are not packed to overflowing; a poor house will spell poor gratitude. Tickets, 3s., 2s., 1s., can be obtained. . . .

But it was not roses all the way between the two women. 'Dear K. H.' is very frequently 'vexed' to learn of yet another meeting fitted into the Despard schedule. Apart from her concern about Charlotte Despard's health, Mrs Harvey was 'troubled about the children and our militancy'. But she was at hand in April 1914 when Charlotte Despard fell seriously ill. A throat infection silenced her at a Trafalgar Square demonstration against 'Loyal Ulster': 'a good crowd, all workers. I could not speak. . . . I longed to speak.' A few days later, in St Ives, she had a temperature and was not allowed to get up. Then the illness, 'which I thought would cover a few days, prolonged itself – cough, fever, pain in the head, weakness day after day. A new experience for me. . . .' At the Plymouth stage of her return to London she thought of that other painful journey, twenty-four years earlier, 'with Fitz when we had left Max behind. Ah me! All those years.' At Paddington Station the League's treasurer, Dr Elizabeth Knight (incidentally a Knight's Castile heiress), was waiting with a wheelchair and Mrs Despard was taken to a London hotel where a throat specialist, to her enormous relief, pronounced that the enlargement on her throat was 'of no moment'.

Eventually she progressed to Mrs Harvey's Brackenhill where, 'surrounded as I am with care and attention, and living, whenever the weather permits, in open air', she had every chance of a complete recovery. But that was conditional upon complete rest for two months. For much of that time books and visitors were banned. Mrs Harvey compensated with Theosophical readings in the morning and so the 'little reverse' was used to contemplate 'those who suffer, the great multitude without alleviations' and to vow that 'if recovery came to devote myself more than I have done to their service'. When a glimpse of the 'outer world' was permitted, via *The Times*,

> To read it one would think that there was nothing but the Ulster question in all politics. Of course the Government have been whitewashed but that they are alarmed by the very threatening aspect of things is very evident. All these days I have been thinking of Mrs Besant, the brave, grand woman, face to face with enemies and always undaunted. . . .

Recovery was marked by frustration:

> I have not been able to hear much but the labourers are still

on strike. There is to be a big 'rally' at the Albert Hall. Delia
Larkin is in England talking about a little company of singers
etc. to help in the formation of a cooperative industry for
Dublin women. . . . I sent a contribution. It is hard to be out
of everything.

By May she could thank well-wishers in her own hand, and
send letters to *The Vote*, which had had a weekly bulletin on
the president's condition. 'I have never studied the branch news
so carefully before. The campaign in Scotland, of which I have
heard from Miss Eunice Murray, and the send-off of the
caravan, have interested me deeply.' She also warned them about
the 'strange thoughts' she had had while very ill, 'which I may
be privileged when health returns to pass on to you'. Whatever
they made of the homilies, the Leaguers were seriously anxious
about their mascot-President, and very relieved when she pulled
through the worst. Accordingly, her seventieth birthday was
made into a very special celebration. On the day itself, 15 June,
there were flowers and greetings from the League, the Builders'
Union and the Battersea 'Mothers'. For the official birthday,
early in July, there was a garden party at Brackenhill, with
a ceremonial planting of a laburnum tree in Mrs Despard's
honour.

The illness had been sufficiently alarming to prompt many
family visits. The surviving elder sister Carrie, and the younger
one nearest her in age, Maggie, found Lottie's politics abhorrent,
but it was nevertheless pleasant to talk of old times. With the
youngest and also widowed sister, Katie Harley, she could have
that pleasure and more, because Katie was an active constitutional suffragist. The 'dear, good Jack' also came to visit. On
the second occasion he came with Lady Clonmel, a friend whose
presence would have caused anyone but the innocently high-
minded Charlotte Despard to nudge and wink. Although Sir
John French was the only member of the family likely to have
been directly embarrassed by Lottie's affiliations, their differences do not seem to have surfaced during those always
'delightful' meetings. But at this stage in his career, Sir John
may well have been seeking the support of his comforting, pre-
revolutionary sister, because in July 1914 Winston Churchill
described him as being, 'for all his composure, a broken man'.
Field-Marshal Sir John French had been racked during the

incident in March 1914 which is still sometimes referred to as the 'Curragh Mutiny'. Anticipating unwelcome orders to 'coerce' Ulster into accepting Home Rule, a group of officers based at the Curragh Camp in Ireland resigned. Sir John French was first and foremost 'the King's man' and himself would never have contemplated disobeying an order, according to his most recent biographer, Richard Holmes. But he was on close terms with several of the leading 'mutineers', who came from similar backgrounds. He behaved relatively honourably, but as the piggy-in-the-middle his response to the crisis was sufficiently ambiguous to make him resign his senior Whitehall position. The outbreak of the First World War brought him back into the active top rank as Commander-in-Chief of the 100,000 men who landed in France ten days after the British declaration of war.

Charlotte Despard was not privy to any of the details of the Curragh crisis, or indeed to the details of other high-powered manoeuvres in her brother's career; she could only supplement what she read in the newspapers with her own knowledge of his personality. But she welcomed the mutual connections with Ireland, particularly with her Franks in-laws. Soon after Jack's visit in July she packed her trunk and set off for a holiday in Ireland designed to complete her convalescence. She stayed with the Franks, brother-in-law Matthew and niece Lucy, at their house in Garretstown, County Cork. She and the beloved Lucy collaborated for this account of Irish rural life, which was duly despatched to *The Vote*'s summer holiday issue.

English people who read their party papers diligently are, no doubt, many of them trembling over the critical state of affairs in Ireland. They imagine Protestants and Catholics, Unionists and Home Rulers, in that unhappy country, facing one another with clouded faces and clenched fists. They imagine the Volunteer armies (Ulster and Nationalist) perpetually under arms, looming large in the towns and villages, when men and women are holding their breath in suspense and fear, and thinking and talking of nothing but politics.

Nothing could have been further from the truth according to Miss Franks and Mrs Despard, who proceeded to illustrate the happy, expectant state of rural, southern Ireland with a sub-Somerville & Ross account of the natives preparing for a dance.

'Good marning, Mrs Ryan,' says Mrs Quinn, 'And what does Terry be doin' down there wid the boards?'

'Shure,' says the better-informed Mrs Quinn, 'the Father Nolan has given him the job of putting up a bit of a floor there for the girls and boys to be dancin' of Sunday afternoons.'

'Well! Glory be! Isn't that grand for them? When we were young, wasn't the cross-roads good enough for us, and ne'er a bit of a board at all? But shure, they say it's all Home Rule is doing it. But indeed the ould time was good enough for us.'

'Jus' so, Mrs Ryan, but the Father must have good raisons of his own, and they say it breaks his heart entirely to have all the growin' boys and girls leaving for Ameriky, and half of them never comes back. So 'tis likely when Home Rule comes, they'll hear out there of the gran' doens here and maybe they'll be settling down again in the old country and buyin' a bit o' land for themselves.'

This cringe-provoking vignette, unmistakably written from the perspective of a liberal big house, is an indication of Charlotte Despard's sentimental relationship with Ireland, a relationship that would be tested and tempered in years to come. But in the warm summer of 1914 she was feeling rather mellow towards the world in general. On 29 July she had one of many glorious days: 'We were able to go to our cove in the morning. They bathed, I paddled and read the melodramatic newspapers.' In spite of that adjective, months of distance from political urgencies, and such an abhorrence of war that a diatribe against all wars had been one of the first things she had penned in June, Charlotte Despard was not as shocked as other Edwardian progressives were by the Great War that broke out within days of that idyllic day in County Cork.

Formally, and without account of the complex political and cultural pressures building up to it, the war declared upon Germany on 4 August 1914 was the result of the assassination of the heir to the Austro-Hungarian Empire in June. That outrage had led to a chain of diplomatic manoeuvres and, on 2 August, to Germany's invasion of Belgium, to which country's neutrality Britain was committed. From that day everything was, in Mrs Despard's words, 'in commotion'. She had recovered from the first serious illness of her life and, with an extraordinary combination of vision, fortitude and efficiency, began to deal with the greatest ordeal yet.

# CHAPTER 9

# THE FIRST WORLD WAR: 'KEEP OUR OWN FLAG FLYING'

Unusually, the mystic Charlotte Despard's line on the war was crystal clear:

> So long as materialism – physical force – is the order of the day, so long as the spiritual considerations which women and honest workers of both sexes could bring to the government of nations are absent, we shall have these epidemics of armed strife, this war hysteria through which peaceful communities are plunged into deadly conflict. . . . Our first object must be to demonstrate everywhere, so long as time is left, against our nation embarking in this criminal war.

Early on the night when war was actually proclaimed more than 2,000 women representing virtually every women's organization, apart from the pro-war WSPU, trade unions, Co-operative Guildswomen, suffragists and internationalists, crowded into the Kingsway Hall in London to rally against war. Charlotte Despard, Helena Swanwick and Olive Schreiner were among the luminaries on the platform and Millicent Fawcett presided over the meeting as a whole. But despite the resolutions passed in favour of mediation and conciliation, most of those present knew that nationalism was stronger than 'Christianity, than Judaism, than socialism, than international feminism . . . .' By midnight, when the women had dispersed and the war was official, Millicent Fawcett gave in to what she perceived as reality:

> Women, your country needs you. As long as there was any hope for peace most members of the National Union probably sought for peace, and endeavoured to support those who were left trying to maintain it. But we have another duty now . . . LET US SHOW OURSELVES WORTHY OF CITIZENSHIP, WHETHER OUR CLAIM TO IT BE RECOGNIZED OR NOT.

Within days all suffragette prisoners were released as part of the government's response to the 'Women's Armistice', and the women's organizations were mobilizing for their contribution to the war effort. The attitude of Charlotte Despard and therefore, for the moment, of the Women's Freedom League was subtly different from that of Mrs Fawcett. Mrs Despard was not prepared to bandage the wounded and think of England, to let a tide of patriotism roll over the demand for women's rights:

> If, or when that [the effort to forestall the war] fails, let us, by every means in our power, while helping so far as we can the innocent sufferers in all such times – the women and children, keep our own flag flying, and emphasize our demand to have a voice in decisions as to momentous events on which hang the destinies of nations.

The mass calling up of reservists and the enlistment of more men meant the removal of the chief breadwinners for an unknown time, and often unknown destination, from families where, at the same time, the women often also lost their jobs due to the sudden cessation of the luxury trades and the general economic disruption. Because of delays and inefficiency in the processing of army separation allowances, this meant that people who normally lived from hand to mouth were in even deeper trouble. To this innocent suffering was added the plight of the very young, the old and the sick for whom welfare provision became even less available than before. Then, from late August onwards, there were refugees from Belgium, eventually more than a quarter of a million of them, and soldiers returning from the front on crutches or stretchers. Many suffra-

gists and individual Women's Freedom Leaguers joined the
nursing and auxiliary military services, but the League concentrated on relief work on the grim home front. This effort was
made through a new organization, the Women's Suffrage
National Aid Corps, President: Mrs Charlotte Despard.

This organization put suffragette administrative and fund-
raising expertise into a wide range of relief projects, such as
cost-price vegetarian restaurants in London and the provinces.
At Nine Elms, Mrs Despard's dynamic cousin, Isabel Tippett,
resuscitated a soup kitchen like the one Rosalie Mansell had
managed. There were many takers for the 'Belgian soup' and jam
puddings. But the punters did not take so readily to vegetarian
delicacies like 'lovely tomatoes with rice'. They sometimes made
off with the cutlery and there were frequent staffing problems,
as with one Swedish cook 'who did not expect to work in such
a rough neighbourhood'. Mrs Tippett's son, Sir Michael Tippett,
was a teenager during the war years and he still recalls ladling
out soup at a halfpenny, pudding for a penny, in Battersea.
Cheap children's clothes were also supplied by the National Aid
Corps. They were made with material bought by that veteran
bulk-buyer of quality produce, Mrs Despard, in sewing work-
shops that occupied some of the unemployed women. In the
first days of the war Charlotte Despard had combined visits to
cloth and boot merchants with the relief committee meetings
and the suffragist peace initiative.

In the war years the Lambeth Board of Guardians' experience
was to prove invaluable, for Mrs Despard was better prepared
than the government for the realities of war privation on the
home front, and a telling critic of their belated attempts to
organize the fair distribution of food. But her illness in 1914
had precipitated more WFL involvement with the Battersea
projects and during the war the Nine Elms 'Settlement' became
the Women's Freedom League Settlement. Even so, on a day-
to-day, *ad hoc* level, Mrs Despard was back on the philanthropic
beat. One moment she was dealing with Mrs Jamfrey, 'who has
three sons at the front and whom the Poor Law are trying to
sell up for debt', the next she was interviewing the 'rather
strange' Mr Forbes who promised the profits from his patent
medicine 'Vundi' for WFL relief work, 'if we would push it'.

Inspired rather than directed by Mrs Despard, who was still
not a good committee woman, the WFL struggled out of the

confusion of the first months of the war with a number of humanitarian initiatives. They ran a milk depot, which supplied cheap pure milk to nursing mothers, and a maternity clinic, and Mrs Tippett's restaurant doubled as a guest house for children whose mothers were recovering from childbirth or suffering from general exhaustion. Leaguers were also busy sending parcels of food and clothing to British prisoners-of-war in Germany. By October 1914 the indefatigable Mrs Harvey had turned her Bromley house into a fifty-bed hospital, complete with lettuce-crate bedside lockers and cots made from Canary banana-cases. Brackenhill Hospital catered for refugees and for women and children displaced from the regular hospitals by military patients. The first baby born in the maternity ward was Belgian and a bevy of WFL fairy godmothers attended the Christening.

When Mrs Despard addressed one of her Catholic Mothers meetings in Battersea she suggested that they 'offer up as a sacrifice to the passing souls indulgence in intoxicating liquor'. In the old days she had frequently lamented those feckless female drunkards called 'soakers', but in wartime the problem appeared to become worse. Although there was no hard evidence of more drunkenness among working-class women, the fact that, when at leisure, women were more conspicuous in the absence of so many men, precipitated a rather sour and censorious official reaction. Despite her pious exhortations to the Battersea mothers, Mrs Despard's response was imaginative and realistic. She opened a teetotal pub, the Despard Arms, conveniently located on the Hampstead Road near the big railway stations of Euston, St Pancras and King's Cross, from where soldiers often arrived in or left London. It was designed to provide the cheerful atmosphere of the public house without any of the odium, 'a public house which shall take away the reproach of the name'. Food and non-alcoholic drinks were sold all day long, there were several public bathrooms, facilities for cheap overnight accommodation and a large clubroom. In due course the young male regulars formed a football club, the Despard Uniteds, and frequent 'entertainments' were also laid on. The Despard Arms was another focus for WFL energy and its progress was recorded in *The Vote*: 'Can any member recommend a strong girl of fourteen or fifteen to be trained as a kitchen-maid?' Lord French himself visited the Despard Arms, to meet some soldiers who were temporarily billeted there, as well as wounded men from the nearby Temperance Hospital. Songs and 'entertaining stories of Tommy' were offered him and the Field-Marshal gratified his sister by expressing his thorough satisfaction with the whole project.

Although Mrs Despard was a keen advocate of temperance, she was never a conventional puritan. When it came to the administration of soldiers' pay, the government, for once acknowledging working-class reality, did not distinguish between 'unmarried dependants' and 'married wives'. Some churchmen objected to this placing of 'marriage and concubinage practically on a level', but for Mrs Despard it was a wholly welcome acknowledgement of fathers' responsibility for their children, whether illegitimate or not. She was to keep a consistently feminist, or as she would have preferred, a 'humanist' perspective on all government actions pertaining to women.

Among the more obnoxious symptoms of the wartime mentality were the repeated attempts to monitor the 'morals' of women at home, particularly soldiers' and sailors' wives. When local Commanding Officers began using the new Defence of the Realm Act (DORA) to impose curfews on women, the WFL was quick to protest against what Charlotte Despard called the 'New Inquisition'. She joined Sylvia Pankhurst in founding the League for the Rights of Soldiers' and Sailors' Wives and Relations, but the WFL's volunteer corps of policewomen, an initiative of Nina Boyle's, came unstuck in the face of the New Inquisition. One of the many employment substitutions to be pioneered during the First World War, Mrs Despard had been very enthusiastic about the women police scheme. She eyed up any 'strapping' young suffragettes she met with as potential policewomen and the corps kept order at suffragist exhibitions and meetings. But official WFL backing for the first women police had to be withdrawn when they were asked to help in imposing the odious curfew. When it came to other substitutions of women in what had been male jobs the WFL insisted on its pre-war principles of equal conditions and equal pay for equal work. A 'straight talk' between a WFL contingent and the Glasgow Tramways Committee, when women were about to be introduced to jobs on the trams, produced what *The Vote* called 'good results'.

Even more offensive than the surveillance of soldiers' wives was the campaign to revive the Contagious Diseases Acts via

Regulation 40D of DORA. These notorious Acts of the 1860s had, until Josephine Butler led a campaign against them, empowered magistrates to order any woman suspected of being infected with venereal disease to be subjected to a compulsory examination. By overwhelmingly misogynist criteria, any woman could be a 'potential prostitute' with, if found to be infected, no redress against humiliation and punishment. Every time such proposals reared their ugly heads, Mrs Despard, Nina Boyle, Sylvia Pankhurst and their like, hotfooted it to Downing Street and mobilized protests. There proved to be many occasions on which it was imperative to 'keep our own flag flying'.

In the first months of the war, before it became obvious that it was not going to be a short, invigorating and glorious affair, there was a certain cheery solidarity in the air. Mrs Despard probably enjoyed a sense of oneness with her family and the friends who dated from her days as the progressive wife of a successful businessman. The relatives who before the war had locked up their daughters for fear that Aunt Lottie would take them on political sprees that would land them in Holloway now nodded benignly and even mucked in with the relief committees. Her sister-in-law, Lady Norah French, contributed baskets of vegetables to the Nine Elms restaurant, and her niece, Lady Essex French (Jack's daughter), found WFL support, notably from Margaret Wynne Nevinson, for her scheme to send a team of trained masseurs, forerunners of physiotherapists, to treat the wounded in France. Various young Lydall relatives surfaced in different Despard-sponsored schemes and the youngest Miss French, Mrs Katie Harley, went off with two of her adult daughters to run a military hospital unit in Serbia.

Outright pacifists were not conspicuous at the beginning of the war, but some people professed at least to a dislike of war, even if there were such a thing as a just one. Mrs Despard never talked of the 'enemy', or as The Vote often did, of 'Teuton fiends'. She refused to help with recruitment campaigns and did her best to attend the Women's International Peace Congress held at the Hague in April 1915, a brave follow-up to the Budapest Congress of 1913. From this venture, for which the heroic organizers earned media vilification as 'folly in petticoats' going to 'pow-wow with the fraus', emerged the Women's International League. Charlotte Despard did not make it to the Hague only because, along with the majority of other hopeful delegates, she failed to get a passport out of the obstructive authorities – passports being a wartime innovation for which ladies had to provide a photograph of themselves 'full face without hat'. The twenty-four British women who did succeed in getting passports were frustrated in any case by a suspiciously simultaneous ban on all civilian sailings across the North Sea.

For all this, Charlotte Despard shared her uncomplicatedly patriotic friends' feelings for 'our splendid men', particularly those Nine Elms old boys who had signed up for the massacre. She was proud to say that her brother had made a special pre-war study of military conditions in Belgium and she was gratified when she bumped into people with news of him, once a soldier who had been one of his bodyguards for several weeks, on another occasion a retired colonel who reported that Jack was 'well and full of hope'. She noted in her diary that it was 'with keen admiration, and a constriction of heart that I heard of Jack's splendid despatch of the retreat that would make history. Joy to think that it is over; but ah! the sacrifice.' That 'constriction of heart' was not just a reference to the fact that her brother very nearly died, and thousands really did, holding the line at Ypres. It also referred to the inner turmoil that usually signalled one of Charlotte Despard's more uncomfortable political positions.

By the time Field-Marshal Sir John French had been removed from his position of exclusive overall command, late in 1915, the 'dread hosts' were, literally, entrenched, and casualties were beginning to be predicted in terms of millions rather than thousands. His removal from the field was well-timed from Charlotte Despard's point of view because it made her emergence as an outspoken, uncompromising pacifist less personally painful. Just when she might have enjoyed basking in the public approval for the suffragette and suffragist contributions to the war effort, she made things rough for herself again.

The peace movement, and her forthright pacifist career, really took off in 1916 because that year saw truly awful carnage and the introduction of conscription for all men between the ages of eighteen and forty. Although provision for conscientious objection was made in a clause of the Military Service Act, the ambiguity of its wording and the ambivalence of its adminis-tration meant that in practice conscientious objectors were treated like criminals. The conscription issue threw dissident young men into the limelight and while Mrs Pankhurst and Christabel upbraided them as 'slackers', women like Charlotte Despard, Helena Swanwick, and Catherine Marshall, to name but a few, campaigned on their behalf. New acronyms now provided the focus for the hectic life of the lady who declared that 'like St Paul's' her war was not 'against flesh and blood, but against principalities and powers'. There was the Hague-initiated Women's International League (WIL); the Union for Democratic Control (UDC), a pressure group drawn mainly from the labour movement for the democratic ratification of foreign policy and a League of Nations; the No Conscription Fellowship (NCF); and the Women's Peace Crusade (WPC). In a letter to Catherine Marshall, Helena Swanwick wrote, 'I am stomping the country again quite a lot for the UDC, ILP, WIL, WPC (do you know your alphabet?).' This last organization, the Women's Peace Crusade, which was started in Glasgow by that Red Clydesider Helen Crawfurd, got a quota of Mrs Despard's energy and commitment equal only to that given to the Women's Freedom League. She wrote its best-selling pamphlet, *An Appeal to Women*, and went the length and breadth of the country speaking on the Crusade's behalf. Halfway into the war she was back on the speaker's road again, looking, if possible, even more venerable, and just as indomitable.

In the frighteningly bitter atmosphere it was expedient for pacifists, especially those based in jingoistic London, to smooth over personality and political differences. For example, in the pre-war past Mrs Despard had found Sylvia Pankhurst unpalatably temperamental and spontaneous in her political doings. Now she found the socialist pacifist Miss Pankhurst 'very much improved'. From the beginning of the war they had made common cause on issues relating to food rationing and distribution, to the treatment of soldiers' wives and dependants, and to the regimentation of industrial workers in wartime. But pacifism brought them together in a new way, and Easter 1917 saw them preparing to address a huge meeting in Victoria Park, Hackney, on the theme 'Spring and Peace Must Come Together'. But the platform had been surrounded by soldiers on leave who were in no mood to listen to peacemongers. 'We don't want German terms: we want our terms!' one of them yelled. To this

Mrs Despard, who was described by a journalist as an exotic visitor from the epoch of samplers and wax fruits, called back, 'You shall have neither the German terms, nor your own terms; you will have God's terms!' Charlotte Despard had a disarming way of bringing God up. But the ugly situation on that particular Sunday in Victoria Park was not unusual. She emerged from it unscathed (Sylvia Pankhurst less so) by telling the soldiers, 'I am not afraid of Englishmen. None of you will hurt me.'

Many of the prominent female pacifists had been steeled by their suffragist days and were therefore better able than many younger pacifists to withstand verbal and physical abuse. It even took a certain courage to be openly sceptical about the German atrocity stories filling up the otherwise censored newspapers, and great anguish was suffered by individuals who stuck to unpopular ideals. In 1916 a dinner was held at the Lyceum Club to celebrate the promise made by the British government to give the vote to women, an as yet unspecific commitment which seemed to vindicate Mrs Fawcett's hope that the women's war effort would show them to be 'worthy' of full citizenship. At this dinner Mary Sheepshanks, who ran the London headquarters of the International Women's Suffrage Alliance, read out a congratulatory telegram from German suffragists. Within days she had been banned from the Lyceum Club and when her fighting brother learned of her 'treachery' he never spoke to her again.

It was a bleak, dispiriting time which no amount of Theosophical rumination could alleviate. Just a month before that Victoria Park meeting Mrs Despard learned of the death of her youngest sister, Katie Harley, from shellfire in Serbia. Nina Boyle, who had met Mrs Harley while doing a stint with the medical unit she was leading, had written back, 'Tell Mrs Despard that it was a real delight to see someone so like her, in person and in spirit.' Then, in the following year, her beloved nephew, George Franks, was killed in action – 'I can hardly think of anything else' – and many of the Battersea boys whose games she had once supervised also perished. On a trivial, day-to-day, level it was hard even for Charlotte Despard to avoid rancour. She had to have strong words with a local priest, one Father Flanagan: 'Alas! He is like most of the clerics – maintains we are fighting for righteousness and that the war must go on until the enemy is completely humbled.'

That simple Father Flanagan of Battersea was not the only Irishman on Mrs Despard's mind during these troubled years. Like many others, she did not immediately absorb the significance of the Dublin Easter Rising of 1916. She wrote almost casually in her diary of the 'bad news from Ireland', of the General Post Office 'in the hands of rebels', and, two days later, that 'the Irish trouble seems to be spreading'. But, as political scientists observe, it is only human to back winners, even retrospectively. Sixteen years later, when the Easter Rising was seen as the debut of a separate, independent Ireland, this is how Mrs Despard recalled her reactions to an Irish radical newspaper, *An Phoblacht*.

> The occurrences of Easter week, for which I was already partly prepared, I remember vividly. Little news came over. It was a time of intense anxiety. On the Sunday that followed my two friends [Eva Gore-Booth and Esther Roper] found me. I heard from them that Con Markievicz with others was lying in a Dublin prison and sentenced to death [eventually commuted to life imprisonment because she was a woman]. My brother, Sir John French, was then the commanding officer in the British Army and they thought it might help if I went with them to the War Office to make enquiries. As a matter of fact, we were met sympathetically and through another department Eva Gore-Booth was given permission to cross to Ireland.

She added that in Ireland in 1932 it was not generally known that on the night before James Connolly was executed protest meetings had been held all over London and in other parts of Britain.

Mrs Despard, and the Women's Freedom League, were shaken most personally when Ireland's most prominent male suffragist and pacifist, 'our friend' Francis Sheehy-Skeffington, was murdered by a deranged army officer after he had been picked up by a patrol while trying to stop looting. From the time of this outrage onwards, Charlotte Despard took a keen interest in the career of Hanna Sheehy-Skeffington, whom she had met at the Budapest suffragist conference and was to 'glimpse' later in 1916 at a London meeting, but who she did not really know until after the First World War. But although

Mrs Despard later attributed her commitment to Ireland to her feelings in the brutal aftermath of the Rising, from her diaries it would seem that those events were a painful sideshow in a generally ghastly world. Sheehy-Skeffington's murder affected her profoundly because he, too, had participated in the pacifist struggle and she coupled his martyrdom with that being undergone at the same time by 'our own young resisters'.

But *The Vote* was fierce about the Irish rebels:

On the situation in Ireland one can speak with no sympathy at all, save for the loyal lives unnecessarily sacrificed and the nation's burden of mourning increased. The plot was not even secret, which makes its own futility, and the idiocy of those who complacently watched it forming, all the more infuriating.

This accompanied accounts of 'heartless rebels' shooting at innocent women and children, and no mention was made of the plight of Constance Markievicz, who was partially rehabilitated by *The Vote* only when she became the first woman elected to the British Parliament. The WFL attitude to Ireland, as expressed in *The Vote*, distressed its figurehead, but for the time being she kept her peace with women whose views increasingly diverged from her own.

The latest country retreat, which replaced Earnshaw Cottage, was the 'sweet' little bungalow which she had had built near a house purchased jointly with Kate Harvey in Sussex. But despite daffodils and evening skies, and the inevitable troops of sick and disabled children who found sanctuary there, the friendship between Mrs Harvey and Mrs Despard was waning. Theosophy, philanthropy and suffragist work had bound them together, so it was not surprising that Mrs Despard's reorientation, via the pacifist movement, towards international socialism should have separated them. Moreover, Mrs Despard's 'women the first' decision of 1906 had now shifted back to her original position: 'I have come to feel that the only way – and the best way on – is adult suffrage.'

Whatever she felt about Ireland, this shift and pacifism served to alienate Mrs Despard from the Women's Freedom League, especially since she was no better than she had been before at separating her individual feelings from the League's official policy. Back in 1915 *The Vote* had been stern on a 'marked tendency of late' to secure the support of suffragists for a number of 'alien aims and interests' on account of that 'well-known energy and organizing ability so constantly displayed in our public work; and we cannot too carefully guard against this insidious danger.' So much for the League's attitude towards the spirit of feminist internationalism. When Mrs Despard publicly regretted the fact that women engaged in munitions work were making weapons of destruction, her speech was reported in *The Vote* with the prefix, 'speaking personally'. By December 1917 things had become tense enough for a terse little 'Where We Stand' paragraph in *The Vote*, signed by Mrs Despard as President, Dr Knight as Treasurer, and Miss Underwood as General Secretary:

> The Women's Freedom League, as a society, takes no part in any form of peace or war propaganda, and anything that might be said or done by a member or official of the WFL in respect of any activities other than woman's suffrage must be understood as being done solely in her individual capacity.

Mrs Despard was now more comfortable with her pacifist socialist friends, but she stayed on as the League's President, though not as editor of *The Vote*, until the first instalment of woman suffrage came in 1918.

Another personal casualty of Charlotte Despard's political principles was Vere Foley. Although her guardian would occasionally down tools when Vere had flu, the unhappy teenager was still shuffled back and forth between schools, Currie Street and Sussex. Mrs Despard arranged meetings with her natural father – 'he was very pleased with her and she was very affectionate with him' – and experimented with having her mysteriously 'unsuitable' natural mother care for her. But otherwise the seventy-two-year-old mother of the world was not much of a mother-substitute for her decidedly unsoulful ward. But before condemning Charlotte Despard for this particular lapse on the home front, it should be remembered that her own memories of girlhood stretched back to the 1850s. If Vere had been a tomboy of intellectual inclination, as eager for causes as she was for new clothes and practical jokes, Granny Despard might have coped more creditably.

There were some suitably world-historic consolations for the League's neutrality and little Vere's deficiencies of character. In March 1917 came the joyful news of the first stage of the Russian Revolution. Maybe something positive would come out of the war, and if tsardom could be toppled, why not British capitalism? In June Charlotte Despard was prominent among the 1,000-plus delegates, including Sylvia Pankhurst, Dora Montefiore, Ramsay MacDonald, Bertrand Russell and Ernest Bevin, who met in Leeds for the 'great Labour, Socialist and Democratic Convention to hail the Russian Revolution and to organize British democracy to follow Russia'. This day-long convention was dominated by Labour Party politicians and, to the chagrin of many of the revolutionary socialists present, they moved the key resolutions on Russia and peace. Mrs Despard reportedly wowed the convention as a whole when she rose, in her mantilla and black robes, to second a resolution calling upon the government

to place itself in accord with the democracy of Russia by proclaiming its allegiance to and determination to carry into immediate effect a charter of liberties establishing complete political rights for all men and women, unrestricted freedom of the press, freedom of speech, a general amnesty for all political and religious prisoners, full rights of industrial and political association, and the release of labour from all forms of compulsion and restraint.

This was a very tall order but such was Mrs Despard's enthusiasm that she was elected to the committee that was supposed to make real the Lenin-inspired local councils of workers and soldiers which were to work strenuously for peace and for the emancipation of international labour. Specifically, her participation in the attempt to get such a council going in Newcastle did not outlast the founding meeting, which was broken up by hostile jingoes. As soon as it was realized that Russia might pull out of the war and 'desert' her allies, a possibility that was confirmed with the treaty of Brest-Litovsk in March 1918, only advanced radicals were left celebrating the revolution.

But Mrs Despard's hopes and her sense of excitement could be shared with fellow members of the 1917 Club, named in honour of the Russian Revolution, to which she repaired every other day when she was in London. As an informal meeting place for male and female progessives, the 1917 Club inspired this scathing piece of doggerel:

> In 1917 they founded a club
> Partly as a brothel and partly as pub
> The members were all of them horrible bores
> Except for the girl in Giotto-pink drawers.

The club was a clearing house for the issues and crises of the day. It was also the place where Mrs Despard could get hold of influential people in the emergencies that were frequently brought to her notice. In 1918 fourteen-year-old Sean MacBride (who looked older) came to London on account of his mother's (Maud Gonne's) incarceration, with Kathleen Clarke and Constance Markievicz, in Holloway as an Irish political prisoner. He stayed with Sylvia Pankhurst on the Old Ford Road. In October he went to Battersea to see what Mrs Despard could do for his mother, and she duly sought out Labour MPs at the 1917 Club to get them to ask awkward questions in Parliament on behalf of the imprisoned Irishwomen. She also took her Irish visitors of these years – Louie Bennett and Mary MacSwiney, for example – to the club to be introduced to sympathetic journalists and politicians.

While women were denied access to the normal channels of political power, the informal 1917 Club was a useful meeting point. But when the vote did come, in January 1918, the excitement was tinged with disappointment because it was only for women over thirty. This insulting qualification reassured those male politicians who feared that 'petticoat government' would accompany any immediate enfranchisement of a homogeneous army of women. (Limiting votes for women by age had been politically more expedient than introducing property qualifications.) Another sting in the tail of this Act was the clause that disenfranchised many of the conscientious objectors for five years. So, January 1918 only represented a 'first phase' and was therefore greeted as something of an anti-climax: 'Let us say at once that it is with no exultation, no rapture of gratitude, that we acclaim our victory, rather with wonder that such an elementary act of justice should have been so long delayed.' Then, as the war came to its close (November 1918), preparations were made for a General Election in December. Only weeks before the election was announced a bill was passed to allow women to be Members of Parliament. The result was that, at the age of seventy-four, Charlotte Despard found herself standing as the Labour Party candidate in Battersea.

To his credit, the old enemy, John Burns, had resigned from the government in 1914 because of his opposition to the war, even though he did not go on to support the pacifist campaigns. But this resignation meant that he could not stand for parliament on Lloyd George's coalition, or 'coupon' ticket, and neither could he be bound by the Labour Party's socialist policies. So, as the ex-King of Battersea bowed out, the local Labour Party turned to the Mother of Battersea, the only other person reckoned to have a chance against the coalition candidate.

Although she was the official Labour Party candidate in Battersea, Mrs Despard's platform showed her personal commitment to the welfare of women and children. Her election address, as summarized by *The Vote*, stressed equal political rights for women and men; equal pay for equal work; the child as a most important factor in the state; children to have the first consideration in all food schemes; boys and girls to start work at a later age and more rigorous inspection of the shops and factories where they worked. She also dwelled on the necessity for adequate welfare provision for the aged and for disabled men and women, the abolition of the Defence of the Realm Act, especially Regulation 40D, free speech, a free press, individual liberty and a League of Nations.

The Women's Freedom League took a proprietorial interest in the campaign, taking over the canvassing work in the Nine Elms part of the constituency and organizing relays of speakers on Mrs Despard's behalf. She was grateful for Mary Sheepshanks's speech but on other occasions was nonplussed by the enthusiastic WFL's insensitivity to the Labour Party dimension of her campaign: 'How often one has to say, "save me from my friends".' *The Vote* waxed lyrical about its ex-President's prospects: 'Judging from the experiences of the past week at Battersea, and the interest and enthusiasm aroused, we anticipate a great victory for Mrs Despard over the Coalition (Unionist) candidate, who is a stranger to the constituency.' In like vein, *The Pall Mall Gazette* reported that 'sentiment' would be a deciding factor in the election:

> Only to mention Mrs Despard's name in the poorer streets of the constituency is sufficient to draw a shower of blessings upon her for all the practical kindness and genuine philanthropy she has scattered through Battersea for years past. Then too must be considered the romantic figure she makes as she addresses the electors with her lace mantilla shading her fine head, her ruggedly beautiful cast of countenance, and her glaring eyes, her startling eloquence, and passionate intensity.

Until recently there were Battersea people alive who could remember working by candlelight in Mrs Despard's campaign 'shop', and she did her best to be worthy of their efforts. But the weather that December was vile – 'windswept and blizzardy' – and, despite the motor car laid on by a supporter, she was handicapped throughout by a bad dose of flu and bronchitis. Fighting her cough, she countered anti-pacifist accusations of 'treachery to our boys' and dealt with the inevitable 'Hang the Kaiser!' hecklers. On her optimistic days she could note that 'things seem to be going well for Labour everywhere' and that there was a general absence of what she called 'flippancy'.

On polling day, 14 December, Ethel Lydall drove her around the constituency which, if Nine Elms had been a larger and more typically poor proportion of it, would indeed have been a walkover. That night she was too tired to sleep and she woke early next morning resolved to rid herself of the heat and passion of the campaign. Then it was off for a recuperative Sussex Christmas with loyal Kate Harvey. (Vere had been sent to her mother, in due course returning to Currie Street to meet, for the first time since their traumatic separation, Rosalie Mansell: 'the child was excited but presently everything became natural.') In Sussex Mrs Despard got over her flu and felt pleased that 'the great struggle is over and I have been strong enough to face it and now we are waiting for results . . . as regards myself I am trying to keep quiet.' The count was deferred until after Christmas to allow time for the votes of servicemen still abroad to come in.

Charlotte Despard went to the Battersea count to be told that it was going against her. Then 'It did not take long.' However, with 5,634 votes to the successful Coalition man's 11,231, she had done remarkably well, even by modern standards, for an old woman of so many outspokenly progressive opinions. This relatively impressive performance became clearer when, with the WFL's Dr Knight, she went to the 1917 Club to learn the full extent of the 'awful slide – not a pacifist in, none but the Jingoes had a chance.' More stoical than many of her supporters – and probably more thrilled than most of her British sisters that the one woman who had been elected was a Sinn Fein candidate, Constance Markievicz – she cheered up *The Vote*'s readers with the thought that, 'After all, in 1911 or 1912 could any of us have imagined that in 1918 no less than sixteen women would even be able to present themselves to the electors as parliamentary candidates?' She closed that momentous and exhausting year of 1918 with a prayer that the 'hate spirit' might depart, and the conviction that 'we shall fight again!'

# CHAPTER 10

# THE CALL TO IRELAND: 'YOU MUST GO YOURSELF'

Charlotte Despard retired from her increasingly uncomfortable presidency of the WFL at the 'victory' conference of 1918, but she was still an incorrigible joiner. Although she was to continue as the League's fond dowager for another twenty years, from that conference onwards she was more available for her other roles. For example, she now became President of the London Vegetarian Society, a body of national weight in that particular movement and one for which she had previously served as a Vice-President.

Ever since dear Max's death Mrs Despard had been vegetarian, along with her heroine, Annie Besant, and other progressive luminaries such as Tolstoy and George Bernard Shaw. Her remarkably vigorous old age was a good advertisement for that decision. Teresa Billington-Greig recalled the incongruity of festive meals, for birthdays and so on, at which, while fellow socialists, suffragettes and members of her family guzzled roast meat, the old lady herself munched dry biscuits. Her lifestyle, food-wise, was a necessarily frugal one in the days when a vegetarian diet usually meant a traditional British diet minus the meat. Even so, the famous sandals showed that her principles did not extend to the use of other animal products, unlike Gretta Cousins, who refused to wear leather shoes, belts or gloves.

Charlotte Despard's vegetarianism was inspired by her commitment to the 'slaying of the self' and by a feeling that the slaughter and consumption of animals were symptoms of a corrupt and unjust society. But she did recommend the fleshless diet for general well-being, and even, on one occasion, for military efficiency. Noting that the movement of the British Army during the First World War was marked by trails of empty beef cans, she suggested that this beef contributed to constipation and skin troubles, and to the deficiency in minerals and vitamins that debilitated soldiers. All this could be remedied by good vegetable soup, 'such as any French housewife makes'. Had the authorities heeded her recommendations 'Despard soup' might have joined watered-down beer as a cause of wartime popular lamentation.

The vegetarian cause, and the Theosophical one, were not particularly combative and in the wake of her retirement from *the* Cause, more urgent issues beckoned. It was all-important to ensure that the post-war peace settlement was not so vindictive as to lay the seeds of further wars (which, despite her efforts and those of like-minded people, the Treaty of Versailles ultimately did). Accordingly, May 1919 saw Charlotte Despard at the Women's International Congress held at Zurich in Switzerland. Old friends among the British delegates were Emmeline Pethick-Lawrence, Helena Swanwick and Helen Crawfurd, while the three Irish delegates included Hanna Sheehy-Skeffington and Louie Bennett. This was an opportunity for the internationalist feminism of Budapest 1913, and of the Hague 1915, to be revitalized. But amdist the joyful reunions there was the sobering, literally ravaged, presence of the delegates from the defeated countries. Mrs Despard shook off the shock of having had her handbag snatched in a Zurich market to dwell upon the means by which women together could force the Allied powers to rise above the victory in order to create a stable and harmonious Europe.

By a coincidence the Versailles peace terms were published on the first day of the Zurich conference. The American Jane Addams, 'Wonderful Miss Addams' to Charlotte Despard, arrived from Paris with a copy of these terms and a committee spent the first night poring over them. For Mrs Despard the 'atrocious' peace confirmed her direst expectations; the conference as a whole announced that the settlement would 'create all over Europe discords and animosities which can only lead to future wars ... by the financial and economic proposals a hundred million people of this generation in the heart of Europe are condemned to poverty, hunger and despair, which must result in the spread of anarchy and hatred within each nation.'

It was decided to send a small deputation to lobby the political leaders still in Paris, to recommend, in addition to the Charter of Women's Rights for inclusion in the League of Nations plans, certain German amendments 'which seem to us quite reasonable'. Predictably, Mrs Despard was one of the five-women strong deputation, which also included Jane Addams. As she strolled along the Rue de Rivoli Charlotte Despard recalled those carefree days with her sister Carrie half a century earlier, and as she sat in the Tuileries Gardens with the Scottish delegate, Crystal Macmillan, she thought about what she now saw as the 'old militant suff days'. There was a hopeless tinge to such nostalgia because although the women were politely received at the French Chamber of Deputies, Lloyd George and Clemenceau refused to even meet them.

Meanwhile, on the post-war home front, it was necessary to fight the immediate effects of imperialist diplomacy, namely the famine that stalked central Europe as a result of the food blockade imposed by the Allies until Germany signed the peace settlement in June 1919. The American and Western European women at Zurich had been shocked both by the gaunt appearance of their counterparts from the defeated countries and by their testimonies on what was happening, particularly the accounts of life in post-war Austria and Hungary. In Budapest the babies who were dying in their thousands were being wrapped in newspapers for burial, while in Vienna in the summer and autumn of 1918, 7 to 11 per cent of the total mortality was strictly attributable to starvation, quite apart from the lethal sweep of the great post-war flu epidemic. Britain's pacifists responded with a 'Fight the Famine' campaign and a young woman called Eglantyne Jebb was tried for distributing a handbill depicting an emaciated Austrian baby. For this unpatriotic behaviour Miss Jebb was fined but as a result of the publicity she was able to mobilize a new charity that refused to be stopped by political boundaries. In the summer of 1920 Charlotte Despard went to Hungary as the representative of the Save the Children Fund. She now revisited institutions that had delighted her in 1913, but 'what a difference. Now, nothing for comfort.' She saw newborn babies sleeping on a coarse sacking made from paper fibre and a general, sickening absence of the 'decencies of life'. 'I knelt and drew a tiny tot to me. She pressed her face against my soft cloth, smiling like an angel. Alas! it is motherhood the world needs.'

But Mrs Despard was wearing a socialist as well as a philanthropic mantilla when she returned from Hungary. In addition to alerting public sympathy and donations for Save the Children's relief efforts, she made no bones about her outrage at the reign of White Terror stalking Hungary under the proto-fascist Admiral Horthy. With Allied collusion, Horthy had crushed Bela Kun's communist revolution, and by now the Western Powers were more worried about the spread of communism than about German militarism. Mrs Despard was one of the many people in the British labour movement who were determined that the same thing should not happen to the Russian 'hope of the world'.

The 'Hands Off Russia' campaign had been launched in the summer of 1919. With massive demonstrations, a concerted refusal by riverside workers to load a munitions ship bound for Poland and the threat of a general strike, this movement successfully dissuaded the British government from continuing to intervene on the White side during the Russian Civil War. As one inspired by the Bolshevik leap forward, Charlotte Despard joined the Communist Party of Great Britain which was formed in the summer of her Hungarian trip. For her, communist was to socialist what suffragette had been to suffragist. At the time, Ellen Wilkinson wrote, 'it was extremely easy to believe that communism was simply advanced socialism, and that the best thing an advanced socialist could do was to become a communist and follow the guidance of Lenin and Trotsky.' Wilkinson, who left the Communist Party a year or so later when formal membership became incompatible with membership of the Labour Party, referred to herself as one of the 'idealists' who joined the CP as a 'ginger group to the Labour Party'.

For all her Catholic/Theosophical woolliness, Mrs Despard was keen to ginger up the Labour Party and fervently committed to the primacy of the workers in forthcoming struggles. The workers of Britain were 'beginning to find themselves' and it was 'out of such material that the better world of the future will be built'. Once again, her Battersea premises became strike headquarters and her belief that politics and economics went hand-in-hand was reinvigorated. This belief harked back to her days in the Social Democratic Federation but it had been submerged when she had put all her eggs in the basket of world regeneration through the enfranchisement of women. The awareness of Russia's transition and of Leninist discipline meant that the local Battersea left was galvanized with the aid of a permanent office and professional organizers – Mrs Despard dipping into her dividends to subsidize the new way forward. It was not a matter of building barricades but of making sure that British traditions for real revolutionary change through the existing political structures could be tellingly mobilized.

Charlotte Despard herself was appointed as an Alderman to the Borough Council in November 1920 and she served on the Health Committee, on the Maternity and Child Welfare Committee and as the Council's representative to the Tuberculosis Dispensary Committee. She also continued her work as School Manager for a group of Nine Elms schools. But in September 1921 she resigned from all these positions and left her London 'Little Ireland' for real Ireland. The Currie Street premises were made over to the Council as a maternity and child welfare centre to be funded from now on by voluntary donations. The mayor of Battersea duly sent out this appeal:

Her work is to be continued at those premises, and the Ministry of Health have sanctioned the Council accepting the gift and adapting the premises so that they can be used to the greatest possible extent for the benefit of the neighbourhood. But the Minister's consent is subject to the institution *being maintained by voluntary contributions* . . . there are many in Battersea who would make further sacrifice rather than allow the good work in which poor children principally benefit to be dropped or even limited in scope, and it is to those I now appeal.

The Sussex house was left to Kate Harvey's philanthropic enterprise, Mrs Despard continuing to maintain some of the children in her friend's care.

Ten years later, Charlotte Despard made her decision to move permanently to Ireland sound like a very sudden fall on the road to Damascus:

It was early in 1921; the news was bad. Two leading papers were making protests and printing letters from Irish men and women about the state of things in their country. I was feeling it all very deeply. One Sunday as I was kneeling at Mass in my club-room at Nine Elms, where Mass was said on Sunday mornings, it seemed to me that I heard a voice: 'You must go yourself'. Purely emotional, some will say. So it may be, I might answer. In my case it was irresistible, and I may add, I never regretted my decision.

Ireland had been creeping up on Charlotte Despard for at least two years before she heard that voice in the club-room. Her special interest and affection for Ireland was well known and she was often described as 'Irish-born' in the British press, but from 1917 onwards her sympathies were more directly and inalienably engaged. She had noted with great satisfaction that, whatever the shortcomings of the male politicians in Paris, the women at Zurich were happy to ratify Ireland's right to independence, and she usually met prominent Irish visitors to London. Back in 1917 she had attended a meeting addressed by Louie Bennett and carefully noted in her diary, 'They would not now be satisfied with Home Rule. They desire to have their *nationality* recognized. All day I was in a dream thinking of the dear folk in Ireland.' On her way to, or from, her in-laws in Laois she usually managed to fit in meetings with individuals such as Hanna Sheehy-Skeffington and in April 1918 she recorded the 'fine news' that one million people in Ireland had taken an anti-conscription pledge. But within a few weeks her brother was installed as the Viceroy with the job of getting conscription going and quashing nationalist aspirations that went beyond Home Rule. Now Mrs Despard's Jack was taking 'strong measures' and 'a number of Sinn Feiners, including Countess Markowitz, have been arrested and interned.'

It was not long before Charlotte Despard knew how Constance Markievicz prefered to spell her name and she had personally to confront the painful reality of her beloved brother's role in Ireland. Late in November 1918 she set off one night for the flat in Woburn Buildings 'where my Irish friend, Maud Gonne, just released from prison on her doctor's report, is staying. A miserable little place! Several friends were there . . . treatment in the military prison was odious. Home through the dark very very sad.'

The miserable little place was tenanted by William Butler Yeats but Mrs Despard's sadness was aggravated by the fact that she was no longer as useful to her Irish friends as they hoped, being neither the President of the Women's Freedom League nor a heeded sister of the Viceroy. There is something dogged and demoralized about her repeated explanations of her relative powerlessness. She told Hanna Sheehy-Skeffington of her 'deep indignation' at her detention, one of Mrs Sheehy-Skeffington's many incarcerations, and promised to give particulars to *The Vote:*

> . . . but I am no longer editor. There have been differences of opinion in the·League with regard to the war and at our conference it was decided to adopt a neutral attitude and as I am so ostentatiously a Pacifist, I thought it better for the WFL to cease to edit the paper. Therefore I cannot say whether what I give will be put in the *Vote*.

Whereas Lady Astor MP was *urged* by concerned Irishwomen 'as a mother' to intercede on behalf of hunger-striking prisoners in Dublin's Mountjoy Prison, and the American ambassador in London was *asked* 'for humanity's sake', Mrs Despard was *begged* for her 'personal intervention' with her brother. Dispiritedly, she responded to those letters: 'I did think of protesting personally, but I do not believe that it would have done any good.'

She was realistic about her brother's attitude towards her Irish friends but that did not make it any easier. She was almost tearful when she found a heap of letters on her Nine Elms doorway appealing for mercy for Kevin Barry:

> Heaven knows I would have done anything and travelled any distance for that poor boy; but I was away from London. . . . Everything was so hurried. . . . But I know only alas! too well – that I could have done nothing. For my beloved country I am doing what I can through *this* country. I feel everything that is happening more than I can possibly express.

Repeatedly, she offers her comradeship: 'You may rest assured that I am doing all I can to make the real state of things in Ireland known to the Labour people here.' She raised Ireland whenever she could, mentioning Terence MacSwiney at her lectures on Hungary 'and at my request they all rose', and addressing meetings outside Wormwood Scrubs where other Irish political prisoners were on hunger strike.

When Mrs Despard had visited Ireland in April 1919 her niece Lucy, bereaved only the previous winter of the brother who had died in a death and glory charge against the Germans, was on her mind as much as the Irish political prisoners. Together they strolled around the walled garden at Westfield House, talking of those who had 'passed' and of 'the possibility of communication with our beloved'. But she avoided the Viceregal Lodge when she reached Dublin and was met by 'dear Madame MacBride' (not yet Maud) and her son: 'She lives in an old-fashioned house in St Stephen's Green. The poet Yeats came to supper.' At the Irishwomen's Franchise League reception laid on for the distinguished visitor from London, Mrs Despard met Constance Markievicz and other leading republican women for the first time. But with half an eye still on the Vice-regal Lodge she kept a low profile. Even the visit she made early in 1921, which was precipitated by the meeting with Dorothy Macardle at Christmas, was at first a guardedly philanthropic one. As such it was reported in an Irish newspaper, probably the *Irish Times*, for a clipping found its way into the scrapbook of the liberal but far from republican Lucy Franks. It is headlined, 'Mission of Lord French's Sister, Children in Distress':

Some time ago Mrs Despard gave her idea of the woman's point of view as one of a mission of mercy. Consistent with this is her coming to Ireland. She has been told by Irish friends that many families are in acute distress throughout large areas in this country, their condition most severely affecting the children. It is her intention to inaugurate an appeal for relief to 'Save the Children Fund' which has already done so much to succour destitute children in the European war-zone. The children, she says, must not suffer, whether through military or industrial warfare; and to this purpose she has already brought some monetary aid.

Mrs Despard, after seeing for herself the state of things in

Ireland, will address many meetings on the matter on her return to England. She has already appealed in some measure to English labour.

Fair enough, the Viceroy and Miss Franks might have said, but they knew better. Mrs Despard's philanthropic motives and expertise were utterly genuine, but they were inseparable from her political perspective, which was very apparent after her fact-finding tour of terrorized Munster in the company of the notorious Madame MacBride. Nevertheless, when Mrs Despard came out in her full republican colours, and set about organizing her departure from Battersea, her brother had been safely removed from his Irish hot seat.

Mrs Despard was seduced by what she later called the real period of Irish administration, that truce period before the treaty was signed in December 1921 and before the outbreak of the Civil War:

> During the brief period of a real Irish administration there came to me what I cherish still, and which was at the back of my mind when I made my final decision, the creation here of a real Commonwealth, a Republic which might be a model to the mighty world.

Constance Markievicz was in charge of an alternative Ministry of Labour and other women friends were serving as justices and magistrates in the republican courts that answered to the interned or fugitive Dáil. These legal roles were justified partly in terms of the ancient Brehon laws, which had so delighted Charlotte Despard in her suffragette heyday. And although there was a certain amount of window-dressing in the Dáil's 'Democratic Programme', which had been put together with the support of a forthcoming International Socialist Congress in mind, it was music to her ears:

> It shall be the first duty of the Government of the Republic to make provision for the physical, mental and spiritual well-being of the children, and to secure that no child shall suffer hunger or cold from lack of food, clothing, or shelter, but that all shall be provided with the means and facilities requisite for their proper education as Citizens of a Free and Gaelic Ireland.

The as yet untested exponents of the Free and Gaelic Ireland were also dedicated to the abolition of the 'odious, degrading and foreign Poor Law system' and 'all rights to private property must be subordinated to the public right and welfare'.

Notwithstanding the distress and bloodshed against which this rhetoric reverberated, it was a hopeful, exhilarating time for Charlotte Despard. Moreover, the woman who replaced Kate Harvey in her life was the romantic new Ireland incarnate. Maud Gonne MacBride's person and personality have been made immortal in the poetry of W. B. Yeats, and otherwise celebrated to an almost monotonous extent. It seems appropriate, therefore, to offer the description of her made by an Englishwoman with political affinities similar to Mrs Despard's, though with no special affinity for Ireland, that of the cool Helena Swanwick:

> I saw at once how she came to be the sort of woman about whom legend naturally grows. Not only because she was indeed singularly beautiful and picturesque as well, but because she had a way of creating a court wherever she went, and everyone became her willing courtier.
>
> She was dramatic, and when she entered a room it was as if a pool had been stirred and the eddies all centred round her tall, elegant figure, with the quick gestures, the eager response, the rapid alternations of pathos and laughter. She had an air of gay gallantry covering tragic experiences, and withal a sweetness and courteous grace including everyone. She seemed in a way lighthearted, having thrown all she had, memories as well as dreams, into the cause she believed in. . . . It is well for me that I have not spent my life within her orbit, for I have sometimes felt as if I might have committed any folly, against my judgement, if she had desired it; or if, alternatively, I had felt compelled to oppose her it would have broken my heart.

Charlotte Despard was too much Maud Gonne's senior in years and still too much of a legend herself to be slavishly starstruck – indeed they had met for the first time at a Women's Freedom League meeting in London in 1917. But Mrs Despard's equanimity in the face of Maud Gonne's rabid Anglophobia might seem to smack of idolatry until we recall those eulogies of the generous, naturally rebellious Celt, as opposed to the cold and calculating Anglo-Saxon, in her novels. And even without much taste for Maud Gonne's charisma, Louie Bennett, who initially found the nationalist movement repugnant, was eventually moved to site her trade union energies in an Irish nationalist context:

> And I, with romance as I thought for ever dead for me, came to a new sense of romance. I have caught the secret and so for me, life has a new beauty. I have come into a new Kingdom. And now I understand. And I understand what it is gives an edge to life for the labourer – and the working man.

The writer Francis Stuart, who married Iseult Gonne, didn't like his matriarchal mother-in-law's 'easy assumption of the absolute rightness and moral purity of the nationalist cause' and he resented the court syndrome: 'It seemed to H they were being hemmed in on all sides, by his mother-in-law and her wide circle of admiring acquaintances (one of whom, the lady he'd had to keep out on the landing when she visited them, lived in the same house and, he imagined, made her reports). . . .' That threatening lady was probably Charlotte Despard; another was the woman gynaecologist with whom the pregnant Iseult often couldn't keep appointments 'because she couldn't be sure that the examination mightn't reveal that they'd made love that afternoon and that her mother, getting to hear of it, would regard it as a further sign of his degeneracy'.

But the sense of rectitude so resented by that impatient young man was probably reinforced by Charlotte Despard, famous for her capacity to imbue campaigns with sanctity. It had been precisely that quality that had made Teresa Billington-Greig so anxious to recruit her to the militant Cause. Together Madame MacBride and Madame Despard were to be a formidable, to some ludricous, pair. But we must leave it to the 'mother of all the Behans', then a young republican widow by the name of Kathleen Kearney, to explain the 'Madame business'. For about a year it was Kathleen Kearney who opened the Georgian door of the house in St Stephen's Green that was Charlotte Despard's first Irish home:

Madame Markievicz got the job for me. (Didn't we have a lot of gentry on our side?). . . . It wasn't a bad job, though Madame MacBride paid very little (my meals and that and a little money besides), but then I wasn't really a servant – more a receptionist. I let the visitors in and answered the telephone. . . . so although I got very little for it, I didn't feel degraded ever, and that was worth something. . . . As I said, we had a lot of gentry on our side – the nationalist side – and they didn't want to use English expressions like Mr and Mrs. On the other hand, if they'd used the Gaelic version, 'Mrs MacBride' would come out as 'Ban MacBride', which means 'MacBride's woman'. And that wouldn't do for them – they thought it was common. So all these grand Irish ladies were Madame this and Madame that, as though they were French.

Madame Despard didn't quite come off for the lady who had been such a prominent Mrs for so long: it was to be an honorific rather than a settled new title. But, for better or worse, Dublin was her new scene and Madame MacBride the most important person in her new life.

As these two beautiful old women entered the drawing room I could not help feeling a thrill; they had been heroines of my girlhood; it was nearly a decade since I had last seen them. Beauty is not as common in Ireland as is personality but these two were not only beautiful; they were incredibly distinguished and full of almost everything that makes a rousing personality. Both had been inspiring leaders. Maud Gonne had been known all over Europe and even in America as 'Ireland's Joan of Arc', she had in Yeats' poems passed into literature. Then Mrs Despard, outstanding figure in the suffrage movement. . . .

Few people in Dublin accorded Mrs Despard equal status with Maud Gonne, and Mary Colum, here recalling a salon of the 1920s, was one of them. It was literally true that the Mother of Battersea and the Women's Freedom League had less stature in Ireland alongside Maud Gonne MacBride. But from here on she was invariably described as a 'little woman' not simply because her partner was six foot tall. Her physical diminution can also be seen as a metaphor for the diminution of what she represented in the brave new Ireland.

# CHAPTER 11

# DUBLIN DAYS: 'MAUD GONNE MAD AND MRS DESPERATE'

Arthur Griffith and Michael Collins returned from London with the treaty they had agreed to under Lloyd George's threat of 'immediate and terrible war'. Early in January 1922 it was debated in the Dáil and ratified by just seven votes. Its leading opponent, Eamon de Valera, then resigned as President of the Republic which, according to the treaty, was to be an Irish 'Free State' within the British Empire. Apart from the offensive stipulation that all officials and representatives of the Free State take an oath of allegiance to the British Crown, acceptance of the treaty meant acceptance of the *de facto* partition of Ireland. During the debates Constance Markievicz spoke for many when she declared, 'I have seen the stars and I am not going to follow a flickering will-o-the-wisp.' But for the moment the opposition was verbal. The country was war-weary and as lorry-loads of Black and Tans and Auxiliaries left, Charlotte Despard and Maud Gonne MacBride, as disappointed as anyone at the prospect of the Free State, faced immediate problems.

There was acute distress, bordering on famine, in parts of Donegal. Maud Gonne went up with Mrs Despard to see what the White Cross could effect and reported to Arthur Griffith that the county was suffering from a lack of supplementary income derived from migrant workers in Scotland, as well as the erosion of fishing livelihoods on account of unrestricted competition from English and French trawlers. To add to the problem, the people of Donegal were too proud to advertise their distress, one man dying alone in his home rather than leaving it to beg. The White Cross set up school-feeding for children, but, according to Madame MacBride's calculations, there was an urgent need for more funds: 'Will the Government or the county committees be able to do the rest?'

But if there was economic distress of the traditional kind in Donegal, there was hell for the nationalist community in the six counties of the north-eastern state. The Catholics of Belfast in particular suffered from the Unionist perception of them as enemies within, in collusion with republican aspirations for a united Ireland. The Treaty negotiators had agreed to stop a very effective republican boycott of Belfast goods, which had been a means of bringing pressure to bear on Loyalist employers to reinstate Catholic workers who had been expelled from their jobs. But while the violence against Catholics escalated in the spring of 1922, condoned and more by the northern authorities, the upholders of the Free State made no effective protest for fear of jeopardizing a partition that might yet be confirmed in their favour. The result was that the beleaguered northern Catholics were seen as fair game for a reign of terror that has been graphically catalogued elsewhere. Many of the victims fled south and the White Cross met trains filled with 'wild-eyed refugees' and 'women half-demented and children sick with terror'. The anti-treaty IRA took the initiative of commandeering the Dublin headquarters of the Orange Order, Fowler Hall, as a refugee hostel, and at the same time occupied the central Four Courts complex as a direct challenge to the Free State government.

Charlotte Despard, who had visited Admiral Horthy's Hungary only two years previously, went up to Belfast to see for herself what the refugees were fleeing from. In the course of this mission she had an encounter with Sir Dawson Bates, northern Minister for Home Affairs and the man responsible for a draconian Special Powers Act. This occasion, which she regaled her friends with for years afterwards, was one of the last on which she used her status as the ex-Viceroy's sister because it was in that capacity that Dawson Bates agreed to meet her. In response to her appeal for protection for the besieged Catholic ghettoes of Belfast, he told her coldly that she was a disgrace to her family and that she should have been expressing sympathy for the forces of law and order. Then he turned his back and so she addressed the remainder of her appeal to the Bates 'posterior'. After that she turned to the Victoria Barracks, where she was probably acquainted with senior British officers, and as a result of remonstrations there did succeed in getting a Company of the Norfolk Regiment, Catholic British soldiers, to guard the Ardoyne. Otherwise, she could do nothing but contribute to the Dublin relief efforts. But while she was addressing Sir Dawson Bates's posterior, things were hotting up in Dublin.

The post-treaty tensions escalated into a Civil War of nearly a year's duration when, in June 1922, Field-Marshal Sir Henry Wilson was assassinated by the IRA in London. Among republicans, Wilson was odious as the British military advisor for security arrangements in the North, which virtually licensed state terror. He was a fervent Unionist and it is easy to see why Mrs Despard thought her own brother really not a bad sort when we read what Wilson thought about his friend Johnnie French: 'Poor little man, he is so weak and pliable and then has such inconsequential gusts of illogical passion. He is an Imperialist, a Democrat, a Home Ruler all at the same time. Poor man.' There is evidence that Wilson's assassination was ordered by Michael Collins but the British government presumed that the crime was the work of the IRA men still established in the Four Courts. Accordingly, pressure was brought to bear on the Free State authorities to move against them, with the help of a loan of British artillery. When the bombardment began there were about 400 people inside the Four Courts, among them Maud Gonne's son, Sean MacBride. This was the first chapter in the Civil War.

With Mary O'Connor of the Irish Women Workers' Union, the ever-practical Louie Bennett immediately set about evacuating the people living around the Four Courts. By the next day the Dublin women's grapevine had mobilized a peace committee which met at the Mansion House. This is Louie Bennett's account of the women's attempt to stop the war.

Among those who came were Mrs Sheehy-Skeffington, Maud Gonne MacBride, and Mrs Despard, and we were sent on as peace emmissaries to Government Buildings, where we saw Cosgrave, Griffith and Collins.

Collins was excited; obviously excited. Griffith was utterly depressed; an old, broken man. Cosgrave was outwardly unmoved, frigidly cold. After a lot of talk we saw that they were prepared, if the others would meet them, to try and negotiate. They didn't go very far, but they were prepared to talk anyway. We went back; and then the difficulty was to get in touch with the Republicans. The Lord Mayor said that as the fighting was going on he would loan us the ambulance to cross town. It was the only way we could go to what used to be the tram parcels office, and which was now being used as some sort of headquarters for the IRA.

We went into some sort of dark room, with sacks all around it. I sat on a sack of flour or something. We couldn't see any of the Republicans, but eventually someone – a General somebody or other, but I could never remember since who he was – had a long talk with Mrs Sheehy-Skeffington. But they would not negotiate on any terms. They said they were in it now, and there was no way out but to fight it out.

Soon the east side of O'Connell Street matched the west side, which had been ruined during the 1916 Rising. In just one week of fighting sixty people were killed in Dublin, and 300 wounded. As the war spread southwards, the Free State, now in harmony with Britain and Ulster, sent troops round the country to deal with it.

Charlotte Despard and Maud Gonne MacBride were politically, the latter also emotionally, in sympathy with the republican side. But they took the most important line of non-combatant action open to them, that of caring for the new population of political prisoners and their families. It seems best to give Maud Gonne's account of how the Women's Prisoners' Defence League, of which, after yet another momentous Mansion House meeting, Charlotte Despard was the President, began:

The WPDL was started in August 1922 informally outside the gates of Mountjoy Jail by the mothers, wives and sisters of Republican prisoners (of whom there were at least 11,000, including 250 women). No visits were allowed or information supplied. One woman was shot in the leg while trying to get news of her husband inside Wellington Barracks. One young lad was killed outside Mountjoy while accompanying a woman seeking news of her son. Terrifying stories, but too tragically confirmed later, of the glasshouse beatings and torture of prisoners for information circulated. The constant sound of firing in the jails and wounding of prisoners made the need of a Prisoners' Defence League obvious and urgent.

The 'Mothers', as the WPDL women were soon known, shared all the available information about conditions within the jails and the fates of individual prisoners. We see them here, we see them there, we see them everywhere: outside the prisons, in courtrooms, at the Dáil and, every Sunday after mass, at the 'ruins' corner' meetings in O'Connell Street. The old suffragette strategies of poster parades, instant street meetings and a constant deluge of letters to the press now came into play. They did everything as flamboyantly as possible, even, on occasion, leading poignant processions of prisoners' children to church to pray for amnesty. They were spat at, hosed upon and even shot at, but nothing stopped the 'Mothers' of the WPDL who, for most of that decade, were to be the only opposition to the Free State at large.

Although Maud Gonne provided the WPDL with its driving energy, as President Mrs Despard lent moral, magisterial authority. One typical letter of hers to *An Phoblacht* described the agony of a mother whose prisoner son had been shot dead: 'Oh the pain, the pain – I shall never be free of it – never! never!' But Mrs Despard's tone must have seemed exotically Old Testament in the Irish context: 'I say to them, I say to Ireland, I say to the world: "Be not deceived. God is not mocked. Whatever a man soweth, that shall he also reap." ' In his portrait of Charlotte Despard for *Rebel Irishwomen* (1935), Dick Fox described her as she led a group of ex-prisoners, who had been on hunger strike, from the train station, where they had arrived in Dublin, to the WPDL's clinic in Harcourt Street.

One afternoon the door of the hospital opened and Mrs Despard walked slowly in. Turning to the entrance, she spoke in gravely welcoming tones: 'Come in, my friends, here you will find food and fire!' Behind her, coming forward at her invitation, were 6 wild-eyed unkempt young men, who had just been released from gaol. They filed slowly into the room while she stood with arms outstretched. The scene seemed to belong to some old Greek tragedy.

It was through the WPDL that Charlotte Despard's Irish image, as the ubiquitous and spectacular Madame MacBride's right-hand woman, emerged. This image is still fresh in the minds of a generation of Irish people. Mrs Colette Quinlan, for example, remembers being brought, as a little girl, by a politically aware aunt to a commemoration service in the military church in Arbour Hill:

> I was walking along, scuffing my shoes in the gravel yard, when my aunt called my attention to two ladies walking just ahead of us. I had an impression of floating draperies and at least one big hat. One lady was tall and slender and had a regal carriage, her companion was smaller and rather dumpy looking. 'Do you see those two ladies,' said my aunt, 'well, remember that you have seen Maud Gonne and Mrs Despard.'

But 'dirty Dublin's' respect is always barbed and for the leading matrons of the republic there was a ready nickname – 'Maud Gonne Mad and Mrs Desperate'. Charlotte Despard sometimes found the speech of her Irish flock, especially poor Dublin women, hard to understand, but she hadn't lost that feeling for the woman in the street, and for urban children, which she had developed all those years ago in the slums of Battersea.

During the fighting in the summer of 1922 the St Stephen's Green house had been turned into an emergency hospital, where Maud Gonne took her turn nursing republican casualties dressed in her First World War nursing uniform. But by then Charlotte Despard had made alternative housing arrangements for herself, for the marble bust of Max that had migrated with her from Battersea, and for her closest Irish friend. In the past she had had her country boltholes and in the still rural environs of central Dublin it was possible to have your cake and eat it, to be surrounded by fields and yet within a twenty-minute car ride of the urban action. Today, Roebuck House has been shorn of the farms that it viewed in the 1920s and Clonskea is a pleasant suburb. But it is still an impressively commodious early Victorian detached house with a short curved drive leading to the front doorsteps and a generous garden full of mature trees. Above the ground-floor sequence of long-windowed reception rooms, Mrs Despard commandeered her own bedroom and bathroom, where she continued to have her daily tepid bath, while Maud Gonne retained an apartment for her personal use.

But the two châtelaines of Roebuck House were incapable of living in such a house in a secluded style. Apart from servants, including Maud Gonne's French cook, Mrs Meagher the housekeeper, Maggie the maid from Belfast, and Michael the chauffeur, Roebuck House swarmed with visitors and casual residents. At Christmas 1923, when 3,000 of the prisoners were released, partly as an amnesty gesture and partly on account of government fears about an outbreak of flu in the jails, there were mattresses in every room at Roebuck. The house was also regularly accommodating for Maud's children, and later grandchildren, for WPDL meetings, for Cumann na mBan meetings, as a halfway house for discharged prisoners, a convalescent home for wounded men, even a congenially rambling house for men on the run. Although Charlotte Despard no longer presided with her Currie Street authority, she enjoyed Roebuck's hivelike atmosphere and was soon acclimatized to the consequences of its status as a safe house: 'Some strange noises in the house. These things affect me very little now.' She did her best to placate Mrs Meagher, who was continually rattled by the fact that she never knew how many occupants to budget for.

Mrs Despard had moved in first and from her new address she wrote, in January 1923, a letter of condolence to Mrs Childers, whose husband, Erskine, had been executed by the Free State authorities for possessing a gun which had been originally given him by Michael Collins. Mrs Despard was sure of Mrs Childers's personal courage and offered her prayers that additional strength and some means of consolation would be given her.

> We, as you will know, have been passing through an anxious and strenuous time. My dear friend Maud Gonne, who is living here now, is, I think, just kept going by her work which leaves little time for anything else but sleep. And she is able to sleep. I hope you can sleep. So far as the body is concerned, that is the one balm.

In anticipation of her visit she politely warned Mrs Childers that she didn't eat meat — 'anything else will suit me well' — and closed her letter with a wish that the new year would be better for 'our sorely tried country' than 'disastrous 1922'.

But, if anything, 1923 was worse, and as she approached her eighties Charlotte Despard was less able to cope with its vicissitudes. The letter she wrote to the unreformed Vere's father a year before reflected her cumulative irritation with her ward, but it has an unusual, extra tartness to it.

> I think it is right to let you know that I have had rather a bad turn and am under treatment for the heart – I am told it is over-strain and may be remedied by complete rest which I am trying to take, but naturally it may not be so and therefore I am setting my affairs in order. . . . I have been looking over my will today. I find I have left her £1,000 with instructions for my executors not to allow her to handle the capital; but to sink it in an annuity for her. This will not be enough to keep her. I do not wish that it should be, it will however prevent her life from being so hard as it might otherwise be. . . . I hoped things would have been different. But indeed there is no use in looking back. I have done my best. Things being what they are with me I think it best to put the exact situation before you.

Of course, that was not the end of Vere Foley in Granny Despard's life, for the high-spirited young woman, a 'gold-digger' in the opinion of Mrs Despard's Belfast friend Jack Mulvenna, regularly came over for holidays at Roebuck. On such trips she had strange adventures, including first-hand experience of one of the many security raids on the household. But she was not political material, not a young Margaret Bond-field in the making. As late as 1935 Kate Harvey was expressing, by letter, the rather fatalistic hope for Vere that 'some good man with a comfortable home to give her would ask her to marry him'. Maud Gonne's daughter and son were much more inspiring representatives of the young generation to Mrs Despard's way of thinking. Sean MacBride had few detailed memories of his mother's friend because, as he so disarmingly reminded me, he was in and out of jail most of the time. But he did remember the £100, a large sum in the 1920s, which she gave him to buy a boat on the Shannon.

The alarming heart trouble of 1922 seems to have abated but

other serious discomforts returned. From now on the pocket diaries are speckled with 'tired', 'depressed' and 'exhausted' and there were frequent confinements to bed. There was recurring pain in one shoulder, for which Dr Kathleen Lynn, of 1916 and Citizen Army fame, gave morphia: 'It was curious. Pain went and I slept much. It was like being slightly and pleasantly drunk.' At other times she had the then fashionable electricity treatment and osteopathy for the shoulder trouble. She even records the life-renewing 'joy' of a Turkish bath at the Minarets in Westland Row (now Pearse Street), where Leopold Bloom also enjoyed a purification. Charlotte Despard now had to make room for a daily siesta and there were frightening moments of sudden giddiness: 'Lasted only a moment. Maud with me or I might have fallen.' Most infuriating was the deteriorating eyesight and it was with great reluctance that she ordered spectacles for herself: 'I wonder if I shall ever use them.' But the remarkable thing is how often Charlotte Despard managed, despite these disabilities, to bounce back to a vigorous involvement with the world outside.

Mrs Despard needed to be well for the great trials that lay ahead. She lost her little book for 1923 and so opened the 1924 diary with a fragmented account of the chief events of 'perhaps the most disastrous year that our country has ever passed through'. It was one of 'great sadness upon our household', which began under 'heavy gloom of executions, Liam Mellows, Rory O'Connor and their like, followed by the trial and execution of Erskine Childers and many more.' Looking back on 1923, it seemed to Charlotte Despard that she, and the other 'Mothers', had been protesting the whole time: 'But we know that agitation has kept up the courage of our boys and girls in prison.' Within weeks of that letter of condolence to Mrs Childers, the WPDL was proscribed as an illegal organisation and Maud Gonne MacBride was clapped into Kilmainham Jail where, with other women republican prisoners, she immediately went on hunger strike.

Yeats rushed off to plead with the Free State Prime Minister, William Cosgrave, only to be told that 'women, doctors and clergy ought to keep out of politics, as their business is with the sick'. Meanwhile Charlotte Despard, moved by a different kind of 'sudden resolve', rushed off to the gates of Kilmainham. There she sat herself down upon a chair and remained for the twenty days and nights that elapsed until her friend was released: 'Oh! the bitter cold and length of those nights.' This vigil didn't do much for her health but at least she didn't have that hopeless feeling, so familiar in suffragette days, that somehow she was immune to the cruellest consequences of her convictions. And she was rewarded with a 'wonderful moment' when, still at the prison gates, she was told of Maud's release. An ambulance was requisitioned and with great joy she bounded into it beside her stretcher-borne friend, off to recuperate at Roebuck House.

Lucy Franks was loyal and affectionate enough to visit her aunt at Kilmainham, when other relatives in Britain shunned the Aunt Lottie who was reportedly 'living in a hen-house in Ireland' and had been disowned by her brother. Though no republican, Miss Franks preferred to think of her aunt as a vagabond saint, and in her own genteel way she supported the new Ireland. She was a founder member, and funder, of the Irish Countrywomen's Association and decades later earned herself the accolade of 'buan chara' to that body. In 1923 West-field House, the scene of Charlotte Despard's honeymoon more than fifty years earlier and the Franks' ancestral home, had been fired. This would have made the temporarily homeless Lucy Franks bitter about her aunt's associates, had she been that way inclined. For her part, Mrs Despard was loath to see that particular big house as a bastion of the Ascendancy and she reassured herself with the conviction that the crime was agrarian rather than political.

Lucy's visits to Roebuck were among the pleasant interludes in the otherwise grim 1920s. But though the household was chaotic and subject to regular raids, it was a warm and welcoming place. Yeats's biographer, Joseph Hone, recalled how, once beyond Maud Gonne's flock of unruly dogs, 'anyone could walk in and ask for dinner or asylum for life'. Apart from the constant stream of ex-prisoners and politicos, there were Christmas parties for prisoners' children and, in summer, garden fêtes (*aeridheacht mor*) in aid of the WPDL. Both the presiding ladies at Roebuck enjoyed the garden, Mrs Despard using her proximity with nature as a kind of restorative therapy. Before rising each morning she liked to study the particularly beautiful copper beech that could be seen from her window and she took great pleasure in planting the little avenue, ordering garden furniture, installing a wicket gate and generally supervising a garden 'full of promise': 'If only,' she mused regularly, 'men could live naturally.'

To Roebuck Con Markievicz regularly rolled up in her motor, as did new friends such as 'Maire' (Comerford), who brought Mrs Despard handspun tweed from one of her political trips to Donegal, and 'Helena' (Moloney), who helped Mrs Despard out in O'Connell Street on the Sundays when Maud was away. Favourite men included Roddy Connolly, son of James Connolly, and a young man by the name of Peadar O'Donnell, who impressed Mrs Despard from the start because he was so 'full of economic schemes'. Of the 'Mr and Mrs Fox' who frequently came to tea, the Mr was the Dick Fox who wrote *Rebel Irishwomen* and the Mrs was none other than Patricia Lynch, author of such children's classics as *The Turf-cutter's Donkey*. Described by Sylvia Pankhurst as a dark-eyed Irish girl who wrote poetry, Patricia Lynch had been an active socialist feminist when she had lived in London and she would have known much about Mrs Despard's pre-Ireland career.

But July 1926 brought a unique and happy opportunity of seeing suffragette friends because in that year Dublin hosted the Fifth Congress of the Women's International League for Peace and Freedom. Many of the 150 delegates from twenty different countries were old acquaintances and Helena Swanwick actually stayed at Roebuck House. The WFL's paper, *The Vote*, usually avoided mentioning political events in the 'Isle of Unrest', sticking instead to such newsworthy gems as the fact that in August 1921 a Miss Shamrock Trench became the first woman in the Irish Free State to secure a pilot's licence. When it came to the Dublin Congress of 1926 *The Vote* therefore provided an uncontentious description of what was on offer in Dublin and of the Congress's broad theme: 'The next steps towards peace'.

The Irish Section is setting up committees to study the subjects of Militarism and Minorities, and to report on them to the Congress Commissions. The problem of the relations between minorities and majorities, in particular, is pressingly important in Ireland, and special attention is being given to it. . . . Every group of women, whether standing for civil reform, labour, or a political party, is to receive the Congress delegates. The Irish Women's Citizens' Association are issuing invitations to a Converzatione at which the work of women in Parliaments will be the subject of discussion. The Trade Union Women are having an afternoon tea party at their seaside club for delegates interested in the Labour movement. . . . The United Irishwomen's Society (whose aim is to draw the women of Ireland together, irrespective of class or creed, for the betterment of rural conditions) intend, through their President, the Countess of Fingal, to invite a group of delegates to Killeen Castle to talk over rural problems. . . . The women of the Republican parties have formed a committee to arrange an afternoon excursion for the entertainment of the delegates. They mean to take their guests by motor to the valley of the Boyne River, to give them an opportunity of seeing the most ancient and famous of Ireland's prehistoric monuments.

Notwithstanding the good show, local tensions hung over this international gathering. Louie Bennett recalled the awkwardness at the opening reception where, for the first time since the Civil War, both Republican and Free State leaders were present. W. T. Cosgrave was there, as she reported to Dick Fox – 'small, stiff truculent' and wearing his official decorations – and in another corner of the room, 'towering above his supporters' and 'lean, gaunt, with grim, strongly-marked features', there was Mr de Valera, not long released from prison. Louie Bennett got up on the plinth to welcome the guests of the evening but when she announced that the 'President' was going to say a few words, the two rival groups of men stiffened and glared defiantly at each other as if they dared each other to advance. But as Louie Bennett stepped down, Jane Addams, the American President of the WILPF, took her place. At a later Mansion House meeting Addams read a statement made by Francis Sheehy-Skeffington in which he had advocated peaceful struggle for social and national justice. But when his widow, Hanna, rose to endorse this statement, she quoted Patrick Pearse, saying, 'Ireland unfree can never be at peace.' According to Swanwick, some of the foreign delegates were puzzled by the divisions between the uncompromisingly republican women and those members of the Irish section 'who pursued the same aims, but by other methods'. Mrs Despard, who had been a party to the Boyne Valley plans, was very firmly with the group referred to by Swanwick as the

'Black women', who boycotted many of the Congress's official functions: 'my old dear friend Mrs Despard . . . never in her life could accept a compromise'. But despite her distaste for the politics of Mrs Despard's group Swanwick was content to listen to tales of her adventures since the treaty and to meet with her 'beautiful friend'. 'As it was, I felt no obligation to do anything but love these friends for their goodness and beauty.'

Mrs Despard had a great time during the Congress, although she was predictably sarcastic about the Governor-General's garden party at the Vice-regal Lodge, which, of course, she did not attend: 'We hear some of the delegates had to pay five shillings for the privilege of going.' (Apart from his occupation of a role that symbolized the inadequacies of the Free State, Governor-General Tim Healy may have been odious to Mrs Despard because he had been the employers' advocate during the 1913 lock-out. On the other hand, he had also served as the legal defender of the Pankhursts in 1908, a role that probably endeared the Governor-General to some of the other delegates.) But Mrs Despard did not dwell on unpleasant things. Instead, she revelled in the 'picturesque' Japanese delegate and the American Miss Pollitz, who was 'desperately keen about a revolution, demanding absolute sex equality. I lunched with her and two or three other enthusiastic girls.' And, despite the inevitable puncture, the Boyne Valley outing was a great success, another 'wonderful day'.

Until she got her own extra-WPDL projects going, Mrs Despard's lifestyle was, when she was in good health, unusually sedate. With the help of a teacher who called to Roebuck she busied herself learning Irish, but despite diligent study she did not make much headway with her *Seana* (sic). Then there was the odd expedition to the 'Pictures', or to a Jack Yeats exhibition. But the only theatre event recorded in her diaries was the *Plough and the Stars* production of February 1926, which she attended as a protester against O'Casey's scornful depiction of the 1916 Rising. Whatever she felt about O'Casey's politics, culturally he would have been too modern for Mrs Despard, whose literary tastes were still Victorian. When she set about reading some of the modern poets she found 'none of the thrills' of her own old favourites. There was cause for further dissatisfaction with the afternoon debates of the 'Optimists' at the 'Ritz' café in central Dublin, which she sometimes attended with Con

Markievicz. Here, such topics as 'Tara as the national metrop-olis' and 'the influence of literature on national life' were debated. But on one occasion Mrs Despard was disgruntled by 'feeble speeches', on another by, horror of horrors, a speaker who misquoted her beloved Shelley.

Since the formal ending of the Civil War in May 1924 the 'Unionists and Free Staters have everything their own way.' The nervous government brought forth public safety measure after public safety measure, but this repression went unchecked by an opposition that was still boycotting the Dáil. Moreover, the Free State vision of the new Ireland fell far short of the quasi-socialist ideals of the first Dáil. It has to be said, however, that as the country stood then it did not have the resources to become an instant Celtic Utopia. Ireland, or rather the twenty-six county Free State, lacked natural reserves of minerals and non-agricul-tural raw materials, while outside of Dublin, Cork, Waterford and Limerick the technical infrastructure for a developed economy was minimal. Meanwhile, in the rural subsistence-economy peripheries, distress was still endemic.

Maud Gonne had helped to set up a fish-curing plant at Balderg in Mayo and Mrs Despard likewise aided 'fisherfolk friends' by providing a lorry to take fish to market. This kind of work was taken up by many republican women. Mrs Cathal Brugha, for example, distributed woollens made by Connemara women, arriving at Roebuck House with 'lovely things' for sale. But the hopeless state of the countryside was brought home to Mrs Despard when she travelled west in the car that was almost comically prone to mishaps. Ever since that wintry election campaign of 1918 she had felt the 'shelter' of her motor to be indispensable, but her adventures with her chauffeur, the feck-less Michael, recall the chorus of that Percy French Song:

Are you right there Michael, are you right?
Do you think that we'll be there before the night?

On one particular journey to Mayo, 1926 they picked up a male pedestrian just outside Dublin: 'He had intended *walking* to Sligo. We took him to a village where he said he had friends about ten miles from Sligo. Food with us – very shy, and modest – nearly starving.'

Mrs Despard had instituted welfare schemes in Nine Elms

before the British Labour Party had been founded, and as a Poor Law Guardian she fought for the rights of the elderly before there were old-age pensions. Not surprisingly, she had decided in 1924 to set up the sort of cottage industry that Irish republican visionaries saw as the basis of a revolutionary new economy. She hoped thereby to set an example and at the same time to provide work for ex-prisoners and their families. Maximilian Despard's shrewd business instincts would have been affronted by the Roebuck Jam Factory, which, after she had toyed for a while with the idea of a bakery, was what she eventually plumped for. While some of the farm outbuildings near the house were commandeered by Madame MacBride's makers of floral shell decorations and other 'fancy goods', Mrs Despard's workers were put to the cooking, potting and labelling of preserves made from fruit grown in the nearby fields she had purchased.

She was full of energy and optimism for this scheme, seeing her bank manager to arrange for the channelling of her dividends, watching how her gooseberries grew, getting in agricultural advisors to inspect her fruit trees and advise her workers, and motoring around tea-shops and grocers to take orders. Significantly, it was 'Roebuck Jam' and not, as it would have been in the days of the Despard Club, the Despard Arms and the Despard Uniteds, Despard Jam. The newspaper started in the summer of 1925 as the organ of republicans who boycotted the Free State Dáil, *An Phoblacht*, carried regular advertisements for her '100% Irish' wares. Its readers were exhorted to 'Eat Pure Jam!' and told that the Roebuck variety contained the best quality fruit, 'pure white sugar only', no chemicals or other artificial substances, and that the pots were sealed with 'special hygienic covers'. 'If your grocer does not stock it, send us his name.' Many a Dublin grocer must have quailed at the thought of having his name sent to Mrs Despard, but that was the least of her problems.

Almost as soon as it got going the jam factory was an exhausting disappointment: 'all expense and no profit'. There were the careless girls who didn't adhere to the high standards of hygiene, the men who didn't have green fingers or resented the strictures of business, and dire weather. The text of the following *An Phoblacht* advertisement was surely written by the jam evangelist herself: 'Do you want to be happy? You can't be happy if you are not healthy, to be really healthy you must eat pure food. If you eat jam, eat pure jam. If you don't eat jam begin today with a pot of Roebuck. It is guaranteed pure.' Between the lines of this frantic copy, which might usefully have recalled that it was through cheap jam that the British working class got its first regular dosage of vitamin C, we can see Mrs Despard's desperation. But the final betrayal and the end of the enterprise came in 1927: 'I have been robbed of money from the house. I believe that two of those who lived with us and whom I trusted have betrayed me badly. My poor girls will be out of work and my factory has gone. It will be all I can do to pay what I owe.'

The ailing jam factory apart, Mrs Despard was increasingly exercised by grander financial matters. Her Theosophical sympathies were to be a casualty of this preoccupation with what she called 'the economic side of things'. Back in 1909, Annie Besant, President of the Theosophical Society, had adopted the two sons of an impoverished Brahmin Theosophist who worked at the Society's headquarters in Adyar, Madras. One of them, Krishnamurti, was groomed as the 'World Teacher', a role akin to a new Messiah in Theosophical doctrine. Spiritually, society was continually evolving and at critical moments in human history great teachers, or avatars, such as Christ or Buddha, had emerged to aid the process. Before Kirshnamurti's hour came in December 1925 Mrs Despard had been optimistic about his destiny. It had been under the auspices of his special society, the Order of the Star in the East, that she had given many of her pre–1914 Theosophical lectures.

Dublin Theosophists met in Dawson Chambers, the 'yogibogeybox' of James Joyce's *Ulysses*, and when Krishnamurti came out they had the benefit of first-hand accounts from the letters of two prominent Irish Theosophists, Gretta and Jim Cousins. They had sat under the great Banyan tree at Adyar and heard Krishnamurti declare, 'I come to those who want sympathy, who want happiness, who are longing to be released, who are longing to find happiness in all things. I come to reform and not to tear down; not to destroy but to build.' Jim was a bit sceptical but Gretta's 'psychic body and emotions were so stirred that she was prostrated for hours in our room in a state of ecstasy and semi-trance.' Back in Dublin, Mrs Despard responded with a cool 'I wonder'.

To be hailed by Charlotte Despard, the World Teacher had

to be politically engaged with the earthly vale of tears. Since Mrs Despard perceived Christ as a first-century communist, Krishnamurti's mystical waffle wasn't good enough: 'If only we could feel that the Master were behind working through and inspiring the great economic struggle. . . . Impossible to believe. If the *Master* were speaking through him, would he not be with the *People*?'

The less exotic local Church was equally uninspiring: 'Never have so many been asking for work or bread and all this the church disregards.' Throughout the 1920s the ex-Lambeth Poor Law Guardian was regularly called upon to remonstrate with the Commissioners of the Dublin Union on behalf of the unemployed and of individuals such as the aged arthritic Dubliner whose wife was blind. The no-room-at-the-inn pathos of the destitute family who called at Roebuck one night to be admitted for shelter and food caused the comment, 'The world's too sad just now.' Many advanced republicans left the Church in the 1920s because it was seen to be simply the Free State at prayer. But that was not the high-minded Mrs Despard's way. She had been a convert to the faith on her own terms, a Catholic who had not grown up under the shadow of clerical authority and who had been uncowed by a jingoistic Battersea priest. So she carried on attending Mass in Donnybrook and managed to find enlightened confessors.

But as the jam factory was floundering and Krishnamurti was being dismissed Charlotte Despard's communist vision reasserted itself. She had not been actively or directly involved with previous Irish communist initiatives. Now she opined, with all the disarming enthusiasm of a person thinking about setting up a bonsai-growing club, 'It would be nice if we could start a Communist group in Ireland. There is no country where it is so much needed.'

# THE GREAT DEPRESSION AND THE IRISH FREE STATE: 'WE MUST GO ON DREAMING THE IMPOSSIBLE DREAM'

It seemed to the eighty-one-year-old Mrs Despard of Roebuck House that

> Abroad and in England communism is growing extraordinarily. We mean to try and start a group here. So far as society is concerned that is the only hope for this tormented world. The trial of our imprisoned comrades in England has done much to quicken the movement. I have read Pollitt's defence. It is very convincing.

Her acquaintance with Harry Pollitt, leader of the British Communist Party, stretched back to the Hands Off Russia campaign. Pollitt gatecrashed the London birthday fête of 1937 (celebrating Mrs Despard's ninety-third birthday) to pay his respects to the 'only real saint' he professed ever to have met. Teresa Billington-Greig remembered him sidling towards the plinth of honour 'like a boy doing honour to his mother'. This was an unknowingly accurate description because Pollitt's worship of his own mother, who was to die within weeks of Charlotte Despard, was probably a factor in his affectionate memories. But on that star-studded occasion the like of Harry Pollitt couldn't even get near the birthday old girl and so he hung around the back of the hall and told the doorman about Mrs Despard's capacity for combining 'revolution with tenderness'.

The trial referred to in Charlotte Despard's 1926 diary was over a charge of 'publishing seditious libel and incitement to commit breaches of the Incitement to Mutiny Act of 1791'. Despite the self-defence that had so impressed her, Pollitt and his comrades were sent down for nearly a year. In September 1926 she was conspicuous among those who gathered at Holborn in central London to greet their release into the bitter aftermath of the General Strike: 'A great occasion. The place throbbing with gay enthusiasm. Hannington and Tom Mann spoke.' On the following Sunday a huge crowd gathered around five platforms in Hyde Park to hear a galaxy of left speakers, including George Lansbury, Shapurji Saklatvala and Mrs Despard 'of the Irish Workers' Party'.

Mrs Despard, who appears not to have been actively involved with previous communist initiatives in Ireland, probably because of ill-health and the demands of the post-Civil War crisis, was an executive member of the new Workers' Party of Ireland. Its leading light was Roddy Connolly, son of James Connolly. He was a regular at the Roebuck political salon and his ancient hostess (and, for a time, paymistress) liked hearing about his experiences in the Soviet Union. He probably also appealed to her because he was an avowed Marxist with an imaginative rather than a dismissive critique of republicanism. She paid Roddy Connolly as the full-time organizer of a movement which she hoped would be 'both political and economic, for if labour and the republicans came together there might be a chance'. Otherwise, all she could look forward to was 'another spate of the Free State and imperialism'.

Previous communist initiatives had been bedeviled by the defeat and demoralization of the urban working class, by internal dissensions about how to relate to the IRA and by the twists and turns of Jim Larkin's career. A colossus of the Irish labour movement before the First World War, in 1923 Jim Larkin had returned to Dublin after eight and a half years in the USA. The charismatic Larkin was perceived by Mrs Despard as the great hope for a Bolshevik revolution in Ireland. She noted his 'great magnetism' and was gratified when, at an early meeting, he honoured her by inviting her up to the platform. But within a couple of years she was sarcastic about the 'great Jim', accusing him of mischief-making and of 'tolerating nothing of which he is not the boss'. This attitude is reminiscent of her attitude towards John Burns and his Battersea machine. But in the case of Larkin, who was no class traitor and whose battles were mainly with the right, it was unfair. That being said, it was undoubtedly very galling that because of Jim Larkin's international status his moribund Irish Worker League got the benediction of the Comintern (The Communist International) at the expense of Roddy's Workers' Party.

If Mrs Despard had had the ear of the Comintern authorities the WPI would have been ratified as the official communist party of Ireland, because it was a lively, agitational organization which within months had set up a parallel Unemployed Workers' Movement. The UWM's inaugural meeting was recorded as yet another day 'long to be remembered'. It lobbied the Poor Law authorities for what there was by way of official relief to Dublin's jobless. It also mobilized voluntary relief efforts and in so doing sought to encourage workers and their families to have a political perspective on their situation. (As usual, Mrs Despard noted that, though subject to local rivalries, the women were, when it came to the distribution of milk for children, 'much more businesslike than the men'.) Mrs Despard contributed funds to such initiatives but she was not comfortable, and even a little distressed, when she found herself on the editorial committee of the WPI's *Hammer and Plough*.

She no longer felt able to be so active and felt that it was as much as she could do to transfer funds from the ailing jam factory to the purchase of some printing facilities for her comrades. But her supportive role almost landed her with a need to make a Pollitt-like defence when comrades Campion, Ferguson and Lynch of the unemployed movement were arrested on a conspiracy charge. She waited for a long time to make her offer of bail for these men and when this was refused they were taken off to the Bridewell. But next day, to her enormous relief, a magistrate dismissed the charge, 'which would have included me'.

It was Mrs Despard's self-imposed task to defend the communist movement against the stigma of godlessness, something that had not been so necessary in relatively secular England. She thought for a while about setting up a socialist Sunday School and in the frequent 'idle, pain-filled days' she composed a lecture reconciling Christianity with communism: 'I need to show how it will express that universal perfect love which exists I believe in the very meaning and basis of creation.' There is no record of how this talk, if it was ever delivered, went down with the Dublin punters.

These Irish developments happened in tandem with similar events in England upon which Mrs Despard also kept her half-blind but still beady eyes. Throughout 1926 she was preoccupied with the 'great battle', the General Strike, across the water and she maintained direct connections with leading figures in the British labour movement. (Bob Stewart and Helen Crawfurd had even spent time in Dublin as communist scouts in 1925.) Her prestige among British leftists was probably higher than it was in Dublin, where few people were aware of her remarkable history. Thus *An Phoblacht* would reprint the speeches made in Mrs Despard's honour at her London birthday fêtes but when it published a life of Mr Gandhi it failed to mention the old lady who was probably one of the few individuals in Dublin to have actually met the man.

Mrs Despard usually combined meetings and campaigns of her British communist friends with her annual visit to the WFL-sponsored birthday parties. Wal Hannington, the leader of the National Unemployed Workers' Movement in Britain, recalled her 'warm place in the hearts of the London unemployed' and that she was always 'enthusiastically received' at their meetings. In 1934, when Hannington stood as a parliamentary candidate in Merthyr Tydfil in South Wales, she journeyed over to join his campaign. Marjorie Pollitt remembered how spectacularly ancient and frail she looked,

> but someone would bring out a kitchen chair or a mineral water box, and willing hands would help her to climb on it . . . although she was then quite old, when most people rely on reminiscence and dwell in the past, she had a complete understanding of every issue which was topical at the time.

Needless to say, she did not voice that complete understanding of topical issues when she met her relatives. She was compatible only in nostalgic terms with the surviving elder sister, Carrie, with whom she had done those pre–1870 Grand Tours: 'Poor darling, sorely outraged about the "wicked strikers" who are making life difficult. I do *not* talk politics.' On such a non-political basis she also managed cordial visits to other relatives during her hectic London seasons. Jack's granddaughter, Lady Patricia Kingsbury, remembers her Aunt Lottie's visits vividly. Her grandmother, Lady Ypres, who had been discreetly estranged from her late husband and who had not accompanied him to Ireland, got on very well with Lottie. But some discomfiture was aroused by Lottie's outlandish Irish comrade-servants, one chauffeur by the name of 'Comrade Tom' being particularly well recalled.

Charlotte Despard never became respectable. By the end of the 1920s she was vehemently disenchanted with the British Labour Party – the Irish version being equally 'futile'. The Labour Party had not backed the miners, who stayed out for months after the short-lived General Strike of 1926, and it was led by a man with a prominent place in her personal gallery of rogues, Ramsay MacDonald. During his by-election fight against MacDonald in 1929 Harry Pollitt received an open letter of support from Mrs Despard. She wrote as 'an old Socialist and for many years an active member of what was at one time the Labour Party of Great Britain' and catalogued MacDonald's misdemeanours thus: 'When I claimed his help for Irish prisoners and deportees, he did nothing, made no protest . . . What did he do for the miners? Was he there when all London was moved with sympathy for the Hunger Marchers?' Whenever her health and the timing of the WFL festivities had permitted, Mrs Despard had been there.

But back at home the Workers' Party failed to sustain its original promise. Despite hard-working and talented leading members it did not take root. With hindsight it is possible to see insurmountable difficulties in the simultaneous existence of Jim Larkin's Comintern-backed Irish Worker League and in the acute demoralization of Dublic workers, but Mrs Despard was most vexed by the WPI's debilitating lack of funds. She regretted that she herself was not wealthy enough to do more, but she had never had the means to subsidize a whole movement. She only had enough to get the ball rolling – to pay the rent for the

Women's Freedom League's offices for a year, or to maintain a Labour Party office in Battersea for a time. She was not a millionaire, and she got no return on her many Irish investments. Back in the Battersea days, Mrs Harvey had stepped in to organize the accounts when, as happened frequently, they got out of hand. But Mrs Despard had no Mrs Harvey in Dublin and as money haemorrhaged away she became even more scatty about its management.

She began 1927 with a feeling of 'general bankruptcy', which was not yet a literal state, and confessed to her bewilderment: 'so many things to arrange for and consider' and 'I have had difficulty in holding my mental balance.' This despondency made her very peevish about the WPI:

> I'm not sure of it. We want stronger and more intelligent men. Are they to be found? . . . None of the men seem able for their big task. One can talk – others can theorize – not practical. They do not appeal to the people and there is not much following.

When Mrs Despard first got involved with the WPI she had told a meeting of 'republican ladies', probably the Cumann na mBan group that regularly gathered at Roebuck House, that 'I had made up my mind to drop politics and to devote myself to economics' – a Despardism for the shift from radical republicanism back to communism proper. But the WPI's campaign to set up rural Workers' Republic clubs was a fiasco because although the communist evangelists were treated politely as opponents of the Free State, the Mayo men did 'not quite grasp our position. The men here are just republicans.' While Mrs Despard and her friends tried to get the WPI going nationally many potential, or indeed actual, recruits had their eyes on Eamon de Valera's doings. His political mission was defined in republican terms but he had stolen many of the left's clothes for his speeches and he was undoubtedly big enough for his task. He seemed to offer the only real hope of a broad opposition to the Free State.

The WPI had tried to fill the vacuum caused by the crisis within Sinn Fein since 1925. In that year the IRA had withdrawn its allegiance in order to pursue independently its aim of a thirty-two county republic, and Mrs Despard, who had belonged to the Donnybrook branch of Sinn Fein, declared, 'I am giving up Sinn Fein. I feel that it is hopelessly dead.' This pessimism was not original or unique to Mrs Despard. While it continued its boycott of Free State political institutions on account of the oath, Sinn Fein was self-willed to frustration. At the 1926 Ard-Fheis (annual conference) de Valera proposed that the party should fight for seats in the Dáil if a way could be found of removing that oath. When he failed to make adequate headway he left Sinn Fein to form his own party, Fianna Fáil. This new party, which had yet to work out a face-saving way of dealing with the oath obstacle, attracted women of the calibre of Constance Markievicz and Hanna Sheehy-Skeffington. These were the kind of people that Mrs Despard had hoped to attract into a communist party, and now she watched their progress with a critical sympathy.

Fianna Fáil duly won three seats less than the government in the 1927 General Election. But what pushed de Valera and his deputies into the Dáil was the aftermath of the assassination of the Free State Minister for Justice, Kevin O'Higgins, in July of that year. Young, brilliant and right-wing, O'Higgins had been the confident architect of much of the repressive legislation inaugurated by the Free State, and it seems that he was murdered by freelance IRA men. But the assassination yielded a new Public Safety Act and, on the argument that abstentionism contributed to such extra-parliamentary crimes, a measure whereby no one could even stand as a parliamentary or local political candidate without being committed to taking the oath. Accordingly, Mr de Valera took the book containing the text of the oath of loyalty: 'I am putting my name here to obtain permission to enter among the deputies elected by the Irish people. Understand that there is no other meaning to what I am doing.' One elected deputy who would not have been able to stomach this was Constance Markievicz, but she died just five days after O'Higgins's murder.

She was fifty-nine and she died in a public ward after a minor operation (appendectomy), probably because of a general ill-health precipitated by repeated imprisonments. The Free State authorities refused permission for her body to lie in state at the City Hall or the Mansion House, so it was taken to the Rotunda, which was not civic property. As the most famous Madame's Fianna scouts formed a guard of honour around the coffin, an estimated 100,000 people filed past. For the funeral procession to Glasnevin Cemetery, there were eight lorry-loads of flowers, seven bands and marchers from every trade union, and from every women's and republican organization. Charlotte Despard and Maud Gonne MacBride headed the WPDL 'Mothers'. But, fearful that such a vast demonstration of mourning might turn into something threatening, the Free State government sent a hundred soldiers to make sure that no republican volley was fired as the coffin was lowered into the grave. That was one consequence of the post-O'Higgins emergency. Another was the immediate arrest of Sean MacBride as a suspected assassin, and Mrs Despard's designation under Section XIII of the Public Safety Act as a dangerous character liable to expulsion from Ireland.

With a somewhat cosy innocence of the reality of their heroine's Dublin scene, the British *Women's Leader* reported on Charlotte Despard's officially nefarious status.

We are at present ignorant of the exact nature of the activities which have led the Free State Government to take this very cautious step, but we surmise that among large sections of the Dublin poor it will be deeply regretted. There are, however, equally large sections of the British public which will welcome the return of this very well loved veteran suffrage leader. Should anything go wrong with our promised Equal Franchise measure there is a lot to be said for having a potential public danger on this side of the Irish Channel.

The classic history of the suffrage struggle, Ray Strachey's *The Cause* (1928), which has recently been reprinted, still has a footnote on Mrs Despard stating that in 1927 she was 'expelled from the Irish Free State as a dangerous character'. In fact, the authorities did not proceed with the deportation of the incorrigible eighty-three-year-old, but she needed the love and support of her British friends even more than ever.

For the exhausted and demoralized Charlotte Despard the yearly London season was a tonic. 'How is it,' she exclaimed with gratitude, 'that I have such friends. May I be more worthy of them.' From the boat-train at Euston she would be met by WFL stalwarts such as Dr Knight or Marian Reeves, who continued to fan the 'First President's' personality cult for nearly twenty years after she had left them for the 'Isle of Unrest'. The Leaguers also gave Mrs Despard a rousing send-off. At one such departure they asked some respectacle looking fellow passengers to take care of Mrs Despard on her return journey, which she generally insisted on doing third-class. These fellow passengers were slightly put out when, upon arriving at Kingstown (Dun Laoire), their elderly charge was met by an Irish welcoming party which contrasted forcibly with the WFL ladies.

Mrs Despard, who was often restless at night in Dublin, always slept well among the familiar sights and sounds of her English bases. She was reassured by her old sitting-room at Nine Elms. At Mrs Harvey's establishment at Hartfield, now an open-air school for children of 'delicate' health or from 'unfavourable' (i.e. fatherless) homes, she enjoyed 'delicious vegetarian suppers'. Here, in 1924, she heard the wireless for the first time, playing jazz. The Hartfield school was part of a movement which had begun in Berlin in 1904 and which sought to emulate ancient Greek and Roman educational practices. With the aid of twelve acres of land, Mrs Harvey's pupils were given a practical schooling to fit them to 'serve the community'. The fees were 'moderate' and Mrs Despard, who had already donated land and her bungalow, funded some of the pupils until the late 1920s.

The show also continued at Battersea and in 1922 a plaque was unveiled in Currie Street by the Mayor: DESPARD HOUSE: FOR MANY YEARS THE RESIDENCE OF MRS CHARLOTTE DESPARD AND PRESENTED BY HER TO THE BATTERSEA BOROUGH COUNCIL FOR MATERNITY AND CHILD WELFARE IN WHICH SHE WAS SO KEENLY INTERESTED. *The Vote* reported on this little ceremony, at which, unusually, the person commemorated was present:

In acknowledging the cheers and greetings of the crowd, many of them bareheaded mothers with babies in their arms, Mrs Despard said that it had been a very real joy to live amongst them, and to try to help them to live a healthier and happier life. She could never forget them. (Here a burly voice called out, 'You remember me, mother?' 'Ah, yes, Jack, my boy, I remember you well,' she replied, although it must have been probably thirty years since 'Jack' was a boy and received her guidance and advice.) Then, instinctively raising her hands as if by way of blessing the children who surged all around her, and speaking under deep emotion, she said, 'I leave my love with you, friends, and I know I also take your love with me back to Ireland'.

In 1960 Despard House and its environs were demolished to make way for the Doddington Housing Estate. The council used the proceeds from the sale of the Currie Street building to endow a charity in its donor's honour, a fund to assist 'older women, widows and otherwise, needing employment so that they can work at more adequate rates of pay'. The fund, the very modest yearly income yielded from an original investment of £1,500, is administered by the Battersea United Charities and today goes towards the cost of child-minding, books, fares and materials required by single mothers doing courses of different kinds. The parlance of good works has changed, and Battersea is no longer red, but Charlotte Despard would have approved of her one tangible legacy.

The highlight of her trip to London every year was the triumphal birthday party, usually held in the first week in July. Mrs Despard's actual birthday was 15 June and since that was also the date of Magna Carta and she was the League's living patron saint, her official birthday was the WFL social event of the year. It was also the focus for all fund-raising activities, the sum raised being presented to Mrs Despard in the form of a cheque which she ceremonially returned to the WFL for the year ahead's expenses. For weeks before the party Dr Knight would exhort *The Vote*'s readers to do their utmost in the First-President's honour. Once again, Alix Clark would make her famous mayonnaise sauce at 9d per pot, while other branches would busy themselves with flower and produce stalls and the entertainments: pianoforte selections, Irish airs, recitations, dramas. The League's new 'tea and politics' club in central London, the Minerva Club, organized the occasion's format, which from the 1920s onwards usually took the shape of an evening at the Caxton Hall. The Minerva Club also offered Mrs Despard a home from home in London, where she could host smaller gatherings of her friends. (Such intimates were favoured with the 'charming Irish hand-made pieces of jewellery' which probably came from Maud Gonne's end of the Roebuck House enterprises.)

Charlotte Despard's improbably active old age, her seemingly miraculous ability, often in defiance of her Dublin doctor's orders, to get to the birthday parties and deliver inspiring little speeches, reflected well on the Women's Freedom League, which itself outlived the other suffrage organizations. As one year of eulogy and emotion followed another, the WFL's executive members and their guest speakers were hard-pressed for new compliments to bestow upon the immortal Charlotte Despard. A regular celebrity guest at these birthdays was Margaret Bondfield MP, who, Mrs Despard quipped, had always been right honourable to her. In 1928 Margaret Bondfield told the assembled gathering, 'If I have gained any laurels, I should be glad to place them at the feet of Mrs Despard.' In 1932 Mrs Nehru declared that she would return to India the richer for the friendship of women in Britain, for which bonds Mrs Despard's life was like the fuel in the engine, supplying the 'motive power not only to the women in her country, but to those of other lands'. At the 1937 birthday party, the one where Harry Pollitt found it hard to get near the dais of honour, Lilian Baylis of the Old Vic made a spectacular gesture of homage. According to the level-headed Teresa Billington-Greig, Baylis 'almost rushed' to the dais and set about kissing Mrs Despard's feet, weeping and proclaiming her a saint. 'Our embarrassed president responded in kindly, quiet appreciation, trying at the same time to end the little scene gracefully.'

It was particularly gratifying for Mrs Despard to be alive and well for the 1928 birthday celebration because it coincided with the passing of the Equal Franchise Act by which women got the vote on the same terms, at the same age, as men. Mrs Pankhurst had been buried on the very day when this measure passed through its final stage in the House of Lords. But the other two prominent widows of the suffrage movement, Mrs Fawcett and Mrs Despard, were in Parliament for that occasion. They were also the guests of honour at the many victory ceremonies. Mrs Despard went to the High Mass at Westminster Cathedral, along with other members of the Catholic women's suffrage group, St Joan's Political and Social Alliance. Their patron had been officially canonized in 1920 and Mrs Despard was extremely fond of the little statue of Joan the Maid which the Alliance had presented her with.

Her thank-you speeches usually had a sprinkling of Shelley, a pinch of encouragement for the younger women who had not been in the fight during the heroic pre-war days and a strong measure of simple gratitude for the 'gift of love'. But even on these mellow occasions she never lost a chance to get some new political priority on the agenda. She continued to denounce war, to demand equal pay for equal work and to draw attention to international feminist struggles. In 1928 when she could have sat back and basked in glory she had this to say:

> We must go on dreaming the impossible dream. In the past I did not think the vote would come in my day. The things that are impossible today, are possible tomorrow. Then, we go on to another impossible dream . . . . The dream must be dreamed until it takes a spiritual hold.

The thing about Charlotte Despard, as her friends well knew, was that for all the flowery vagueness of her revolutionary language, she really meant it. Lucy Franks probably preserved a little newspaper item headed 'Mrs Despard is a Grand Old Woman' because she agreed with its reluctant admiration for her incorrigible old aunt:

> She is misguided from our standpoint – fanatical even, but one cannot help admiring an octogenarian who might have lived in comfort – she is a sister of the late Lord Ypres – but who still prefers to go tramping through the streets in labour demonstrations with unemployed men and women young enough to be her grandchildren.

Mrs Fawcett had become Dame Millicent Fawcett and in 1930, at Sir Stanley Baldwin's press of an electric button, the drapery fell from a life-sized statue of Mrs Pankhurst in the shadow of the Houses of Parliament. But Mrs Despard was not writing her autobiography and she was not a candidate for any conventional honour. She was in Ireland pursuing another impossible dream.

# CHAPTER 13

# A VISIT TO RUSSIA: 'DARK AND MENACING ARE THE SIGNS OF THE TIMES'

As the Great Depression hit the already miserable Free State, Soviet Russia was Charlotte Despard's oasis of hope. She loved hearing about the Soviet experiment from friends who had visited Russia and in the summer of 1930 she made her own pilgrimage to the New Order. She went with Irish fellow 'Friends of Soviet Russia'. This society had been founded in April at a meeting chaired by Helena Moloney at which were present, in addition to prominent left republicans, a Free State general, who remained unnamed by *An Phoblacht*.

From the point of sailing early in August Mrs Despard's six-week hadj was completely reassuring. Unlike the exclusive cruise liners on which she had sailed with her invalid Max, there were 'no classes, no separation of interests and no superiorities' on board the Soviet ship that started its five-day voyage to Leningrad from Hays Wharf in London. With typical thoroughness, she inspected the crew's quarters to satisfy herself that their food and conditions were every bit as good as those of the passengers. Indeed, she thought with motherly comradeliness, some of the young worker passengers were enjoying regular square meals for the first time in their lives. It was a very sociable voyage. As well as the Irish FOSR contingent, there were a number of British communists bound for a Moscow trade union congress. (When Mrs Despard reached the Moscow stage of her tour she had the benefit of the solicitude of old friends like Willie Gallacher and 'Comrade Rothstein', the latter dating back to her SDF career.) Wal Hannington was one of the British friends on board. He recalled finding cushions so as to settle the parasol-holding eighty-six-year-old comfortably on deck. The Scotswoman, Helen Crawfurd, with whom Mrs Despard had first allied herself during the pacifist campaigns and who had been a communist organizer in Dublin in 1925, was also an attentive companion. The Irish delegation included Hanna Sheehy-Skeffington and Sheila Dowling.

The versatile crew put on entertainments and there was even a ship orchestra. But being the sort of tourists they were, the company's pleasures included daily political discussions. Miss Dowling opened the Irish debate, which Mrs Sheehy-Skeffington thought very necessary in view of the misguided attitudes of some of the British comrades. Mrs Despard followed with a short account of the WPDL's activities, and the 'late scenes at the Bridewell'. To her great satisfaction the discussion precipitated much useful 'self-criticism' and ended on the consensus that 'republicans and revolutionaries must come together, think together, work together, if ever such an uprising of the people as will fully destroy the present evil conditions is to be brought about'. It was a harmonious and stimulating voyage. Two days into it and Mrs Sheehy-Skeffington was already low in her stocks of Irish revolutionary mementoes, portraits of the 1916 leaders proving to be particulrly popular. Later in the trip Mrs Despard's patriotic feelings were touched when Helen Crawfurd, who generally read aloud to her, commented that *An Phoblacht* gave 'a better and truer picture of things than is generally found in the *Daily Worker*'.

Once Leningrad was reached, and the 'tedious' business of customs examination of baggage done with, it was on to the real business of the trip. Helen Crawfurd and Mrs Despard went to stay in a former tsarist mansion outside the city, which was now a sanitorium for overworked members of the government as well as a retirement home for aged veterans of the revolution. One of the old female veterans wept spontaneously 'at the thought of my having come all this great distance at eighty-six years of age to see and hear about the revolution'. But the next three weeks were full of equally moving and 'indescribable sensations'. While other members of the original party dispersed to see the progress of the collective farms and to attend trade union functions, Mrs Despard concentrated on a systematic inspection of facilities for children, the disabled, mothers, old people and prisoners. These were the social needs that had first made a socialist of her and her inspection was informed by her experience as a London Poor Law Guardian.

Day in, day out, she visited homes, hospitals, schools, prisons and crèches attached to women's workplaces. The open-air school philosophy practised by Mrs Harvey was officially endorsed in Soviet Russia, particularly for children with tuberculosis, and Mrs Despard noted the 'scientific diet' provided in these institutions: vegetable soup, a little minced meat, grain foods and milk. She also noted that the front compartments of trains were reserved for mothers and small children and was delighted by the sight of toddlers napping in cots placed under trees in beautiful gardens. After her memories of Holloway, how humane it seemed that female prisoners' babies were housed in specially equipped nurseries, that their mothers saw them once a day, for a whole day every five days. Everywhere she met with 'bright eyes, solid limbs, happy small faces, breaking readily into smiles'. They would crowd round her as she entered and 'when I kissed one child's little hand, all the others wanted to be kissed. No shyness at all. One could see that they had met with kindness only.' Although the regime at an institution for young offenders was more grim, allowing solitary confinement as a punishment, it was all relative, and everywhere there was a great emphasis on the importance of education and recreation.

It was the same story at the boy scouts' centre, where she provided, with the aid of an interpreter, an account of the Irish Fianna scouts; it was the same at the old people's centres, in the home for the blind and even in the prisons that her very conducted tour allowed her to visit. She was impressed by the female staff of the women's prisons, with whom she could converse in French, and struck particularly by the efforts being made to rehabilitate prostitutes. They were not 'despised' according to Mrs Despard: 'On the contrary, everything is being done to encourage them. The feeling is that in a few years prostitution will pass away forever.' As a whole, the judicial system was pleasing because of its theoretical emphasis on the innate goodness of humankind, the criminal as a victim who would respond to care and education. Moreover, the judges were specially trained workers, both men and women, and there was a conciliation court for family disputes. But while younger, non-Catholic commentators on Soviet Russia in this period tended to be impressed by the ease and dignity with which divorce was obtained, Mrs Despard preferred to dwell on the incidence of remarriage among divorced couples, and the happy fact that there was no legal inequality between children born in and out of wedlock.

There is nothing to sneer about in all this enthusiasm. Coming as she did from Ireland, and knowing the system in Britain, Mrs Despard had every reason to be bowled over by the Soviet educational and welfare system. It was not yet, she knew, the 'workers' paradise' but it was certainly convincingly nearer that state. Nevertheless, as the tint in her spectacles got rosier she was inclined to take a less than complete picture on trust. She enquired about how political prisoners were treated, mindful of the WPDL's business, but was too easily satisfied with the answers.

Of course, there is a residue – there must be until the new order is completely established. These, with others who have deliberately tried to subvert the new order, are sent, I hear, to an island settlement, concerning which, as I cannot visit it, I am trying to get certain information.

Many more tough-minded visitors, the Webbs for example, succumbed just as easily to official blandishments. With regard to the progress of collectivization, Mrs Despard was satisfied that it was being carried out 'gently' and that the small farmers' resistance had 'quite broken down'. This was music to the ears of one who envisioned an Irish workers' and peasants' republic.

Again, anyone who imagines that Mrs Despard would be offended by the Doddington Estate in Battersea, which is intersected by an avenue named for her, can rest assured that she would, initially at least, have approved of austere tower blocks. When she saw a new housing estate going up in Moscow, with women builders at work on it, she was pleased by the 'quiet dignity of it all – no superfluous ornamentation. White, black and grey the principal colours – a garden and a crèche for small children will be added by and by.' Conscious as she was of the sanctity of the Soviet experiment, she could be puritanical. She could not enjoy the sight of the tsarist treasures on display at a mansion turned into a museum, preferring to delight in the sight of groups of workers being led around by a guide.

As a Friend of Soviet Russia from Ireland she was particularly interested in church-state relations. While in Moscow she attended an Orthodox service in the 'very splendid and still very rich' Church of St Saviour. This proved that 'the Soviet State is not a robber of churches' but in any case the congregation was very elderly: 'Old superstitions take long to slay.' But when she went to Mass in a Catholic church in Moscow, she was struck by the numbers of young children who clearly knew the structure of the service and were good at singing. It can be concluded that somehow the Orthodox Church was an old superstition but that the Catholic Church was an acceptably ongoing phenomenon in any context. This was good stuff for the propaganda battle back home.

Although Mrs Despard's health, like that of most people, improved when she was happy, she was frequently exhausted by her round of Soviet institutions. Her friends, notably Helen Crawfurd, shepherded her about and she frequently had to retire to the car, and once to an open-air bed in an old people's garden, completely worn out. But the trip included conventional holiday pleasures, the ballet and a performance of Eisenstein's *Battleship Potemkin* at an open-air cinema. (She remembered in particular the telling image of a 'rich kulak refusing help to a starving women'.) Her shopping expeditions were less satisfactory because the lace and fine antiques available were beyond her means, though the 'useful' Russian blouses which appealed to the dress reformer in her were less so. But Mrs Despard the political saint was in her element at a gala open meeting of the Trades Union Congress which many of her British comrades were in Moscow to attend. (She herself addressed a meeting of women trade unionists.) As the band struck up with the International she was transported by the 'happy life – light, radiant activity, colour'. It did seem that the impossible dreams could be realized, and the inevitable Shelley welled up inside her. 'I thought of Shelley and his Revolt of Islam and breathed within myself a fervent wish that this grand nation – risen from the depths of humiliation – may not have this progress retarded by the capitalists and imperialists who are bent on her destruction.'

Soon after she returned to Dublin her nephew Bertie, who admired his eccentric aunt as a 'persistent upholder of the down-trodden', enquired of Lucy Franks, 'Have you ever made out if Aunt Lottie really saw anything of the real life in Russia or if she was just shown what Bernard Shaw has seen?' In the same year Shaw had signed his Moscow hotel's visitors' book, 'Today I leave this land of hope and return to our Western countries of despair.' Though a somewhat maverick enthusiast for the great Soviet experiment, Shaw's opinion was given great publicity. Like Mrs Despard, he had been politicized in the late nineteenth century, though in Fabian rather than revolutionary ways, and he had not expected any breakthrough in tsarist Russia. But the future there was working, according to him and Mrs Despard, who peppered her little speeches to the WFL with references to the progress she had verified for herself. It was too early yet to gauge the stubbornness of the pyschosexual oppression of women, which would in due course stimulate the later twentieth-century feminism, but in the meantime equal pay and equal access to the powerful institutions of society would resolve everything. In Russia, she opined, there was no longer a need for a feminist movement. At the same occasion, the WFL faithful were treated to a blistering attack on the vigour of the 'anti-feminist snake', with particular reference to the Irish Free State, by Mrs Sheehy-Skeffington.

Back at Roebuck House things were not improving, and Mrs Despard's new year greetings to *The Vote* for 1931 were suitably apocalyptic: 'Dark and menacing are the signs of the times. Mighty changes which will bring desolation to many are impending. My hope is that the young women of the new era will face them . . .' At the end of that trying year she confessed to a young British communist, Charles Wilson, that political pressures and illness often made her long for 'easeful death'. 'But it seems as if I am to live on a little longer.' Mr Wilson was continually trying to get her over to address unemployed workers and anti-fascist meetings in his native Durham and when she was well enough she obliged him. For his information she summarized the latest situation in the Free State:

You may have read in some of the English papers something about the very bad times we are having in Ireland. Meetings proclaimed, the most innocent societies made illegal, arrests, raids (I have been raided twelve times), our best men in prison or on the run, and judge and jury superseded by an all-powerful military tribunal.

Despite her eighty-seven years, 'a time when most people would think to give up public life', the oppositional fight had to go on: 'much anxiety and much work fall upon us the women.' The fate of George Gilmore was a spectacular instance of the impact of Free State repression. Like other prominent IRA 'politicals' such as Peadar O'Donnell, David Fitzgerald, Michael (Mick) Price and Sean MacBride, and republican women such as Helena Moloney and the Sheila Dowling who had been to Russia with Mrs Despard, George Gilmore was a member of the newest republican socialist group, Saor Eire (Free Ireland). Along with the IRA itself, Cumann na mBan, the Friends of Soviet Russia and other communist-sounding groups, Saor Eire had been declared unlawful in October 1931, on the same day that the Special Powers Tribunal consisting of military officers had been set up. Having been imprisoned by this martial machinery, Gilmore protested his political status by refusing to wear prison clothes and spent from October 1931 to February 1932 naked in a windowless cell. (In due course his brother Charlie was also arrested.) The George Gilmore case was one of the *causes célèbres* of the WPDL and Mrs Despard, who found it therapeutic to write poetry in times of crisis, dedicated this 'Song of Liberty' to Mrs Gilmore.

> I arise, I arise, I the dream of the Peoples
> Cleaving the darkness, eternally free.
> I am here, I am there, no power can restrain me,
> And my name it is Liberty, sweet Liberty!
>
> Hearken, oh! hearken, Earth's sorrowful children
> From the slave-sleep of ages, the call is – Arise!
> Fighters and workers linked closely together
> Fire in your hearts, and joy in your eyes.
>
> I alight, I alight on my limitless journey
> On a fair little isle in the western sea

Tis a land that has oftentimes struggled and suffered
For seeking and loving sweet Liberty.

I descend to find still the old battle raging.
Fear's at the helm: power-lust draws the bolt
'Once for all, and forever, by pious endeavour'
They cry out together, 'we'll strangle revolt.'

In the heart of the tempest my children are waiting.
They yield not an inch, firm and dauntless they stand.
Tortured, imprisoned, sent homelessly wand'ring,
Ah! they are to-day the Felons of their land.

Day after day, from township and hamlet
Into icy cold prison they're secretly driven
At the gates stand pale women, wives, sisters and mothers
To be turned away hopeless. No news can be given.

Breathe not a word – the tribunal is sitting,
Three men of mystery, secret as hell.
To them and their minions full power has been given
They can sentence to death those who love me too well.

Men and women of Ireland! I pray you consider,
Is it your will that such things should be?
It is not; it is not, you cry out in chorus
Oh! we seek thee, we love thee, sweet Liberty.

*Chorus:*
Breathe not a word : the tribunal is sitting,
Three dark men of mystery, secret as hell.
To them and their minions full power has been given
They can sentence to death those who love me too well.

While it would have made Maud Gonne's friend Yeats wince,
Mrs Despard's verses scanned better than those by other authors
which regularly found their way into *The Vote*. In any case, as
Madame Markievicz once commented on one of her patriotic
hymns, 'It may not be great poetry, but it *is* good propaganda.'

A wearying hazard of life at Roebuck House was the frequent
raids by the men of the Criminal Investigation Department.
(December 1926: 'They were unusually civil and, in fact, the
raid was perfunctory.') In the aftermath of a raid, the inmates
of Roebuck often discovered that it was some IRA incident

elsewhere that had sent a vengeful CID round to do over the household. According to Madame MacBride, the sergeant at the local police station was embarrassed by CID 'blackguardism' and because of his criticism he was transferred to another station. Most of the raids of the 1920s were perfunctory compared with those of 1931. In May of that year, the CID arrived so early in the morning that they disturbed Mrs Despard and young Mrs MacBride while they were still in bed, and July saw the worst raid of all. This was an all-day event involving thirty to forty CID men. Ignoring the doorbell, they hammered on the front door with their gun butts to secure admission. Then, armed with revolvers, electric torches, iron rods with wooden handles and ordinary walking sticks, they systematically ravaged every room in the big house. 'Drawers and presses were turned out, letters and papers read, walls rapped, floors thumped, boards lifted, grates removed from fireplaces, chimneys sounded.' When one internal wall yielded a suspiciously hollow sound, it was actually gutted in the hope of finding an arms dump.

Since Maud Gonne was away, it was Mrs Despard who saw the pictures ripped from their frames, the vases of flowers overturned, the memorabilia of long and multi-faceted lives tossed out into the garden to blow across the fields. This is how *An Phoblacht* reported the incident:

> 'At one o'clock operations were suspended for lunch. The main body picnicked on the lawn but eight settled in the drawing room until Mrs Despard "froze" them out. The species are rather shy and dislike being examined at close quarters.'

At six o'clock they left, having failed to find their dump. The house looked as if 'a party of particularly destructive chimpanzees had run amok in it' and one garden wall had been completely levelled. There was only one way of ridding Roebuck of such attentions, and that was a change of government. Mr de Valera's political programme fell short of Mrs Despard's communist vision – indeed for more orthodox Irish communists he was a 'green fascist' – but he did support the campaign against payment of the land annuities and was sympathetic to the 'Release the Prisoners' movement. She had met him personally once, at the offices of the WPDL. Accordingly, she did her inimitable bit for his campaign in the General Election of February 1932.

Mrs Despard dogged the Minister for Defence, Desmond Fitzgerald (father of Garrett) as he toured Kilkenny. At Graignamanagh she set up her portable platform just a few yards away from the Minister's lorry. Apart from attacking her (verbally) as a communist, he called Mrs Despard an associate of the 'murder gang' which he alleged to be de Valera's real boss. To this the old lady responded with a reminiscence of how she had once intervened on behalf of Desmond Fitzgerald when he had been a political prisoner of the British at the Curragh. But what was he doing about the current political prisoners? 'In volume of voice the Minister had the advantage, but Mrs Despard, who is eighty-eight, apparently scored more frequently with those who could hear her, so that was the only section voicing its feelings in bursts of cheering.' Soon after two o'clock Mrs Woods insisted on relieving Mrs Despard, but the duel continued at different locations over the next few days.

When de Valera was swept to power there was jubilation. Although she had recently suffered 'a heart attack accompanied by severe pain' Mrs Despard told Charles Wilson that 'the people have triumphed, our brave prisoners were released and tumultuously welcomed. We have entered we hope upon a better era.' She sat beside a standing Maud Gonne on the platform that rose above the 30,000-strong meeting in College Green to welcome the prisoners released by the new government. She heard her tell the crowd, somewhat prematurely as it turned out, that at last the 'Mothers' could take a rest.

In the mid–1920s Maud Gonne had shared Mrs Despard's trust in communism as the 'apotheosis of Christ's teaching'. But as the Irish Church set about systematically denying any such thing in the early 1930s that view became hard for anyone but a Catholic of Mrs Despard's idiosyncrasies to sustain. The full weight of the Church was now down on all manifestations of socialist or even liberal thought. To add to clericalist red-scaremongering, Ireland also had its own visitation of fascism in the shape of an Army Comrades Association which, from February 1933, was led by the ex-commissioner of Police, General O'Duffy. In image at least this body looked to Italy and Germany and it adopted the blue shirt as its uniform. The

Blueshirts mirrored the articulate and overtly socialist republican movement which had, albeit temporarily, been liberated by de Valera's victory. In the polarized atmosphere Sean MacBride felt it pragmatic to keep the political energies of the IRA on a carefully republican course. His mother's political orientation had always been coloured primarily by nationalist values and her son's direction confirmed her in a new distance from communist republicans.

But Mrs Despard, who had started out in the Social Democratic Federation, was offended rather than disabled by church disapproval and predictably uncompromising both in identifying and opposing fascism, at home and abroad. In 1933 she addressed an anti-fascist rally in London's Trafalgar Square and was in demand at similar meetings all over Britain. She felt most at home in the company of overtly communist republicans such as Peadar O'Donnell. This affinity and her precarious health influenced her move in 1933 to the nurses' home in central Dublin run by one of O'Donnell's sisters-in-law, Geraldine O'Donel. She soon recovered enough to rent and then purchase another building in the same street – incidentally, the Eccles Street of Leopold Bloom – for use as her own residence, as a Workers' College and as the headquarters of the Friends of Soviet Russia. Her share of rambling Roebuck house with its wonderful garden was sold to Maud Gonne.

Books about Maud Gonne talk of a rift between her and Mrs Despard in the 1930s which was precipitated by incompatible politics. Though Mrs Despard was 'too left-wing' for Maud Gonne, and Maud Gonne too impartial about fascism for Mrs Despard, such accounts deny the complexity of this relationship, indeed of all Charlotte Despard's relationships. One suspects, too, that because Maud Gonne's political career is underestimated at the expense of her role in W. B. Yeats's career, the great man's known dislike of Mrs Despard is hidden within the notional quarrel. Had there been some conclusive row, it is unlikely that Roebuck House would have been so amicably parted with, that Maud Gonne would have continued to speak respectfully of her friend long after the separation and that she would have been the distraught chief mourner at Mrs Despard's funeral in 1939. For a better understanding of the parting of the ways in 1933, from the less famous personality's point of view, it is useful to recall Margaret Bondfield, the adult suffragist so openly suspicious of lady suffragettes who never lost her friendship with Charlotte Despard. It was likewise with Kate Harvey, the philanthropic Theosophical feminist who disapproved of her friend's militancy in the labour movement. Mrs Despard's women friends could not be permanently alienated because she refused to reciprocate their disapproval. (We can see her refusal to make the political personal most spectacularly in the case of her brother, about whom she thought so fondly long after he had washed his hands of her.) Even Mrs Pankhurst, whose dictatorial vagaries and jingoism disgusted Teresa Billington-Greig and Helena Swanwick, never lost Charlotte Despard's esteemed affection.

But in Eccles Street Mrs Despart was more vulnerable than she had been in the homely chaos of Roebuck House. The very existence of the Workers' College was like a red rag to the bull of Irish anti-communism, which was being fuelled by a preacher at the Jesuit church in nearby Gardiner Street. Inspired by his sermons, and probably also by Blueshirtism, a body of men from this congregation set out in March 1933 to burn down Mrs Despard's latest base. Such a group had already fired Dublin's other conspicuous communist centre, Connolly House, but according to the reminiscences of Brendan Behan, the old lady did not realize that the crowd was hostile. She imagined that they were revolutionary workers coming to greet her and for several hours was effectively trapped within the building. This image of a doddery old lady, though benign, is not consistent with the still lucid letters, the occasional speeches and her general awareness of the consequences of Irish crypto-fascist activity. She may have been given to over-optimistic flights of revolutionary fancy, but she probably knew that the mob in the street was not friendly. It seems more likely that she girded herself in her spiritual armour when she heard them. She could not escape and so she would gladly stand her ground, just as she had done when those Maidstone thugs had advanced on the WFL caravan, when anti-Pacifist, anti-German groups were stalking Nine Elms: 'Each one should try to do his or her best and leave the results to Higher Powers.' As it was, lower powers in the form of gunshots from a hastily mobilized IRA guard got the eighty-nine-year-old mystic warrior out of that particular scrape, though the building was looted and wrecked.

# CHAPTER 14

# LAST DAYS IN THE ORANGE STATE: THE WINDY NEST

Most of Charlotte Despard's Irish dreams evaporated long before there was any hope of their realization. One by one, her fondest revolutionary groupings dispersed and the most promising political campaigns lost momentum, but still she expected something to rise from the ashes. Despite this incorrigible optimism, it might have been expected that after the sacking of the Eccles Street Workers' College, she would, at last, settle down to her memoirs. Not so. Even in her ninth decade Mrs Despard refused to retire from the bitter world:

> People think that because of my age I should take things easy now. Why should I? I find life interesting even at ninety-two, and beautiful. I love getting about, meeting people. Often I am asked to talk of the past, of my experience with suffragette days. But I do not like talking of the past. It has gone. It's the present we should live in. . . .

Her next 'present' was Unionist north-east Ireland. The World Depression of the 1930s was particularly acute in Belfast, so acute that the marginal advantages enjoyed by Protestant workers, by which the government preserved their Loyalism, were seriously eroded. The number of Belfast unemployed, always high and disproportionately Catholic, rose to an unprecedented extent (approximately 45,000) and the Belfast Poor Law relief rates were lower than those of any comparable indus-

trial city in Britain. But in 1932 the unemployed workers on
Outdoor Relief (a sort of supplementary benefit), Catholics and
Protestants, reacted to their predicament by going on strike.
(These were the men working on outdoor relief schemes, which
usually involved heavy manual labour.) This October ODR
strike was 100 per cent solid and its jubilant organizers – among
them Tommy Geehan and Betty Sinclair - saw a class-based,
revolutionary potential in the fact that workers had organized
across sectarian lines. Among left republicans in the South there
was a genuine, active solidarity with this unprecedented display
of unity between Catholic and Protestant workers, and Cumann
na mBan organized a national flag day in aid of the distressed
families of the strikers.

But it was not long before the alarmed government pulled out
its orange trump card to disperse this non-sectarian movement.
Thus rioting was deliberately channelled into Catholic areas so
as to portray the whole unemployed movement as an IRA front.
A wave of repression accompanied these divide and rule tactics,
with many arrests and meetings banned. Hanna Sheehy-Skeffington, the assistant editor of *An Phoblacht*, defied an exclusion
order banning her from the Six Counties to speak at a meeting
in Newry demanding the release of prisoners. For this she
received and served a one-month jail sentence. At the end of
January 1933 Mrs Despard was on the platform in College
Green for her triumphal return to Dublin. Despite her imprisonment, Mrs Sheehy-Skeffington was very positive about political
developments in the North, and Mrs Despard was very eager to
listen. As Dublin became more and more impossible for her, it
seemed that Belfast, where such brave new things were
happening, might be the right base for a communist-pacifist-
feminist like her. There she could combine her sympathy and
familiarity with the aspirations of left republicanism with her
forty-year-long ties with the British labour movement. Maybe,
she thought for the umpteenth time, 'this was it.' As Brendan
Behan, then a teenage rebel, reported, 'Madame Despard had
always said – and I'm inclined to agree with her – that the
next move in Irish revolutionary politics would be made by the
Northern worker.'

Throughout her life, Mrs Despard kept in touch with
hundreds of people, but materially she always burnt her bridges.
As she prepared to move north early in 1934 she sold the Eccles

Street building for a nominal sum to another O'Donel sister, and it became a nursing home. Taking minimal belongings, including that much-travelled marble bust of the dear departed Max, she went to Belfast, living first on the Newtownards Road and within less than twelve months in the more central Glenburn Park. When she left Roebuck House for central Dublin her affectionate Despard nephew had urged her to take more care of herself: 'It really is time someone helped you who have spent your whole life in helping others.' She had always had a household staff, though only in the manner of a person with a tendency to turn her home into a refugee centre-cum-dispensary-cum-welfare centre-cum-political headquarters. Until now she had not, like most women of her class and generation, depended on the intimate care of servants. But the ninety-year-old Mrs Despard who in cold weather resorted to stout leather shoes instead of the famous sandals had to take this nephew's point.

Since the turn of the century she had been used to having the word 'venerable' attached to her person. But by 1934 she really was frail as well as venerable. She was very nearly blind so that she could only read and write intermittently, or with the help of a secretary. Apart from the recurring heart trouble, she was vulnerable to winter chills and viruses, to dizzy spells and falls on uneven pavements and on stairways, and rheumatism and arthritis regularly crippled her. These problems sometimes had the effect of souring what had been a legendary sweetness of temper – she had never been, in the Irish sense of the word, a cranky old lady. Now she could be irritable at times. Even so, as her Belfast companion, Mollie Fitzgerald, told Hanna Sheehy-Skeffington in 1939, she still had her moments:

> Yes, she is really wonderful at her age. Once she's over an illness she picks up very quickly but owing to my being ill and in and out of hospital I've had to have a nurse staying at the house since last August. It looks as if the cold weather agrees with her – she hasn't had the least setback the whole time.

Though subject to occasional lapses of memory, only to be expected in a woman of her phenomenally long and active career, she could sit bolt upright in a wooden chair at political meetings and, with the aid of a microphone, inspire an audience with a few well-chosen words.

For the Belfast households she employed three people. Minnie Doherty was the maid her nephew had hoped for and Mollie Fitzgerald was the secretary-companion that the ongoing political career and social life demanded. A good-looking, high-spirited young woman, Mollie hailed from the South and the Dublin progressive scene. She was a sister of David Fitzgerald, the left-wing IRA leader who had died in the first O'Donel Eccles Street home in September 1933 at the age of thirty-six. According to the *An Phoblacht* obituary he had been a man of 'liberal culture and wide reading' and he, too, had gone to Russia with Irish FOSR in 1930. His Tipperary family had, it was noted, been associated with the separatist movement since Fenian times. Mrs Despard was probably herself at Eccles Street when he died and her wreath at his funeral bore the inscription 'to my friend and dear comrade'. Mollie was to be Mrs Despard's eyes and hands, helping her to keep up a voluminous correspondence and to plan the agenda that took her, in her capacity as honorary chairman of the Belfast UWM, to meetings and crisis points all over the north-east. Secretarially trained, it was Mollie Fitzgerald who took down the poems, which Teresa Billington-Greig referred to as 'red flag doggerel' and which were printed and published in 1935. Apart from Mollie's practical skills, Mrs Despard enjoyed her company. 'I am very, very proud of the young generation,' she once told the WFL, 'I like to see these young girls with their long legs and short skirts. When I was a girl, we were not allowed to show our ankles.'

The car, now a solid Lanchester 14 hp, was more indispensable than ever and its driver, as well as the 'man of the house', an all too necessary figure in the violent Belfast of the 1930s, was Jack Mulvenna. Apart from his endearing first name and great personal charm, the thirty-year-old Mr Mulvenna had other attributes to recommend him particularly to his ancient employer. A northerner and an electrician by trade, he had been politically schooled in the war against the Black and Tans, the struggle against the treaty and the turbulence of the 1920s. But he was not simply a nationalist republican, having joined Saor Eire in 1931, and he participated in the next regroupment of left republicans, the Republican Congress.

So Charlotte Despard's companion-comrades, to whom she

always referred as 'my dear friends' were not cap-touching servants. They were, however, not only from a different class, but also several generations younger. When she reminisced about her Victorian childhood in a Big House – she was rarely directly nostalgic about her married youth or even about her early political work – the world she described was as far away from Mollie and Jack as was the world of Charlotte Brontë's novels. Inwardly, and discreetly, Mrs Despard's optimistic spirit had been dented by her Dublin experiences. In Belfast she was trying to live again as she had in Battersea twenty-five years earlier. She was back among the people in the heart of the city in a house that was only modestly comfortable. (She had the carpet removed from her own bedroom.) But the latest ménage caused raised eyebrows among some of her relatives because now that Aunt Lottie was such a very old lady they felt a more overweening concern with her welfare.

Mrs Despard was, however, still very much her own woman, free to make her own friends, to run her own household, and to be spontaneously generous with what remained of her fortune. When it came to charity she had never been the kind of revolutionary who believes that every penny to the needy delays the revolution. (She was probably too experienced to imagine that a hungry person has more energy.) In Belfast she was as open-handed as ever. She even endowed an unemployed workers' brass band. But such enterprises could not be sustained as well among the jobless of inner Belfast as they were among the solid artisans of Lancashire mill-towns. Within less than twelve months the beautiful instruments had been dispersed among the local pawnshops. Her personal fortune (dowry) had dwindled after her almost profligate funding of every worthwhile Dublin cause over the previous fifteen years. But she still had the dividends from investments, which made her relatively well-off in Belfast, where, as in Dublin, there were few revolutionary philanthropists. Sometimes Jack Mulvenna felt called upon to protect Mrs Despard from people who were more interested in what she might have rather than who she was. Her reputation as a soft touch could have farcical consequences. When an unemployed man hawking fire-sticks knocked on the door, she would say, 'Who is it Jack?' and when told, 'give him a pound.' Paying way over the odds for the stick vendor's entire stock was one way of guaranteeing an army of hopeful stick-sellers on the next morning. Meanwhile the daily post brought more calls upon her generosity. Hanna Sheehy-Skeffington would write, 'sure that you will want to help this latest victim of clericalism'; Dorothy Macardle and Mary Twamley would inform her of a committee being set up to aid the Coughlan family, on the 'tragic death of Nancy' and in consideration of the 'services of the family in the Republican movement'. In thanking 'Madam Despard' for a loan, Alice Delaney wrote to express the regret of 'all the people' at her leaving Dublin: 'Your home was always open to the Poor and Needy.'

Such gestures went hand-in-hand with building for the revolution that would remove a need for them. But even as Charlotte Despard reached Belfast, the great promise of the ODR movement was being dissipated into sectarian violence. Back in 1922 there had been the terrible events which had exercised Maud Gonne MacBride and Charlotte Despard on the provision of shelter for northern Catholic refugees. There had been minor outbreaks in 1932 in Armagh, Lisburn, Portadown and Belfast, when people travelling to the Dublin Eucharistic Congress had been attacked, and in 1934 there were more incidents. But May 1935 was the Silver Jubilee of George V and the occasion was treated as a Loyalist binge. Tension escalated sharply during the celebrations and up until, and after, the Orange marches in July, so that in the summer of 1935 Belfast witnessed the worst pogrom against Catholics since 1922.

An official, and therefore conservative, estimate of the violence in November listed eleven murders and two attempted murders, 574 cases of criminal damage to persons, 133 cases of arson and 367 cases of malicious damage. Needless to say, in only a very token number of cases had it been possible to hold someone responsible for these crimes.

In her 1934 Christmas letter Kate Harvey, still embattled with the needs of the children in her care, had written to her old friend, 'We must not faint or be weary of helping those who need our help badly, so long as we have our share of strength to give.' In the midst of the horror of the summer of 1935 Charlotte Despard did not faint, but the revolutionary timetable had to be put back. Maud Gonne MacBride, who got regular news of her activities, wrote to a friend about the crippled and wounded children who were finding sanctuary in Mrs Despard's Glenburn Park house. This was romanticized hearsay, for although Mrs Despard contributed to such relief efforts, she was no longer capable of direct, practical involvement à la Currie Street.

One of the people determined to make the truth known to the world generally and the British Establishment in particular was Ronald Kidd, Secretary of the newly established British Council for Civil Liberties, ancestor of the National Council for Civil Liberties, and incidentally a son of the Church of Ireland Bishop of Limerick. He was in Belfast to observe the Special Powers Act then in operation and it is a measure of Mrs Despard's links with the British left that he stayed with her for about a month while doing so. Having simultaneously observed the pogroms, Ronald Kidd wrote to the Prime Minister, Sir Stanley Baldwin: 'Long before the 12th it was freely prophesied that there was going to be trouble on that day and it was believed that the anti-Catholic speeches of ministers heralded a so-called porgrom of the Catholic population.' (These were speeches along the lines of Sir Basil Brookes's infamous 'I have not a Roman Catholic about my own place' utterance of 1933.) Mr Kidd complained of the RUC turning a blind eye on Orange mobs attacking Catholic homes and demanded what would never be forthcoming, 'a strictly impartial enquiry' into 'misrule and abuse of authority by the Northern Ireland government'.

Mrs Despard's house in Glenburn Park was vulnerable that summer. But the authorities would have been greatly embarrassed if any harm had come to the late lamented Lord Ypres's sister. So, for a few particularly tense days when Loyalist gangs were haunting its vicinity, the house was guarded by B-Specials. Jack Mulvenna drove home with Ronald Kidd one evening to see, on his approach, these unlikely protectors. Had these guards suspected what lay beneath a tarpaulin behind Mrs Despard's front hedge they might have been less routine about their job. Jack Mulvenna had to disguise his discomfiture and salute them neutrally, to restrain himself from inviting the sort of attention that, as a republican, he was more used to.

But that violent summer in Belfast made Mrs Despard think about moving on again, to a house with that therapeutic 'country' or gardenly dimension. Innocent of the fact that Mrs Despard's own money was almost gone and of the fact that the capital of Max's legacy was entailed, so that upon her death it was to be inherited by Despard and Franks relatives, her bank manager encouraged her to borrow money to build a brand new house. (The dividends from the Hong Kong & Shanghai Bank and from the Cawnpore Muir Mills – the enterprise of her sister Maggie's husband in India – still yielded an income that was beguilingly impressive to the manager of a provincial bank.) So the loan, which would lead to trouble later, was procured and work began on a house on a clifftop overlooking the small town of Whitehead, about twenty miles out of Belfast.

Whitehead was little in more than one sense. It was a solidly Unionist enclave of twitching lace curtains and severely clipped hedges, where Charlotte Despard was at best regarded as an eccentric old lady with an interesting past. To use Mulvenna's memorable phrase, one in which the old Irish respect for cows rather than modern misogynist insults should be recalled, she was a wandering cow, the beast that refuses to move with the herd, in her case her class, and is found scrambling over the mountainside. Whitehead was a curious location for the nearest Charlotte Despard got to a retirement home, but there she had a garden, and an occasional gardener to plant McGredy's famous roses, which she could still smell at least, as well as bracing sea air. It was also true that at Whitehead Jack Mulvenna, always liable to being lifted on account of his known political allegiances, was relatively safe, and that mattered a great deal to his employer.

When Peadar O'Donnell came to visit, he was asked to suggest a name for the new house and came up with 'Nead na Geabhai' (Ulster Irish for 'the nest of geese'). A subtle man, he may have had the migratory habits of geese in mind, and their mythical place in Irish history – Mrs Despard being an honorary wild goose who had returned to Ireland. (She had also, it must be said, laid quite a few golden eggs for Irish progressive forces.) But the others, Mollie, Jack and Mrs Despard, did not have O'Donnell's knowledge of Gaelic and so, through a phonetic confusion, they arrived at 'Nead na Gaoithe', which means 'the Windy Nest'. That name turned out to be very appropriate, for although Mrs Despard always had her nests, they were seldom sheltered from the stormy weather of politics.

Fewer visitors than before made their way to the Windy Nest in Whitehead. But from Belfast there came regularly Dr O'Prey and Father McCloskey, medical and spiritual advisors who were considered friends and whose visits were all the more enjoyable now that she was so often bedridden and comparatively isolated. Still, there was the occasional visitor from her outside worlds: Lucy Franks from Dublin, Marian Reeves from the WFL and the Minerva Club and, once, Sir Stafford Cripps. She took him on an outing to the Giant's Causeway, where he and his wife enjoyed their lunch of fruit and nuts. In 1938 Stafford Cripps, the British statesman now chiefly remembered for his rigid austerity programme as Chancellor of the Exchequer (1947–50) was advocating a popular front against fascism in co-operation with anyone from 'Churchill to Pollitt'.

For this anti-appeasement campaign Mrs Despard found a distinguished local ally. The Earl of Antrim was a liberal aristo-crat who organized a shipment of medical supplies and food to the Spanish Republic as it resisted the forces of fascism under Franco. The Earl threw a garden party in aid of this venture, at which Mrs Despard was the guest of honour. With some amusement Jack Mulvenna recalls how Mrs Despard's reported presence at this gathering earned her invitations to tea from Whitehead worthies who now decided that she might be kosher after all. But the invitations stopped coming as soon as it was realized that she never separated her tea from her irredeemably unpalatable politics.

Whenever possible Mrs Despard did more than write letters of encouragement or send donations to the causes she supported. With Jack Mulvenna at the wheel of her car she got to meetings in Dublin, London, Manchester, Bristol, even Antwerp and Paris, as well as venues all over the north-east. One newspaper account of her arrival at the 1937 WFL birthday party, her ninety-third, referred to Jack as her son, a journalist's mistake that infuriated Lucy Franks. On another occasion, while he was escorting Mrs Despard on a visit to a convent, the Mother Superior kept calling him 'Captain French'. Again, he did his best to live up to the part.

The same progressive personalities were often prominent in different but complementary campaigns, but Spain prompted a greater degree of unity and urgency within the ranks of the organized labour movement in Britain than any other issue. As Michael Foot has written, 'Spain cut the knot of emotional and intellectual contradictions in which the left had been entangled ever since Hitler came to power. Suddenly, the claims of inter-national law, class solidarity and the desire to win the Soviet

Union as an ally fitted into the same strategy.' Since 1931, when the Spanish Second Republic was founded, Charlotte Despard had taken a great interest in Spanish affairs. How the radical and secularist republican government dealt with the power of the Church, for example, was very relevant to the crozier-bashed Irish Free State. But in 1936 Franco, backed by Hitler and Mussolini, launched his rebellion against the Republic and La Passionara's cry rang out: 'It is better to die on your feet than live on your knees.' Charlotte Despard watched and prayed as many of her friends, including Peadar O'Donnell, George Gilmore and Frank Ryan, as well as many Belfast republicans and communists, volunteered for the International Brigades.

Charlotte Despard's pacifism did countenance physical resistance to repression, even though she herself could never have been a combatant, and that was the spirit with which she viewed the Spanish Civil War. She desperately wanted to go there herself, telling a *Manchester Guardian* reporter in 1937, 'I feel I might be able to encourage them.' Indeed, representing as she did so many different radical traditions, Mrs Despard was well suited for exhortative roles in the epoch of popular front politics. She had not been well enough to make it to the 1936 birthday party in London, so her arrival at the 1937 event was a cause for great jubilation. When asked by another journalist what she regarded as the most important achievement of her long life, she said 'surprisingly' that it was not women's suffrage but 'the improvement in the treatment of children'.


Not that Mrs Despard is satisfied with things as they are. 'Was women's fight for freedom finished?' I asked.

'No, not while equal pay is denied to women for equal work to that done by men,' she said, 'the whole basis of society today is wrong and cruel. Everything is considered from the point of view of some selfish interest – collective, or racial or national. We need the universal outlook so that all mankind can live together with affection.'

Mrs Despard dislikes the appellation 'feminist'. But it is still the cause of woman's equality with man that most engages her sympathies.

'I remember at a meeting many years ago,' she said with a twinkle in her eye, 'that a man interrupted me with the question, "Who is it mans the army and the navy?" I retorted at once, "Woman." '

'There were roars of laughter but the truth of it went home. It is true, you know. Every soldier and sailor once lay a helpless infant in his mother's arms, owing his life and continued existence to her.' She took up her stick and moved briskly off to lunch.

Ill-health frustrated Mrs Despard's desire to go to Spain but she did make it to a Brussels Congress in support of the Second Republic, from there going to Paris where she met with leading French communists and addressed a few workshop meetings. But she was not well enough to go to her 1938 birthday party, and so the Windy Nest was deluged with telegrams and flowers from distant well-wishers. Meanwhile the Western powers stood by Spain's agony in the name of appeasement and so, early in 1939, the Republican movement collapsed before Franco. Charlotte Despard often spoke of the 'spiritual darkness in high places' and the year of her death was a very dark one indeed. Over Spain the storm clouds for another world war had begun to gather. When Stalin signed the Soviet-Nazi Non-Aggression Pact Hitler felt free to invade Poland, and Britain declared war in September.

Charlotte Despard's last year was also a dark one on a personal level. Her financial situation, aggravated by the loan for the Windy Nest, had become very confused. Now very sick, she was unable to keep track of her affairs and Mollie Fitzgerald, herself unwell, had to be straight with the people who still solicited help.

About the little matter of Miss Delany. I don't know if I can make this quite clear but it's difficult to explain in a letter Mrs Despard's position with regard to things of that sort. She is and has been for some time in the hands of her trustees and although Madame MacBride wrote on the same thing a good bit ago she was obliged to let the matter drop, hoping that later on she could manage. However perhaps I should let her explain this herself only her affairs are rather complicated at the moment and everything is in the hands of her solicitor for to be cleared up.

Jack Mulvenna, in whose favour she had signed power of attorney, bore witness for Mrs Despard when she was declared a bankrupt in the very month when the Second World War broke out. The magic dividends had been frozen or reduced as a result of the war emergency and when Mrs Despard's bank realized that she was not uncomplicatedly wealthy, her cheques bounced and there was panic about the house loan.

During the bankruptcy an effort was made to incriminate by innuendo Mrs Despard's republican staff. Queries were raised about the expense of her 'world-wide correspondence' and about the cigarettes that she bought on account from a local tobacconist even though she herself never smoked. Lady Essex French was alarmed enough to enquire about whether it would be wise to take steps to place her aunt in the care of the Lord Chief Justice of Ireland. But her solicitor adivised that such a step would be too complicated to be practicable. Mrs Despard was too old and too out of it now to defend her lifestyle and her friends. The Whitehead household was isolated but she knew she was in good hands. Years before no one could have dared to challenge the satin frocks for Vere, the boat on the Shannon for Sean MacBride. Now her lawyer, who had worked for every radical cause in Dublin and who was a brother of her doctor there, Alex Lynn, journeyed up to plead her case in the bankruptcy court.

About six weeks afterwards, Charlotte Despard, drugged for pain and sleeplessness, fell down a blacked-out step (a war-time measure) in her specially adapted annexe of the house. She was found, unconscious, by Jack Mulvenna at about 1 a.m. She never came to, despite the efforts of the local doctor summoned by Jack and Mollie and those of Dr O'Prey, who had come from Belfast. With Lucy Franks by her bedside, she died in hospital three days later, on 10 November 1939. A verdict of accidental death arising from shock due to multiple injuries was recorded. The squalidness of the bankruptcy proceedings was followed by an even more squalid dispute over the will in which she left the little she had to her Irish friends, in particular Mollie Fitzgerald and Jack Mulvenna. Apart from them, she remembered – with degrees of generosity ranging from the £100 to Dr O'Prey and the £20 to each of Jack Mulvenna's three sons – George Gilmore, Roddy Connolly, Alexander Lynn, Buddy Fitzgerald and Norman Shaw. Though temporarily suspicious of the circumstances of Charlotte Despard's death, her family held aloof from any dispute about the friends she chose to thank. It was the local Unionist establishment which determined that 'not a penny of Lord French's sister's money will go to a republican'. And so the lawyers had their way with the will, dragging the case out for fifteen years, by which time the modest legacy had been used up in legal fees. Jack Mulvenna had another fight to honour Mrs Despard's wish for burial in Glasnevin Cemetery in Dublin. This request stuck in the craw of the undertaker appointed by the lawyers, who had no inclination to organize a full republican funeral for Mrs Despard. Through sheer persistence Jack Mulvenna managed to transfer the arrangements to a Catholic and therefore more sympathetic undertaker. It should not, though it did, have surprised anyone that Mrs Despard wanted a Catholic funeral in Dublin. Despite her otherworldliness she liked the Papist way of death. Immediately after her widowhood she had been impressed by Catholic forms of bereavement and the funeral rituals of the Irish poor in Nine Elms. The magnificent procession accompanying Terence MacSwiney's body to its entrainment at Euston had contributed to her conclusive embroilment with Ireland. Moreover, she wanted to be buried near Constance Markievicz, the great 'Madame' whose funeral in 1927 had been another deeply moving occasion for her. Besides, after the bleakness of her last years at Whitehead, only Dublin could do justice to the Irish dimension of Charlotte Despard's life.

On the cold wet morning of 13 November 1939 the hearse, accompanied by about ten individuals, including Jack Mulvenna, Mollie Fitzgerald and Dr O'Prey, left Whitehead. Just outside the town a few more cars joined on, a few more at Lurgan, Newry, and so on until, by Dundalk, the cortège was half a mile long. At St Joseph's Church in Haddington Road in Dublin, it was hard for the pall-bearers to clear a path for the mourners gathering outside, among them a distraught Maud Gonne MacBride. The men who bore the coffin on Jack Mulvenna's request represented the full spectrum of Irish republican and communist politics: Peadar O'Donnell, Roddy Connolly, Sean MacBride, Frank Hugh O'Donnell, Sean Murray and Mick Price. Hanna Sheehy-Skeffington represented the Women's Freedom League at the graveside and laid their wreath upon the coffin, while Maud Gonne, in tears, made the peroration in which she described her friend as a 'white flame in defence of prisoners and the oppressed', and her death as the 'loss of a great light'. In due course Lucy Franks arranged for the erection of a headstone that accorded with the detailed instructions left with Mollie Fitzgerald and Jack Mulvenna: 'Mrs Despard impressed it upon us that any headstone or other memorial must be of the simplest design.' The Glasnevin grave now bears the following inscription:

> In Loving Memory of
> Charlotte Despard
>   née French
>   widow of
> Maximilian Carden Despard
>   Born 15 June 1844
>   Died 10 November 1939
>   She tried to do her duty.
>   'I slept and dreamed that Life was Beauty,
>   I woke and found that Life was Duty.'

The quotation from a poem by the Victorian Ellen Sturgis Hooper provides as good a summary as any of Mrs Despard's long and valiant life. She had lived at least four lives and had what her Nine Elms friends would have rated as a good funeral. But few of the mourners gathered in Glasnevin on that November day could have imagined the ghostly hordes from the past who jostled among them to pay their respects.

# CHRONOLOGY

1839    Maximilian Carden Despard born.

1844    Charlotte French born.

1854    Captain French died.

1860    Mrs French confined to a mental home.

1864    Garibaldi, the hero of the Italian unification movement, made a triumphal visit to London. Max Despard was in Shanghai.

1865    Margaret (Maggie) French married Gavin Jones. Charlotte and her unmarried sisters began touring the Continent.

1867    Mary French, the eldest sister, married John Lydall.

1870    Charlotte and Caroline (Carrie) French left Paris after the outbreak of the Franco-Prussian War. Charlotte met Max Despard, who had an office in London, and they were married. John French left the Navy to join a cavalry regiment.

1874    *Chaste as Ice, Pure as Snow*, Charlotte Despard's first novel, and *Wandering Fires* were published.

1879    *A Modern Iago* was published.

1882    The Married Woman's Property Act allowed wives to have independent property.

1884    *A Voice from the Dim Millions*, Charlotte Despard's overtly political fiction, was published.

1886    *Jonas Sylvester* was published. The Married Women (Maintenance in Case of Desertion) Act was passed.

1888    County Councils set up in Britain.

1890    *The Rajah's Heir*, Charlotte Despard's most successful novel, which used her experiences of the East, was published. Max Despard died and she emerged from a reclusive widowhood to join the Nine Elms Flower Mission. The Irish Nationalist Party was split by Parnell's divorce scandal.

1891   Madame Blavatsky, founder of the Theosophical Society, died. The first Despard Club in Battersea was started.

1892   John Burns was elected as Member of Parliament for Battersea and Charlotte Despard made her first public speech in Wandsworth Town Hall.

1893   John French's family lived at Courtlands. The Independent Labour Party was founded and Charlotte Despard, also a member of the Social Democratic Federation, joined it.

1894   The abolition of the property qualification for Poor Law Guardians meant more working-class and female candidates for the office. At the end of the year, Charlotte Despard was elected as the Guardian for Vauxhall to the Board of the Lambeth Poor Law Union.

1896   Charlotte Despard was an SDF delegate to the International Socialist Workers' Trade Union Conference in London.

1897   Queen Victoria's Diamond Jubilee celebrations marked the peak of Britain's imperial ambitions.

1898   Death of Eleanor Marx.

1900   Labour Representation Committee, direct ancestor of the Labour Party, was formed. John French's military career took off with the Boer War (1899–1902).

1901   Death of Queen Victoria.

1902   Charlotte Despard visited Canada to see what had become of the Lambeth boy emigrants sent out under the auspices of Dr Barnardo's organization. The Education Act of this year put the responsibility for education in the hands of local authorities and Charlotte Despard was prominent in the local campaign for school meals.

1903   She resigned from the Lambeth Board, only to serve briefly on the Wandsworth Board. The Women's Social and Political Union was founded in Manchester.

1905   Annie Kenney and Christabel Pankhurst were imprisoned after their sensational disruption of a Liberal political meeting.

1906   Charlotte Despard was recruited to the Cause of votes for women and became joint hon. secretary of the WSPU. She probably resigned from the SDF at the same time. Liberals won a landslide victory and Labour Members of Parliament appeared.

1907   February: first spell in Holloway after suffragette demonstration. September: split within the WSPU which led to the formation of the Women's Freedom League. The Qualification of Women Act allowed women to be councillors.

1908   *Outlawed* was published. Herbert Asquith, who was unsympathetic to women's suffrage, became Prime Minister.

1909   Mrs Despard's status as President of the Women's Freedom League was ratified. The suffrage campaign hotted up as prisoners began hunger-striking. The Lords' rejection of the 'People's Budget', which provided for social expenditure financed from income tax, provoked a constitutional crisis. Old age pensions introduced. Beginning of cheap motor cars. As President of the Theosophical Society, Annie Besant adopted Krishnamurti to be groomed as the World Teacher.

1910   The promise of the first Conciliation Bill yielded a short-lived truce in the militant suffrage campaign.

1911   The Edwardian 'Labour Unrest' began. The Parliament Act limited the power of the House of Lords. National insurance was introduced and MPs were paid for the first time. Asquith torpedoed the Conciliation Bill.

1912   While the WSPU made its 'war' on the government, the WFL stuck to non-violent militancy and Mrs Despard made suffrage tours of Ireland. Rosalie Mansell's breakdown resulted in a closer responsibility for ten-year-old Vere Foley.

1913   Emily Wilding Davison became the most famous suffragette martyr when she died after throwing herself under the King's horse at the Derby. Mrs Despard attended the 7th Congress of the International Women's Suffrage Alliance in Budapest.

1914   Sir John French resigned his senior military position after the Curragh Crisis. Charlotte Despard underwent her first serious illness, recovering for the outbreak of the First World War.

1915 Military operations were extended from the main front in France and Belgium to the Russian plains, the Balkans, the Middle East and the German colonies in Africa. Charlotte Despard failed to get to the Hague to meet with other feminist pacifists.

1916 After conscription had been introduced in Britain the peace movement gathered momentum. The Easter Rising in Dublin triggered off a new phase in the struggle for Irish independence.

1917 Katie Harley (youngest of the French sisters) died from shellfire in Serbia. The strain of the war brought revolution in Russia. Mrs Despard met Maud Gonne MacBride for the first time.

1918 January: the vote was granted to some women. Mrs Despard resigned as President of the WFL and became President of the London Vegetarian Society. May: Sir John French became Viceroy of Ireland. November: the end of the war. December: General Election. Mrs Despard stood as the Labour candidate for Battersea but was not elected. Sinn Fein won the election in Ireland.

1919 May: terms of the Treaty of Versailles, the peace settlement, were published. Mrs Despard attended the Women's International Congress at Zurich. Lord French survived an assassination attempt.

1920 The Black and Tans arrived in Ireland. Mrs Despard went to Hungary on behalf of Save the Children. The Communist Party of Britain was founded. October: Terence MacSwiney died in Brixton Jail after a marathon hunger strike. Mrs Despard was appointed as an alderman to Battersea Borough Council.

1921 Mrs Despard wound up her Battersea affairs and in the summer moved permanently to Ireland. December: Anglo-Irish Treaty signed.

1922 The Anglo-Irish Treaty was ratified by the Dáil and de Valera resigned as President of the Republic. The White Cross mobilized relief for victims of the war. Mrs Despard visited Belfast. June: a full-scale civil war started. The Women's Prisoners Defence League began its work and an increasingly infirm Mrs Despard moved into Roebuck House.

1923 Maud Gonne moved into Roebuck. The WPDL was

proscribed and Maud Gonne imprisoned. Mrs Despard's vigil outside Kilmainham. A year of 'great sadness upon our household' was marked by executions and raids and by the firing of Westfield House.

1924　After the formal ending of the Civil War Charlotte Despard started the Roebuck jam factory. Lenin died.

1925　Mrs Despard joined the republican protest against O'Casey's *The Plough and the Stars*. Sir John French died in England. *An Phoblacht* was started as a newspaper for abstentionist republicans. December: Krishnamurti declared himself as the World Teacher.

1926　The General Strike in England. Dublin hosted the 5th Congress of the Women's International League for Peace and Freedom. De Valera left Sinn Fein in order to set up a non-abstentionist republican party. Mrs Despard's political hopes were pinned on the new Irish Workers' Party.

1927　The assassination of Kevin O'Higgins resulted in a new Public Safety Act and Charlotte Despard was officially deemed a dangerous subversive. Constance Markievicz died. The jam factory collapsed.

1928　The Equal Franchise Act gave the vote to women on the same terms as men. Mrs Pankhurst died.

1929　The Wall Street Crash led to economic recession throughout Europe.

1930　Charlotte Despard travelled to the Soviet Union with the Irish Friends of Soviet Russia.

1931　Intensified repression of the opposition to the Irish Free State. July saw worst raid of all on Roebuck House. Ramsay MacDonald split the British Labour Party over economic measures. A republic dominated by socialists and liberals was set up in Spain.

1932　Charlotte Despard campaigned for de Valera, who won General Election. WPDL disbanded. The men on outdoor relief in Belfast went on strike.

1933　Mrs Despard moved to Eccles Street and in March her house was attacked by an anti-communist mob.

1934　Charlotte Despard moved north, first to Belfast. She participated in British anti-fascist demonstrations and campaigned for Wal Hannington in a South Wales by-election. Left republicans rallied at the Republican Congress in Dublin.

1935    Pogroms in Belfast. Soon after, Mrs Despard arranged to move to her 'Windy Nest' in Whitehead.

1936    Outbreak of the Spanish Civil War. Illness prevented Mrs Despard from going to Spain herself, but she went to solidarity conferences in Belgium and France. Edward VIII abdicated.

1937    Charlotte Despard made it to her London birthday party.

1939    Defeat of republican Spain. Bankruptcy proceedings against Mrs Despard. Outbreak of Second World War. 10 November: died in hospital after a fall at home. 13 November: funeral and burial at Glasnevin.

# SOURCES

Nine of Charlotte Despard's diaries for the years 1913–26 are in the Public Record Office of Northern Ireland, Belfast. The PRO also has a short autobiographical fragment by Mrs Despard, 'In the Days of My Youth', several of her novels and about thirty letters. But the diaries are small, pocket-sized books in which day-to-day activities are usually summed up in a few cryptic phrases and so they do not offer much to students of her lifetime's general history.

Clues to Charlotte Despard's marriage came from the box of miscellaneous family papers which originally belonged to Lucy Franks and which was lent to me by one of her grand-nephews. Here I found material relating to the history of the Franks and Despard families, two of Max Despard's letters home and a scrapbook containing some newspaper clippings about Charlotte Despard. The Imperial War Museum in London has an autobiographical fragment by Lord Ypres (John French), but since it is so very circumspect about his childhood and moves so quickly to the beginning of his military career, it was not very useful for a biography of Charlotte Despard.

Apart from the autobiographical essay in the Belfast PRO, the closest Charlotte Despard got to a memoir of her life was the article 'How I Became a Suffragette' in *Women's Franchise* of July 1907. This can be found in that treasure trove of feminist history, the Fawcett Library in London. The Fawcett also houses the organ of the Women's Freedom League, *The Vote* (1909–33). Mrs Despard edited and contributed to *The Vote* and so it forms the main printed source for her life story. But such printed sources are more than supplemented by the unpublished notes of Teresa Billington-Greig on the genesis of the

Women's Freedom League, and by the folder of notes which she assembled in the 1960s when she was thinking about writing a memoir of Mrs Despard. The Fawcett Library now also has Charlotte Despard's Russian diary, which Andro Linklater, author of a monumental biography of Charlotte Despard, *An Unhusbanded Life*, acquired from the son of her Belfast doctor.

The minutes of the Lambeth Board of Guardians can be seen in the Greater London Records Office, while Battersea District Library has newspaper clippings and material relevant to Charlotte Despard's local career.

For Mrs Despard's Irish career the printed sources are sparse and insubstantial. There are two letters in Trinity College Library in Dublin, many more in the National Library of Ireland, and a couple of articles and small references in *An Phoblacht*. For the period from June 1925 to July 1936 this is available on microfilm (Reels 39–43). Mr Jack Mulvenna did all he could to compensate for the paucity of Irish sources with his own recollections of Charlotte Despard.

# BIBLIOGRAPHY

**Works by Charlotte Despard**

*Novels*
*Chaste as Ice, Pure as Snow*, London, 1874.
*Wandering Fires*, London, 1874.
*A Modern Iago*, London, 1879.
*A Voice from the Dim Millions*, London, 1884.
*Jonas Sylvester*, London, 1886.
*The Rajah's Heir*, London, 1890.
*Outlawed* (with Mabel Collins), London, 1908.

*Articles and pamphlets*
'Women's Franchise and Industry', pamphlet, 1908.
'Women in the Nation', pamphlet, 1909.
'Women in the New Era', pamphlet, 1910.
'Theosophy and the Women's Movement', pamphlet, 1913.
'The Christ that is to be', Notes of an address given at Queen's Hall, January 1917 (Fawcett Library).

**Select Bibliography of books about Charlotte Despard and her times**

Anon, *Edward Marcus Despard: Memoirs of a Life*, London, 1803.
Behan, Brendan, *Brendan Behan's Island*, London, 1962.
Behan, Brian, *Mother of All the Behans*, London, 1984.
Bondfield, Margaret, *A Life's Work*, London, 1948.
Booth, Charles, *Life and Labour of the People of London*, 3rd series, vol. 5, London, 1902.
Cardozo, Nancy, *Maud Gonne*, London, 1979.
Caute, David, *The Fellow Travellers*, London, 1973.
Chaplin, Charles, *My Autobiography*, London, 1964.

Colum, Mary, *Life and the Dream*, London, 1947.

Coogan, Tim Pat, *The IRA*, London, 1970.

Cousins, James and Margaret, *We Two Together*, Madras, 1950.

Cullen Owens, Rosemary, *Smashing Times: A History of the Irish Women's Suffrage Movement 1889–1922*, Dublin, 1984.

Dangerfield, George, *The Strange Death of Liberal England*, London, 1935.

Davidoff, Leonore, *The Best Circles*, London, 1973.

Dinnage, Rosemary, *Annie Besant*, Harmondsworth, Middlesex, 1986.

Farrell, Michael, *Northern Ireland: The Orange State*, London, 1976.

Fox, R. M., *Rebel Irishwomen*, Dublin, 1937.

Fox, R. M., *Louie Bennett*, Dublin, 1958.

French, Gerald, *The Life of Field-Marshal Sir John French*, London, 1932.

Hobsbawm, E. J., *Labouring Men*, London, 1964.

Holmes, Richard, *The Little Field-Marshal: Sir John French*, London, 1981.

Hone, Joseph, *W. B. Yeats*, London, 1942.

Housman, Laurence, *The Unexpected Years*, London, 1937.

Kapp, Yvonne, *Eleanor Marx*, 2 vols, London, 1972.

Kenney, Annie, *Memories of a Militant*, London, 1924.

Kent, W., *John Burns: Labour's Lost Leader*, London, 1950.

Lansbury, George, *Looking Backwards and Forwards*, London, 1935.

Levenson, Leah, *With Wooden Sword: A Portrait of Francis Sheehy-Skeffington, Militant Pacifist*, Dublin, 1983.

Liddington, Jill and Norris, Jill, *One Hand Tied Behind Us*, London, 1978.

Linklater, Andro, *An Unhusbanded Life*, London, 1980.

Lydall, Edward, *Enough of Action*, London, 1949.

Lydall, Edward, *Lydall of Uxmore*, London, 1980.

Lyons, F. S. L., *Ireland Since the Famine*, London, 1971.

Macardle, Dorothy, *The Irish Republic*, London, 1937.

Mac Manus, Francis (ed.), *The Years of the Great Test 1926–39*, Dublin and Cork, 1967.

Mahon, John, *Harry Pollitt*, London, 1976.

Milotte, Mike, *Communism in Modern Ireland: The Pursuit of the Workers' Republic since 1916*, Dublin, 1984.

Mitchell, David, *Women on the Warpath*, London, 1966.

Mitchell, David, *The Fighting Pankhursts*, London, 1967.

Mitchell, David, *Queen Christabel*, London, 1977.

Mitchell, Hanna, *The Hard Way Up*, London, 1968.

Montefiore, Dora, *From a Victorian to a Modern*, London, 1927.

Morton, A. L. and Tate, George, *The British Labour Movement*, London, 1956.

Nevinson, Margaret Wynne, *Life's Fitful Fever*, London, 1926.

O'Connor Lysaght, D. R., *The Republic of Ireland*, Cork, 1970.
Pethick-Lawrence, Emmeline, *My Part in a Changing World*, London, 1938.
Polak, M., *Mr Gandhi, the Man*, London, 1931.
Pollitt, Harry, *Serving my Time*, London, 1958.
Ramelson, Marian, *The Petticoat Rebellion*, London, 1967.
Rosen, Andrew, *Rise Up Women! The Militant Campaigns of the Women's Social and Political Union 1903–14*, London, 1974.
Rowbotham, Sheila and Weeks, Jeffrey, *Socialism and the New Life*, London, 1977.
Ryder, Vera, *The Little Victims Play*, London, 1974.
Stedman Jones, Gareth, *Outcast London*, Oxford, 1971.
Strachey, Ray, *The Cause*, London, 1928.
Stuart, Francis, *Black List Section H*, London, 1975.
Swanwick, Helena, *I Have Been Young*, London, 1935.
Thompson, Paul, *The Edwardians*, London, 1975.
Tuchman, Barbara, *The Guns of August – August 1914*, London, 1962.
Vernon, Betty D., *Ellen Wilkinson*, London, 1982.
Wagner, Gillian, *Dr Barnardo*, London, 1979.
Ward, Margaret, *Unmanageable Revolutionaries*, London and Dingle, 1983.
Webb, Beatrice, *My Apprenticeship*, London, 1928.
Wells, H. G., *The New Machiavelli*, London, 1911.
Wiltsher, Anne, *Most Dangerous Women*, London, 1985.

## Articles about Charlotte Despard and her times

Balliet, Conrad A., 'Michael MacLiammoir Recalls Maud Gonne MacBride', *Journal of Irish Literature*, University of Delaware, May 1977.
Thane, Pat, 'Women and the Poor Law', *History Workshop Journal*, no. 6, Autumn 1978.
Vellacott-Newberry, Jo, 'Anti-war Suffragists', *History*, vol. 62, October 1977.

# INDEX